# TIGER TRAP

# ALSO BY DAVID WISE

# TIGER TRAP

## America's Secret Spy War
## with China

## David Wise

*Houghton Mifflin Harcourt*
BOSTON   NEW YORK
2011

For information about permission to reproduce selections from this book,
write to Permissions, Houghton Mifflin Harcourt Publishing Company,
215 Park Avenue South, New York, New York 10003.

www.hmhbooks.com

*Library of Congress Cataloging-in-Publication Data*
Wise, David, date.
Tiger trap : America's secret spy war with China / David Wise.
p. cm.
Includes bibliographical references and index.
ISBN 978-0-547-55310-8
1. Espionage, Chinese — United States — History. 2. Intelligence service —
China — History. 3. Intelligence service — United States — History.
4. United States. Federal Bureau of Investigation. I. Title.
UB271.C6W56    2011
327.51073 — dc22    2010042025

Book design by Brian Moore

Printed in the United States of America

DOC 10 9 8 7 6 5 4 3 2 1

*To Natalie, Ambrose, and Ben*

There are no walls which completely block the wind.
— FROM A CHINESE GUIDE ON ESPIONAGE

# CONTENTS

# TIGER TRAP

# PRELUDE

## Scene 1

November 1997.

Katrina Leung made a striking figure, standing there at the microphone in her brightly colored *cheongsam* Mandarin dress and jacket, her jet-black hair swept up in a tight bun as usual, the high cheekbones accenting her thin, angular face. She was joking with Jiang Zemin, the president of China, joshing and cajoling him to sing for the VIP audience of one thousand at the Biltmore Hotel in Los Angeles.

"I will sing a song from a Chinese opera," President Jiang finally agreed, to the delight of the assembled dignitaries.

*"One silver moon over the window sill,"* he warbled in Mandarin, choosing an aria from *The Capture and Release of Cao Cao,* the classic tale of a conniving, murderous third-century warlord who is caught and sweet-talks his way out of trouble.

Katrina Leung, at the time a prominent member of the Chinese American community in Los Angeles, had organized the 1997 dinner in honor of Jiang and was acting as his interpreter and emcee of the affair, basking in the spotlight, where she liked to be. Leung's persuading the president of China to burst into song was the high point of the evening, and her coup created a major buzz in the room.

If there had been any doubt before, the night at the Biltmore solidified her position as the most powerful Chinese American personality in Los Angeles. Leung appeared to move easily at the top of the worlds of politics and business in both the United States and China. How she managed to do so confounded even her many admirers.

But there was something that the distinguished dinner guests did not know: Katrina Leung was a spy, code-named PARLOR MAID.

## Scene 2

December 1990.

Bill Cleveland, chief of the Chinese counterintelligence squad in the FBI's San Francisco field office, was checking into the Zhongshan Hotel in Shenyang, in northeast China, when he saw him.

Dark-haired, cool, handsome enough to be a Hollywood actor, Cleveland was not someone easily rattled. But now he looked like a man who had seen a ghost.

He turned, crossed the hotel lobby, and spoke urgently to I. C. Smith, a fellow FBI agent. As Smith recalled the moment, Cleveland approached him looking "sort of wide eyed."

"You won't believe who I just ran into," Cleveland said. "It was Gwo-bao Min."

For more than a decade, Cleveland had relentlessly pursued Min, an engineer with a Q clearance who had worked at the Lawrence Livermore National Laboratory in California, one of two national laboratories in the United States that design nuclear weapons. Cleveland — and the FBI — were convinced that Min had betrayed critical US nuclear secrets to China. Yet the proof, enough evidence to make an arrest, seemed always, maddeningly, just out of reach.

In the closed world of FBI counterintelligence, only a small group of insiders knew about the highly classified case and the lengthy pursuit of the former Livermore scientist. Min had become the great white whale to Cleveland's Captain Ahab. The FBI gave its TOP SECRET investigation a code name: TIGER TRAP.

Cleveland could not let go of the case; he had delivered dramatic closed lectures on TIGER TRAP at the lab, at the FBI training facility in

Quantico, Virginia, even at CIA headquarters, using it as an illustration and a warning of subtle Chinese intelligence methods.

At the time of the unexpected encounter in Shenyang, Cleveland was the bureau's preeminent Chinese counterintelligence agent. For an FBI counterspy to get into China was tricky enough, but Cleveland, a Mandarin-speaking student of Chinese history, had managed it.

He had slipped into the Communist-controlled mainland as a member of a State Department team inspecting the security of US diplomatic installations in China. I. C. Smith, the other FBI agent on the team, was on assignment to the State Department and traveled as a diplomat. He recalled that they were closely watched. Well before the inspection team arrived in Shenyang, Smith thought he had detected an unusual amount of surveillance.

"In Beijing one day," he said, "it was late in the afternoon, a cold dry wind blowing, and I went into a park called the Temple of the Sun to stretch my legs." The park, near the American embassy, was deserted, but as he turned to go back he suddenly came upon a man who quickly looked away and began studying a mural nearby. Smith continued on a short distance, discreetly photographed the man, and kept walking. As he left the park he saw a black limousine, the motor running, with two Chinese men inside. He had no doubt that the car and its occupants were from the Ministry of State Security, the MSS, China's intelligence service.

"Later in a market, I saw a guy and the same guy kept showing up. We were even followed on a trip to see the Great Wall." Smith was surprised at all the attention. "Usually diplomatic security people don't get that kind of coverage."

And now, incredibly, Cleveland had run into Min, the target of the prolonged TIGER TRAP investigation, in remote Shenyang! Cleveland knew Min; he had questioned him more than once. The two spoke briefly in the hotel lobby. It turned out that both were scheduled to leave Shenyang on the same flight two days later, but Min never showed up at the airport.

Cleveland was shaken by their encounter in the hotel. In a country of more than a billion people, what were the odds of Bill Cleveland running into Gwo-bao Min?

"Neither one of us believed in coincidences," I. C. Smith recalled in his gumbo-thick Louisiana drawl. Was the MSS trying to rattle the FBI? Was the People's Republic of China sending a message from Shenyang to the J. Edgar Hoover Building in Washington?

Cleveland could not be sure. But as matters turned out, the encounter was a dark harbinger of what awaited him.

## Chapter 1

# A THOUSAND GRAINS OF SAND

FOR ALMOST HALF a century during the Cold War, the world focused on the global espionage battle between the United States and the Soviet Union. The duel between the CIA and the KGB, portrayed in countless books, films, and news stories, captured the public imagination.

Espionage became a kind of entertainment, in no small measure due to the fictional exploits of James Bond, first popularized when President John F. Kennedy let it be known that he enjoyed Ian Fleming's stories. John le Carré's George Smiley provided a more authentic, if less glamorous, rendering of the spy wars.

Fiction masked the cold reality. In the actual conflict, spies and their agents died. Lives were shattered. The CIA plotted to overthrow governments and assassinate political leaders. The KGB's supermoles, Aldrich Ames in the CIA and Robert Hanssen in the FBI, stole US secrets by the trunkful and betrayed agents working for US intelligence, many of whom were executed.

As the East-West intelligence battles played out in the cafés of Vienna, in divided Berlin, and in back alleys across the globe, scant attention was paid to the espionage operations of a rising global power—China—and the limited efforts of US counterintelligence, not always successful, to block Beijing's attempts to acquire America's secrets. Inside the FBI, Soviet spies were regarded as the principal quarry; Chinese counterintelligence was relegated to a back seat. After the Soviet Union collapsed in 1991, Russia's spies continued to target the United States, as was demonstrated by the arrest in 2010 of ten "illegals" sent by Moscow to pose as Americans and gather intelligence in the United States. The KGB's espionage arm simply became the SVR (Sluzhba Vneshnei Razvedki), and US counterintelligence efforts against Moscow continued much as before.

Yet China has in many ways become America's chief rival. And China has spied on America for decades, with some spectacular results, little known outside intelligence circles. At the same time, the end of the Cold War enabled the FBI to rethink its counterintelligence priorities. The bureau shifted its focus to China, to the espionage war with the MSS, the Ministry of State Security—China's foreign spy agency—and the intelligence branch of the PLA, the People's Liberation Army. This book offers a history of China's spying within the United States, focusing chiefly on recent decades, but also looking at some earlier episodes from the post–World War II era. It is a story of interlocking agents and cases, centered around the two particularly dramatic stories of PARLOR MAID and TIGER TRAP. It is a history largely undisclosed, and yet no less significant than the parallel story of Soviet and Russian penetrations. There have been no major films, no best-selling thrillers, and relatively little press coverage about Chinese espionage. Yet the drama, and the stakes, are just as high.

America and China are locked in an uneasy embrace. China needs the United States to buy its exports, and American companies long to expand their sales in the huge Chinese market. Washington looks to China for help in dealing with intractable foreign policy issues, such as the nuclear ambitions of North Korea and Iran.

Despite their interdependence, both countries actively spy on each other, a fact that has not been widely understood. During World War II,

Soviet spies penetrated the Manhattan Project and stole US atomic secrets. That history lesson was not lost on China. In the decades after World War II, Chinese espionage was principally aimed at stealing US nuclear weapons data. To the extent that China could acquire those secrets, it could bypass years of research and testing and speed its own development of nuclear weapons, in particular small warheads.

China, its modernization devastated by the chaos of the Cultural Revolution, coveted those shortcuts. It had ample motive to spy. And the United States, particularly the nuclear weapons labs at Los Alamos and Lawrence Livermore, became its prime target.

Another priority of Chinese intelligence has been to penetrate US counterintelligence. Spy agencies work constantly to uncover and disrupt one another's operations. Today, Chinese intelligence also targets a broad range of US military technology, from the Navy's most sophisticated weapons systems to the Air Force's stealth bomber.

Given American preoccupations with Russia, the first thing that must be understood about China is that its spycraft differs in crucial ways from that of the Russians. Some of the techniques — including "honey traps," the use of attractive women to lure targets, and sophisticated electronics — are the same. But the differences are at least as telling as the similarities.

The secret headquarters of the Ministry of State Security is located in Xiyuan, the West Garden section of Beijing, near the Summer Palace. Unsuspecting crowds of foreign and Chinese tourists visit the palace daily, not realizing that they are passing China's spy headquarters.

The MSS — the Guojia Anquan Bu — is China's equivalent of the CIA. Many of its officers live in the headquarters complex in an apartment building called Chien Men, which means "front door." Its location, too, is supposed to be secret, but the neighbors know that the spies live there.

For thirteen years, starting in 1985, China's top spy, the head of the MSS, was Jia Chunwang, an English-speaking Beijing native with a degree in physics. Jia, who was popular among Communist Party members, was chosen in 1998 as China's procurator-general, a post similar to that of the US attorney general. His successor as MSS director was Xu Yongyue, a party hack from Henan Province. Xu opposed corruption in the MSS but also cracked down on Tiananmen Square demonstrators and other dissidents. In 2007 Xu's deputy, Geng Huichang, fifty-six, a bespectacled native of Hebei Province in northern China, moved up to become MSS chief as part of a government shakeup by President Hu Jintao, who sought to consolidate his power by naming five political allies as ministers.

The spy agency is organized into a dozen bureaus. The first bureau operates for the most part inside China, but it also recruits people who are heading overseas for study, business, or vacation. The second bureau manages the spies, sending intelligence officers abroad under diplomatic cover in Chinese embassies or under commercial cover, including officers posing as journalists. The third bureau runs operations in Taiwan, Hong Kong, and Macao. In the latter two locations, the MSS spies are assigned to a group code-named Winter Chrysanthemum, which is tasked with gathering intelligence on Taiwanese organizations and foreigners. A second group, code-named Autumn Orchid, has overlapping responsibilities in the two locations but concentrates on collecting intelligence about the media, political and commercial figures, and the universities.

The fourth bureau, the technology bureau, is in charge of wiretapping and communications, as well as photography. The fifth bureau is internal, responsible for domestic intelligence. The sixth bureau runs counterintelligence. The seventh bureau writes intelligence reports; the eighth is in charge of research; and the ninth runs countersurveillance and works to prevent defections by spies and students. The tenth bureau collects scientific and technical intelligence. The eleventh bureau runs the MSS computers and is charged with protecting the agency from foreign computer hackers. Finally, a foreign affairs bureau cooperates with friendly foreign intelligence services.

MSS spies are trained in the agency's own university, the Institute of International Relations in Beijing. The institute is a huge think tank with more than five hundred researchers. It provides the Chinese leadership with major English-language newspapers, summaries of political and economic trends, and documents issued by foreign governments. It is divided into ten offices covering the geographic areas of the world, as well as sections for international relations and the global economy.

Although the institute teaches foreign languages and geopolitics, it does not teach other courses in espionage tradecraft. For that, students are reportedly sent for specialized training at the Institute of Cadre Management, a school for spies in Suzhou, a city of ancient pagodas and beautiful bridges in the Yangtze River delta, near Shanghai. For up to a year, the recruits learn firearms, martial arts, driving, communications, and surveillance skills.

The size and budget of the MSS are secret, as is true of most of the world's spy agencies. But in September 1996, at a conference of the MSS and other Chinese intelligence agencies, called Strengthening Intelligence Work, China's vice premier, Zou Jiahua, alluded to the number of MSS agents around the world. In an address delivered to the conference, "Salute to Comrades on the Special Duties Front," Zou spoke of the "tens of thousands of nameless heroes who cherish and loyally serve their motherland [and] are quietly fighting in their special posts abroad." If his figure is at all accurate, it would mean that the MSS literally has tens of thousands of agents around the world.

The MSS is not the only Chinese intelligence arm that spies on other countries, including the United States. The Military Intelligence Department (MID) of the People's Liberation Army also conducts espionage abroad. It is the MSS, however, that runs most of the intelligence operations against the US target.

The MSS is only the latest intelligence apparatus of a nation that is hardly a newcomer to espionage operations. China has been in the spy business for some twenty-five hundred years. Around 400 B.C., Sun Tzu, the general and military strategist, is credited with writing the classic treatise *Ping-fa*, or *The Art of War*. In a chapter entitled "Employment of Secret Agents," Sun Tzu describes five kinds of spies that are remarkably close to those still plying their trade in the twenty-first century.

Sun Tzu's typology includes "agents in place" (he calls them native, or inside, agents), double agents, deception agents, expendable agents (who may be killed if their role in passing false information is discovered), and penetration agents. A clever spymaster, Sun Tzu writes, may employ all five types simultaneously, much like a fisherman who uses a casting net, pulling in his catch by a single cord connected to the other strands.

Mao Zedong and the other modern Chinese leaders of Communist China borrowed from *Ping-fa* many of the tactics they used to fight the Japanese and then the Chinese Nationalists. Sun Tzu emphasized that it was supremely important to know the enemy's forces, to have accurate advance intelligence. "Know the enemy and know yourself," he wrote, "and you can fight a hundred battles with no danger of defeat."

In the twentieth century, Kang Sheng was the sinister and powerful spymaster who helped Mao Zedong gain and maintain his power. Born into the family of a wealthy landowner in Shandong Province, Kang joined the Communist Party at age twenty-five and was trained in Moscow in intelligence and security. He became a key member of Mao's inner circle, and by 1937, the evidence suggests, he had become chief of intelligence. A thin man with thick, round glasses and a pencil mustache, Kang was feared, and with good reason, since he was both powerful and ruthless. Kang supported Mao in the chaotic Cultural Revolution but died in 1975 before its backers, the so-called Gang of Four, were arrested and tried.

Kang Sheng, Jia Chunwang, and their fellow spymasters have developed a uniquely Chinese approach to spycraft, and to the penetration of America's crucial military and espionage secrets. The point is best illustrated by an anecdote that has long circulated inside the counterintelligence division of the FBI about a concept known as "a thousand grains of sand." Paul Moore, the former senior China analyst for the bureau, has often used the story to illustrate the belief that the Chinese gather intelligence differently from the Russians and other countries.

As Moore tells it, "If a beach was an espionage target, the Russians would send in a sub, frogmen would steal ashore in the dark of night and with great secrecy collect several buckets of sand and take them back to Moscow.

"The US would target the beach with satellites and produce reams of data.

"The Chinese would send in a thousand tourists, each assigned to collect a single grain of sand. When they returned, they would be asked to shake out their towels. And they would end up knowing more about the sand than anyone else."

There is an element of truth to the tale. Unlike China, Russia and the United States employ many of the same traditional methods to spy. Even their headquarters are the mirror image of each other. During the Soviet era, Lubianka, the KGB's headquarters and infamous prison cells in Moscow's Dzerzhinsky Square, was well known, but the KGB's foreign spies were housed in a modern complex in Yasenevo, in a wooded area off the Moscow ring road. When the Soviet Union collapsed in 1991, the KGB's foreign espionage arm became the SVR, and the SVR headquarters remained in Yasenevo.

The buildings bear a remarkable resemblance to the CIA headquarters in Langley, Virginia. Like the CIA, the Russian spies are out in the woods, away from the capital. Its officers call their headquarters the *les,* meaning "the forest," or "the Russian Langley."

The two countries use similar espionage tradecraft. For example, the Soviets, and now the Russians, typically assign most of their intelligence officers to embassies around the world under diplomatic cover. The CIA does the same.

Like the CIA, Russian intelligence officers under embassy cover attempt to recruit agents, individuals in the host country who have access to military, intelligence, or diplomatic secrets. Usually, the agents are paid for their services. They may betray their country for a variety of reasons; for money, because they feel their talents are undervalued, for ideological or other reasons, or a combination of motives.

When an agent is recruited, the intelligence officer, or IO, faces the problem of how to communicate with the agent. In the wiretap age, telephone and e-mail are hardly secure modes of contact. So various methods have been developed to allow spies and their handlers to communicate undetected.

One method used by both the Russians and the CIA is the dead drop, a hiding place in a hollow tree, under a rock, or in a wall, for example. The agent places documents, microfilms, or a computer disk or digital memory card in the dead drop, which is later "cleared" by the intelligence officer. The dead drop is also used by the IO to relay instructions to the spy. Often when a drop is cleared, a signal is left, a piece of tape or a chalk mark on a telephone pole, for example.

China does not use dead drops. Its spies do not spend their time putting chalk marks on mailboxes, as the CIA's Aldrich Ames did to signal the KGB that a drop in which he had hidden documents was ready to be unloaded. China's intelligence officers under diplomatic cover are rarely caught spying, for a simple reason — they normally do not recruit and run agents.

"China has a different approach to intelligence," said Paul Moore, who has spent a lot of time studying the difference between Chinese espionage tradecraft and that of other countries. "There is also the question of what China is not doing," he explained. "For example, China normally does not pay money for intelligence. The Russians pay money, everybody pays money, but as a rule the Chinese don't.

"The typical Chinese way is, you help the Chinese, they help you to develop an export business to sell cheap salad bowls to Kmart. Ordinarily China doesn't give money in return for information.

"We are looking for intelligence relationships," Moore said, "but the problem we ran into is that China doesn't really develop intelligence relationships with people. China develops general relationships with people that may have an intelligence dimension."

Instead of recruiting agents, the MSS often relies on informal contacts to collect intelligence. It co-opts some of the thousands of students, tourists, business travelers, trade delegations, and scientists who visit the United States every year. It also rolls out the red carpet for American scientists visiting China, hoping to nudge them into revealing secrets.

According to Moore, the Chinese employ a technique against visitors that is carefully designed to leave them exhausted and weaken their defenses. "It's been common enough for the Chinese to arrange a grueling day of tourism for visitors, followed by an evening cocktail reception," he said. Fortified by a drink or two, the visitor might be approached "by a graduate student seeking research assistance, repeating a question that the visitor had previously been unwilling to answer when asked by a senior Chinese colleague.

"In other words, China doesn't so much try to steal secrets as to try to induce foreign visitors to give them away by manipulating them into certain situations." The visitor, Moore adds, may be pitched with statements such as, "Scientific information should recognize no political boundaries."

In Moore's view, "the principle that the Chinese apply is simple: people will almost never commit espionage, but they will often enough be indiscreet if they can be put in the right circumstances. The root problem is people making mistakes, rather than people committing espionage."

That in turn creates a hurdle for US counterintelligence. "The problem for American investigators and prosecutors is not to determine whether someone under investigation has provided information to China, but to prove somehow that he told the Chinese three things when he was authorized to discuss only two."

John F. Lewis Jr. was assistant director of the FBI in charge of the national security division, and worked in counterintelligence for nearly three decades. In dealing with Chinese operations, he said, "You may be talking about a different kind of espionage, where scientists get together and there may not even be an exchange of documents. An exchange of ideas and ways to solve problems. There is the heart of the problem. With unfettered travel back and forth to mainland China, in many cases scientists may not even be aware of what the hell is happening."

Nicholas Eftimiades, a China analyst for the Defense Intelligence Agency, told the congressional Joint Economic Committee that it is easy to tell the difference between a Chinese intelligence officer and a co-opted scientist — intelligence officers sent abroad generally lack technical knowledge, and the scientists co-opted by the MSS usually have no training in clandestine work. "For example, at a trade show in Paris, French military investigators observed members of a Chinese scientific delegation discreetly dipping their ties in a photo processing solution made by the German firm Agfa. The goal of this clumsy act of espionage was presumably to obtain specimens of the solution for later analysis."

The DIA analyst testified that foreign visitors in China are subject to the "aggressive use of technical surveillance measures." Many of the better hotels that cater to foreigners are equipped with bugs and cameras to record their activities. "Surveillance of foreigners in these and other Chinese hotels is carried out by the MSS's technical operations department," he said. "According to Chinese prostitutes who frequent the Jianguo Hotel, the guest rooms used by foreign businessmen there also contain microphones."

Spying is often described as the world's second oldest profession. And China, like many other countries, has used sex for purposes of espionage or blackmail.

By far the most bizarre example of the use of sex by Chinese intelligence is the case of Bernard Boursicot, a French diplomat in China who for twenty years carried on a love affair with Shi Peipu, a famous singer at the Beijing Opera, where female roles are often played by men. There was one little problem with the woman Boursicot considered the love of his life: she was a man.

Boursicot was arrested in Paris in 1983 and tried with Shi, who had moved there and was living with him. The diplomat testified that an officer of Chinese intelligence, whom he knew only as "Kang," had approached him in Beijing and said he would be allowed to continue the affair only if he provided information from the French embassy. He did, giving 150 documents to Shi, who passed them to Kang.

At his trial, when the judge asked how Boursicot, a Frenchman, after all, could have been fooled for twenty years, he testified, "I was shattered to learn that he is a man." Their sexual encounters, he explained further, had been fast and always in the dark. "He was very shy," Boursicot said. "I thought it was a Chinese custom."

Boursicot and Shi Peipu were sentenced to six years in prison. In 1987 President François Mitterrand pardoned Shi, but not Boursicot. The following year their affair became the basis for a hit Broadway play, *M. Butterfly*, by David Hwang, with a musical nod to Giacomo Puccini. In 1993 it became a film starring Jeremy Irons.

Diplomats who stray make easy targets, but Chinese intelligence operations are rarely that predictable. Because of the way China spies, it is harder for US counterintelligence to discover evidence of espionage. "If they don't pay money that means there's no money trail to follow," Paul Moore points out. "Bank accounts don't help you. If a case moves into a criminal investigation, how are you going to prove it to a jury?

"China is not interested in working with people motivated by revenge. We [the United States] love revenge as a motivating factor. Historically, the number one reason people betray the US is money, and the second reason is revenge. It is not normal Chinese practice to deal with people who have psychological or emotional problems, people who are misfits, or lonely."

Whenever a mole is discovered inside US intelligence, the counterintelligence experts try to determine what factors led to the betrayal and might have been detected in advance. Aldrich Ames, the CIA Soviet counterintelligence officer, had a severe drinking problem. So did Edward Lee Howard, the CIA officer who fled to Moscow in 1985 after betraying the agency's secrets to the KGB.

But looking for employees inside American intelligence who have a severe drinking problem or some other personal aberration would in all likelihood not help to uncover a Chinese mole inside the CIA, the FBI, or the national weapons labs. Because China would normally prefer not to deal with them.

Moore elaborated on the point. "To protect our country we have all the CI [counterintelligence] units in the government, and the security guys, the polygraph operators, and they ask about drinking and money, and talk to neighbors for background information. All the security guys are looking for vulnerabilities. If the Chinese are not looking for people with vulnerabilities, when we screen out people with vulnerabilities we don't find the people they are using."

For twenty years, Moore was the FBI's chief China analyst, toiling away in the bureau's CI-3B unit at headquarters. He developed a set of two dozen rules that he believed could apply to Chinese intelligence cases. Three are of particular importance.

First, China does not, in most instances, offer money in exchange for information.

Second, China does not accept typical walk-in cases, because of the possibility that "volunteers" are being dangled as bait by an opposition intelligence service. By contrast, some of the KGB's biggest coups came from walk-ins, not only Ames but John A. Walker Jr., a former Navy chief warrant officer who, with his son, brother, and a friend, sold the Navy's codes and spied for the Soviets for eighteen years.*

Moore's third rule is that China "collects information from good people, people who don't have financial problems, don't have emotional problems, who are not motivated by revenge, not unsuccessful in their lives. Not someone who is lonely, needs a friend, needs a woman.

"China is looking to get good people to do bad things. How do you recruit a good person? You get a good person to do this by convincing him it would be good to help China. China is a poor country, they say, and somebody has to help them modernize, improve their defense system. We need people to help us a little bit. The idea is to convince someone that what he is actually doing is good. You don't talk about the fact that he would be betraying a trust. They say, 'We think you have an affirmative obligation to help China modernize.'

"The metaphor is sex: you are trying to woo a woman and get her to go to bed. At least in my time, if you said would you go upstairs and have sex, the answer was usually no. But getting a kiss, the answer might be different. You would try to build from that kiss onward to greater things. That's what's going on here, seduction. The targets are being led astray in small increments. You have little bits of espionage."

According to Nicholas Eftimiades, China's economic espionage follows a three-pronged pattern. First, persons are recruited in China and asked to acquire specific technological information when they travel abroad. Second, some American technology companies "are purchased outright by Chinese state-run firms." And third, high-tech equipment is purchased by front companies, often operating out of Hong Kong.

One survey prepared for government agencies, the *Intelligence*

---

* Walker was arrested May 20, 1985, pleaded guilty, and was convicted and sentenced in 1986 to life in prison, as were his brother Arthur and friend Jerry A. Whitworth. Walker's son Michael was sentenced to twenty-five years. All had served in the Navy. Boris A. Solomatin, a gray-haired man with hawklike features, was the KGB *rezident* in Washington in the mid-1960s when Walker appeared in the Soviet embassy to offer his services. Interviewed by the author in Moscow in 1991, Solomatin was asked when he knew for sure that Walker was not a plant. "After he showed me the code keys," Solomatin replied.

*Threat Handbook,* estimates that China has more than 2,600 diplomatic and commercial officials in the United States, of whom a "substantial percentage" are "actively involved in collecting intelligence." More than 127,000 students from the People's Republic of China attend schools in the United States, "and many of these students have been tasked to collect information by the Chinese government," the handbook asserts. In addition, "over 25,000 Chinese visit the United States each year as members of official delegations."

American technology continues to be a major focus of Chinese espionage in the United States. A great many cases of espionage or technology transfer to China are centered in California, with its large defense and aerospace industries, and the computer-technology companies centered in Silicon Valley. All are tempting targets for Beijing.

California also has by far the nation's largest ethnic Chinese population, a total of 1.2 million people, by the latest Census Bureau survey released in 2010. That in turn creates a delicate problem for FBI counterintelligence agents investigating possible espionage cases in California that involve ethnic Chinese. Without question, the vast majority of the 3 million people of Chinese background in the United States are loyal Americans.* It is a fact of life, however, that China often tries to enlist ethnic Chinese in its intelligence efforts.

A joint CIA/FBI report to Congress in 1999 touched on the sensitive issue. "Because most Chinese share a common cultural and historical background, Chinese leaders refer to all individuals of Chinese ancestry as 'overseas' Chinese. When approaching an individual of Chinese origin, the Chinese intelligence services attempt to secure his or her cooperation by playing on this shared ancestry."

Bruce Carlson, a Chinese counterintelligence specialist who headed the China section of the FBI from 2006 to 2008, makes a distinction between immigrants and later generations. "It's true that China targets ethnic Chinese," he said. "When immigrants first come here they have 'one foot in each boat,' or so China thinks. They may be more

---

* According to the Census Bureau survey released in December 2010, of the total of 3,204,379 Chinese in the United States, 994,041 are native born and 1,342,973 are naturalized US citizens, so a total of 2,337,014, or 72.9 percent, are American citizens.

approachable by the PRC. It's easier to appeal to the motherland with immigrants. But it's much harder to appeal to the motherland with the second generation, and with those who do not speak Chinese. They are no more likely to commit espionage than any other American."

Paul Moore said that Chinese intelligence has been successful in persuading some people to "help China modernize." According to Moore, "It turns out in agent cases where China developed someone to provide information, 98 percent were ethnic Chinese, 2 percent were not. Even the 2 percent felt an obligation to help China modernize. Normally these were people who had studied Chinese, traveled to China, or bought into Chinese culture.

"Chinese agent cases, where they recruit an agent, are mostly ethnic. Are we looking for the Chinese espionage gene? Everybody realizes that's ridiculous. The Chinese are running in their mainstream ops a program that collects intelligence but is not really an intelligence program. They want to develop relations with people who think they have an obligation to help China modernize. And who will make a little contribution. This is their sales pitch. And it turns out it will only resonate with people who have Chinese ancestry. It won't resonate with the McGillicuddys because the McGillicuddys don't give a shit about helping China modernize. What's really going on here is a marketing campaign, to sell China. It doesn't work very well, the answer usually is no. It's about as successful as telemarketing. This is a campaign which is not very efficient.

"Most who do cooperate with China are FOB, fresh off the boat, first-generation immigrants. Their grandchildren are no more susceptible than the O'Reillys or the Kowalskis. This is not a Chinese thing — it is a Chinese-immigrant thing. They are doing it because they feel it's the right thing to do."

US counterintelligence officials pursuing a spy suspect may overlook a broader point, Moore contended. "China was collecting information from the national labs and they were very successful in doing that. When the Chinese collect we lose, they gain, and they create a capability to do it again. We usually are so focused on the specifics of what they may be getting that we lose sight of the most important part — which is they are developing a capability to do it again."

Moore offered a final thought about the difficulties of catching China's spies. "Normally the Chinese are able to commit espionage against the US without leaving evidence behind," he said. "If you do have enough evidence to make a case, normally somebody in China has made a mistake."

## Chapter 2

# PARLOR MAID

IN DECEMBER 1990, their work in China done, Bill Cleveland and I. C. Smith returned to the United States. Several weeks later, Cleveland called Smith from San Francisco. "I. C., they knew we were coming before we even left," he said.

It was true. The proof was contained in an audiotape, made months earlier, that the government possessed but had not yet analyzed. Counterintelligence agents didn't realize what they had. The tape was an intercept by the National Security Agency of a conversation in Mandarin between a woman in Los Angeles, who used the code name Luo, and her MSS handler in Beijing, named, of all things, Mao.

The NSA, based in Fort Meade, Maryland, forwarded the tape to FBI headquarters in Washington. From there, it was sent on to the San Francisco field office, where most of the bureau's Chinese translators are based. Which is why, early in 1991, the tape eventually made its way to the desk of Bill Cleveland, chief of the Chinese counterintelligence squad in San Francisco.

Among other matters, the woman on the tape revealed to Mao that William Cleveland of the FBI was planning a trip to China — the trip from which he had just returned. The words on the tape were a bombshell.

Cleveland's heart sank, because he instantly recognized the woman's voice as that of Katrina Leung. Her friends knew her only as a high-profile leader of the Chinese American community in Los Angeles. But for almost two decades, she would serve as the FBI's premier secret source of intelligence on China, the Communist Party leadership in Beijing, and the MSS. For her services, the FBI would pay her more than $1.7 million.

Cleveland knew the voice on the audiotape right away because he was familiar, in fact intimately familiar, with the voice. He had become Katrina Leung's lover three years earlier.

Leung had been recruited in Los Angeles in 1982 by another FBI man, Special Agent James J. Smith, and given the code name PARLOR MAID. Since bureau informants are assigned a secret three-digit code name, Leung was also carried on the FBI rolls as "Bureau Source 410." She was thirty-one; J.J., as he was universally known, was eight years older.

Almost from the start, J.J. had begun a sexual relationship of his own with Ms. Leung, whose biochemist husband, Kam, would later insist that he was unaware as the years rolled by that he was sharing his wife with not one but two agents of the Federal Bureau of Investigation.

It was J.J. who introduced Katrina Leung to Cleveland. Whether Cleveland or J.J., both of whom were married, knew of each other's simultaneous affairs with the same woman is uncertain, although apparently they did not. What is clear is that PARLOR MAID frequently strayed from the parlor into the bedroom.

Whether PARLOR MAID acted on her own in having sex with the two FBI agents who worked with her or whether she was encouraged to do so by the MSS is unknown. But the sexual relationships did give her leverage over the two FBI men, who wanted the affairs to remain secret.

Although J.J. would give her instructions, questions to ask Chinese officials, and tidbits of information she was authorized to disclose to Chinese intelligence, Cleveland's trip to China was not among these items. She knew about the trip because Cleveland had told her he was going. The voice on the tape also revealed details of FBI counterintelligence operations.

The tape was a chilling discovery for reasons that were immediately obvious to Cleveland. First, it indicated that PARLOR MAID had been doubled back against the FBI and was working for Beijing. Second, it might explain why the target of the TIGER TRAP investigation had turned up in Shenyang.

Running into Gwo-bao Min was unsettling enough to Cleveland, but this was a lot worse. Who knew where it might lead? If PARLOR MAID had been flipped by the MSS, it was a counterintelligence disaster for the FBI. But it might also drag him down if the truth about his personal relationship with a bureau asset should ever become known. Not to mention what might happen if his wife found out.

Cleveland knew there could be no innocent explanation of why his lover, the FBI's top spy against China, was using a code name and spilling secrets to her MSS handler in Beijing. He was in big trouble, and he knew what had to be done.

He reached for the telephone.

Cleveland spoke elliptically, but his message was clear: Katrina Leung, using an alias, had switched sides. She was working for the Chinese intelligence service.

In Los Angeles, J.J. Smith was stunned by the call. He trusted Katrina Leung. They had been lovers for eight years now, and he cared about her. In addition to their emotional and physical bond, she was his golden source.

If PARLOR MAID was now a spy for the MSS, it raised all sorts of extremely awkward problems for Special Agent Smith. J.J.'s career and reputation in the bureau had been built on his extraordinary recruitment, Katrina Leung. Because of PARLOR MAID, J.J. was a star. The FBI had already paid her well over half a million dollars in expenses and salary.

Leung traveled to China to gather intelligence for the FBI as often as two or three times a year. But Washington regarded her reporting as well worth the money — Katrina Leung was the US intelligence community's secret pipeline into the leadership in Beijing.*

The dilemma Smith now faced was excruciating. PARLOR MAID's highly classified information had, in some cases, gone all the way up to the president of the United States. Her reporting, through J.J., had undoubtedly influenced America's China policy. Now it was all suspect; who knew how long she had been an asset of the MSS?

Only a year earlier, J.J. had received a prestigious secret CIA medal for his recruitment and handling of PARLOR MAID. He had flown to Washington for the ceremony. At a CIA safe house near the White House, in recognition of his intelligence coup, a high CIA official had pinned on him the HUMINT Collector of the Year Award (HUMINT is the CIA's acronym for human intelligence, as opposed to ELINT, electronic espionage).

To shut down the operation now would be a personal and professional catastrophe for J.J. And, not least, it would almost certainly mean the end of his long-running frolic with PARLOR MAID. Smith headed to the Los Angeles International Airport and scrambled aboard the next plane to San Francisco. Once there, he huddled with Bill Cleveland. They began to contrive a plan to deal with the disaster.

The fact that PARLOR MAID was being run by the bureau as a double agent might contain the seeds of salvation for the two FBI men. As such, she was authorized to tell the MSS that she had contacts in the FBI and to pretend to help the Chinese service while remaining under the FBI's control. So there was the key. After all, J.J. knew, double agents sometimes got a little confused about whom they were work-

---

* It is commonly assumed that the CIA is confined to operating overseas and the FBI to activities in the United States. In reality, the lines are blurred. The FBI has attachés in seventy-five foreign cities and, as the PARLOR MAID case illustrates, it can run intelligence agents abroad. Although by law the CIA has no police, law enforcement, or internal security powers, it maintains offices in major cities across America that recruit foreign students, debrief travelers returning from places of interest overseas, and conduct other operations related to foreign intelligence.

ing for. The nature of the game was to give away information to see what could be learned in return. Katrina Leung was six thousand miles from home when she visited China. There were times when double agents had to think on their feet, improvise. They might reveal to the opposition a little more than they were supposed to tell. It was a long shot, but perhaps, after all, this thing could be smoothed over.

In May 1991, a month after the unwelcome tape surfaced, J.J. and Cleveland flew to Washington to discuss the PARLOR MAID problem with their FBI superiors. The meeting took place on May 14 in a conference room at FBI headquarters. Other than the date, the details are enveloped by fog. Bureau officials say they have no record of who was at the meeting, and — with one exception — none of those who might logically be expected to have attended can remember being there. Despite the rampant amnesia, somebody must have met with the pair, because a decision was made.

The one exception was Paul Moore, then the FBI's top China analyst and a thirteen-year bureau veteran. A thoughtful, soft-spoken man, Moore had a PhD in Chinese literature and spoke Mandarin.

J.J. and Cleveland reported to the meeting how PARLOR MAID, using a Chinese code name, had told her MSS handler in advance about Cleveland's trip to China. There was no mention made of the ongoing FBI operations she had discussed on the tape, which actually contained a series of conversations between Luo and Mao.

Moore and the other officials in the room were unaware that both J.J. and Cleveland were sexually involved with their asset, a gross violation of bureau rules.

Weighing the risks and benefits of continuing the PARLOR MAID operation, Moore reached a conclusion he was later to regret. "I made the recommendation we move forward with the case. I asked, 'What's the worst-case scenario?' That was a mistake on my part because there was a worst case. But I didn't know that."

There was much more that Moore did not know. In 1988 China

had opened a consulate at 443 Shatto Place, in the Wilshire district three miles west of downtown Los Angeles. Officials in China's San Francisco consulate consulted Katrina Leung on the project, and she advised them on the best location for the facility. One of the officials from San Francisco, Wang Do Han, came to Los Angeles and worked with her on preparations for the consulate, which was housed in a new building with Fort Knox–like security.

The FBI was elated that PARLOR MAID had become involved in the location and planning of the consulate. She was told to try to persuade the Chinese to purchase cars with sunroofs, to make it easier to identify and track them from the air.

For the FBI, the new consulate offered a target too tempting to ignore. In an operation orchestrated by Lance Woo, a supervisor in the FBI's Los Angeles office, the bureau's electronics experts, using super-sophisticated technology that is still highly classified, managed to penetrate the consulate. Every phone call, fax, e-mail, and communication leaving the building was broadcast to the FBI. It was one of the bureau's most successful technical coups.

But in June 1990 the FBI received intelligence that PARLOR MAID had learned about the electronic operation directed at the consulate and tipped off the People's Republic of China. The PRC must have discovered that the consulate had been compromised, because the FBI's listening devices suddenly went silent.

There was no real investigation of Leung's suspected role, in large part because of J.J. Smith's exalted stature in the Chinese counterintelligence program. PARLOR MAID was considered a supreme source, and Smith's superiors hesitated to challenge him.

But the Chinese did not discover all of the FBI's surveillance techniques. Well after 1990, the FBI was able to obtain copies of checks and documents written inside the consulate. The implication was that the FBI's technicians had even managed to bug the consulate's copying machines. The Chinese finally figured out what was happening, because in the fall of 1999 consulate officials, suspecting that the machines had been compromised, shipped them back to China to be analyzed by their own experts.

The fact that the FBI's technicians had succeeded in bugging the consulate's copying machines almost leaked out in 1998 when *Newsweek* published a one-paragraph item in its issue of March 2. The brief story, headlined "A Check from China?" reported that a Senate committee headed by Senator Fred Thompson discovered that the Chinese consulate in Los Angeles had written a $3,000 check to a hotel owned by Indonesian-born businessman Ted Sioeng, one of the figures in the investigation of alleged illegal money flowing into President Clinton's 1996 reelection campaign. The Senate committee suspected Sioeng of having acted as an agent of China in funneling money into the campaign. The FBI held its breath, because its secret was teetering right on the edge of disclosure. How could a check written inside the consulate be floating around on the outside? No one realized the obvious answer. The Chinese had meticulously photocopied the check for their records — and they had unwittingly transmitted a copy to the FBI. Despite the *Newsweek* item, the bureau's secret held.

In the meeting at FBI headquarters, Moore was unaware that the FBI had evidence that Leung had blown the consulate eavesdropping operation. His expertise on China was well respected in the bureau and his recommendation that the bureau continue to run PARLOR MAID carried considerable weight.

He recalled the position he took at the 1991 meeting. "Here's a woman who's traveling to China, she has established contacts with senior people, including President Yang Shangkun's assistant for intelligence, she's bringing back a lot of information from China to us. They know she gets interviewed by the FBI. The argument I made is, OK, we close this case down — and obviously she has something going with the Chinese she hasn't told us about — if we close it down, does she stop going to China? The impact is she's going to stop telling us stuff out of the president's office in China. So I said let's go forward, and other people in the room were OK with that."

J.J. Smith and Bill Cleveland were ecstatic as they left FBI headquarters. They had dodged the bullet. From their point of view, the meeting could not have gone any better.

Back in California, however, there was still one detail remaining. J.J. needed to deal with PARLOR MAID. She would have to be told that the

FBI was now aware that she had been secretly slipping information to the MSS.

On May 31, J.J. confronted Katrina Leung. In an angry, emotional shouting match in the kitchen of her home in San Marino, he told her that he knew about her conversation with Mao. The CIA had identified Mao as an intelligence officer. And PARLOR MAID's MSS handler was no ordinary spy. Mao Guohua, as he called himself — that may or may not have been his real name — was regarded as the MSS's leading US expert, roughly equivalent to the chief of a CIA geographic division. How he rose to that position was unclear, since his English was atrocious and he had, as far as is known, never traveled to the United States.

J.J. produced the transcript of the telephone call. If Leung had entertained any doubt, she now realized that her incautious call to Beijing had been intercepted. J.J. and the FBI knew exactly what she had said to Mao. There was no place to hide; she had to come up with an explanation for Smith.

She then confessed that Mao Guohua had learned some years earlier that she was an FBI asset. She claimed it happened when, on a trip to China perhaps around 1986 or 1987 — the date is unclear — she took with her notes that she and J.J. had prepared about a Chinese defector to the United States. The notes were in her luggage.

When Leung, en route to Beijing, crossed from a province in southern China to the next, the internal border guards pulled her aside, searched her luggage, and found the notes. On another trip to China a month later, Mao confronted her. He had her notes in hand. They were more detailed than what she had told him about the defector.

By Leung's account, she then admitted to Mao that she was working for the FBI. She also agreed from then on to provide everything she knew about FBI operations to the MSS. Mao ordered her to tell the MSS in advance of all plans by FBI agents to travel to China.

Since she had been working for the FBI since 1982, it was dubious that Chinese intelligence had tumbled to that fact only after four or five years, particularly since J.J. and Leung were often seen together at dinners and other functions around Los Angeles. Hobnobbing in public with the FBI raised Leung's stature in the Chinese American community. But by fixing the mid- to late 1980s as the probable date that the MSS had discovered her role, Leung avoided the issue of whether she had been passing secrets to Beijing even prior to that time.

She admitted that she had told the MSS about Bill Cleveland's pending trip to China. For this infraction, J.J., bizarrely, made her apologize to Cleveland in a San Francisco hotel room. And that was it; PARLOR MAID, the swinging spy, was back in business.

# Chapter 3

# THE RECRUITMENT

GUANGZHOU, FORMERLY CANTON, known as the Flower City or, less poetically, as the Goat City, is a bustling port on the Pearl River in South China, not far from Hong Kong. It was there that Katrina Leung was born, probably in 1952, although she was known to shave two or three years off her age. Her name at birth was Chen Wen Ying; like many Chinese who immigrate to America, she later chose an English first name.

She was the youngest of four children of a dam engineer who traveled a good deal. When she was an infant, her aunt and uncle lost a baby. Her mother, Chen Wu Yueh, offered them Katrina as a replacement, a practice not unknown in China. As a result of the Gilbert and Sullivan–like baby switch, Katrina was raised largely by her aunt, Shuet Ying Young, who was married to her mother's brother.

When Katrina was around three, she moved with her aunt, an older brother, and her grandmother to Hong Kong. "Katrina sleepwalks," according to her husband, Kam Leung, a tall, handsome man with a graying crewcut and cultivated manner. "In Hong Kong they lived on the fourteenth floor, in a penthouse. Her aunt would find her sleeping on the ledge of the balcony of their apartment." Even at that early age,

Katrina was living on the edge; had she rolled over the wrong way, the FBI would have been deprived of its most celebrated Chinese intelligence asset — and, as matters turned out, an unwelcome spy scandal.

Her family background had elements of a soap opera. In the 1930s Katrina's grandfather had immigrated to New York. He opened a laundry on Long Island and eventually owned two restaurants in lower Manhattan. His son, Jimmy Gai Chin, Katrina Leung's uncle and surrogate father, joined him in New York. With his wife back in Hong Kong, the uncle took up with a barmaid and sired two boys. The barmaid moved to England with the children, became ill, and died; the boys, ages six and four, were returned to New York. The uncle, suddenly finding himself a single parent, called on his wife for help, and Katrina, her aunt, and grandmother joined him in Manhattan in 1970. Katrina traveled on a Taiwanese passport that said she was born on May 1, 1954, in Canton, China.

They moved into an apartment at 137 Chrystie Street. "She enrolled in Washington Irving High School, and from three to midnight worked in a sewing factory," Kam Leung said. "She got mugged twice walking home at night."

In 1972, the same year Katrina graduated from high school and became a permanent resident, she was accepted at Cornell University on a scholarship. There she met Kam Leung, a graduate student in biochemistry. He recalled the moment.

"The first weekend I went there I saw a flyer, 'Upper Buttermilk Falls, Chinese Student Association Picnic.' I went, and there was a little girl wearing almond-shaped tinted eyeglasses and pigtails. She said, 'I'm very cold.' So even I could figure that out so I took off my pea coat and gave it to her.

"A week later I found her crying in the lobby of the International Student House. She was lonely and homesick, so that is how we went on our first date. We went to see the movie *Butterflies Are Free*."

They lived together for three years before marrying in 1975. "I was too poor for a wedding ring so neither of us wear wedding rings."

Kam Leung was born in Hong Kong in 1951; his father, a graduate of a military school in China, had been posted to a train station near

Canton. "When the Japanese invaded, he was in charge of the last train out of China. He rescued the safe of Ho Tim, who founded the Hang Seng Bank in Hong Kong, and probably saved his fortune."

In 1969, when Kam Leung was eighteen, he came to the United States to study chemistry at Sam Houston State University, in Huntsville, Texas. He went on to Cornell in 1972 to earn a PhD in biochemistry.

In lengthy interviews over two days, Kam Leung came across as both astute and sophisticated as he described in great detail his life with Katrina. He was also, to all outward appearances, and despite his wife's infidelities, still hopelessly in love with her.

"She is brilliant," he said. "She was always the head of the class. She is generous to a fault." What had attracted him to her? "She's helpless," he replied. "She is extremely insecure inside. I recognized the little girl inside of her, crying out."

There is, of course, a startling disconnect between Kam Leung's gauzy view of the helpless little girl in pigtails who captured his heart at Cornell and the tough-minded, deceptive, and ambitious woman who ended up earning millions as a double agent and a spy for both the FBI and Beijing.

Katrina Leung graduated from Cornell in 1976, and her husband won a research fellowship at the University of Chicago. "She just followed me and hung around the Chinese student center." But 1976, Kam said, "was the beginning of her troubles. Katrina helped to found the Chicago chapter of the National Association of Chinese Americans. It was considered a pro-Beijing group."

And it was in Chicago that Katrina met and became a close friend of Hanson Huang, a smooth graduate of Harvard College and Harvard Law School who had landed a job in that city with Baker & McKenzie, a prestigious international law firm. Huang, who was born in Hong Kong in 1951, and Katrina Leung were both active in support of China in the Diaoyutai Islands student movement.

The islands—in Chinese, *diaoyutai* means "to catch fish"—are a string of eight barren and uninhabited isles in the East China Sea about one hundred miles northeast of Taiwan. They are claimed by China, Japan, which calls them the Senkaku, and Taiwan. During the

1970s, Chinese students around the world joined in a movement to protest Japan's claims to the islands.*

In 1976 Kam Leung completed his PhD and moved to Cincinnati to take a job at Procter & Gamble. Katrina remained behind and earned a master's in business administration at the University of Chicago. Kam visited her on weekends.

In 1980 the couple moved to Los Angeles and took a studio apartment in Azusa, in the foothills of the San Gabriel Mountains east of downtown. Kam went to work as a research scientist for a medical equipment company. "I was killing mice, fifteen hundred mice a week for the lab, injecting them." Katrina got a marketing job with an HMO.

Before that, however, she briefly worked as general manager of an import-export company. The FBI investigated the firm because it was suspected of illegally transferring technology to China. Early in 1981 the FBI began a full field investigation of Katrina herself, who was "believed to be engaged in clandestine intelligence gathering on behalf of the PRC." That investigation languished in the FBI bureaucracy and the case was closed, with no action taken, in November of that year.

At the same time, the bureau learned that Katrina Leung had a close relationship with the target of another case of suspected technology transfer to China, this one in San Francisco. William Cleveland was the case agent; in Los Angeles, J.J. Smith was assigned to the investigation.

A year later, in August 1982, J.J. knocked on the door of the apartment in Azusa. He identified himself as a special agent of the FBI.

It was the beginning of the dance, an intelligence tango that sometimes ends with the recruitment of a useful source. It might seem astonishing, even reckless, that the FBI would try to recruit someone who it believed might be spying for China. But in "the wilderness of mirrors," as counterintelligence is often called, it was not entirely

---

* More than three decades later, the islands were still a flashpoint. Tensions flared anew over the Diaoyutai/Senkakus in September 2010 when Japan's coast guard arrested the captain of a Chinese fishing trawler whose boat collided with the Japanese patrol vessels in the disputed waters near the islands. The Chinese captain was released after sixteen days, but the incident touched off mass protests in China and angry diplomatic exchanges between the two countries.

strange. The recruiter looks for a person who already has contacts with the target. And calculates the risk.

Over the next four months, J.J. interviewed Katrina several times. By December, she had accepted J.J.'s offer.

Soon afterward, according to Kam, "We were sitting by a lake. She said, 'I'm going to quit my job to work for the FBI.'"

# Chapter 4

# DOUBLE GAME

THERE ARE TIMES when a single act can be a turning point in a life. Everything else that happens flows from that moment. J.J. Smith's recruitment of PARLOR MAID was just such a pivotal juncture. He had been a special agent of the FBI for a dozen years. He was thirty-eight; Katrina Leung had just turned thirty-one a month earlier.

J.J. was a big man, almost six feet, stocky and muscular, proud of his blue-collar background. His father was a bricklayer for forty-five years. His grandparents on his father's side were German farmers; his maternal grandmother, who was Mexican, had married a Scotch-Irish fireman.

He and his wife, Gail, a former Daffodil Queen in Washington State, were married in 1966. In the summer of 1967, after graduating from the University of Puget Sound, he was about to be drafted when he encountered a buddy, Doug Walker, who had an idea.

"Let's sign up for Army Intelligence," Walker suggested, "and we'll both end up drinking beer in Germany." Instead, they were trained as intelligence officers and sent to Vietnam. J.J. was assigned to the 515 Military Intelligence Group in Quang Ngai, a Viet Cong stronghold, running double agents in a program code-named 97 CHARLIE.

Back at Fort Bragg, North Carolina, a local FBI agent in Fayetteville recruited him for the bureau, which he joined in 1970. He wound up in Los Angeles, and by 1975 he was handling Chinese counterintelligence cases.

Foreign counterintelligence, or FCI, in bureau terminology, was not a popular career path inside the FBI. "Young agents out of Quantico, all full of piss and vinegar, they wanted bank robberies, criminal cases," said John L. Hoos, a former FBI agent who worked with J.J. "But J.J. was a rare duck, he went into FCI and stayed in FCI."

J.J., he added, "was very likable, with a good sense of humor, he was very dedicated to his work, respected by the other agents. He was well versed in Chinese counterintelligence — a walking encyclopedia on cases, procedures. If you had a question, ask J.J."

By the time J.J. recruited PARLOR MAID in 1982, he had achieved an unusual degree of independence within the FBI field office. His supervisors indulged him and deferred to his expertise on matters Chinese. Although FBI agents are often moved around, because of J.J.'s stature he was able to remain in Los Angeles. With his wife, Gail, and their young son, Kelly, J.J. settled down in Westlake Village, a comfortable suburb.

Although at first Katrina Leung was only an IA, the FBI's designation for an informational asset, J.J. quickly realized her potential as a bureau source. It did not take long for their professional relationship to turn personal. By August 1983 they had hopped into bed.

One of the reasons that J.J. had recruited Katrina was her friendship from Chicago days with Hanson Huang, who had gone to China to work for Armand Hammer and the Occidental oil company. Although Huang was a loyal pro-PRC activist, the Chinese authorities had, ironically, begun to suspect him, perhaps because of his curiosity about the location and size of the country's oil reserves, matters considered state secrets in China. He was arrested, and in June 1983 convicted of espionage in a Beijing court and sentenced to fifteen years.

J.J.'s interest in Huang, and the FBI's, was based on more than Huang's activism in the Diaoyutai Islands student movement. For Hanson Huang had emerged as a key figure in TIGER TRAP, involving nuclear weapons, which Bill Cleveland was actively pursuing in San

Francisco with the help of J.J. in Los Angeles. Now that Huang had run afoul of Chinese intelligence, perhaps he might be willing to help the FBI.

As J.J.'s first major assignment for Katrina, he instructed her to go to China and try to wangle her way into the prison where Huang was being held. It was a tall order. In a tightly controlled Communist state, how could a foreigner manage to visit a prisoner serving time for espionage? That she accomplished that feat might have been expected to raise an eyebrow both with J.J. and the bureau. It did not; J.J.'s first reporting to headquarters from PARLOR MAID was a summary of what she had learned on her prison visit.

I. C. Smith, who was not related to J.J., was then working in the China unit at FBI headquarters in Washington. "J.J. had sent me an airtel and she, Katrina Leung, had all this reporting on her first trip to China in 1983 about Hanson Huang, who was in jail. I said this was a bunch of crap because it's got sex and intrigue and everything but intel. I said, 'Dammit, J.J., where's the fucking beef?'"

"Don't worry, it's coming," J.J. assured him.

I.C.'s annoyance may have been partly rooted in the fact that J.J. seemed to walk on water in the bureau. "J.J. had an LA attitude," I.C. said. "He flaunted the rules. He could get by without wearing a coat and tie. He had this great source, and it made him bulletproof."

By this time, PARLOR MAID had graduated to the status of an OA, or operational asset in FBI jargon. As an IA, she provided information to the bureau; as an OA she was given specific tasks. At the same time, Leung was solidifying her contacts in the Chinese American community in Los Angeles.

In March 1984, with J.J.'s help to speed up the paperwork, she became a US citizen. That year, or soon after, Katrina moved into the big leagues as a full-fledged DA, or double agent. The bureau's plan was to let the MSS think she was working for China, while in fact she was directed and controlled by the FBI.*

---

* In Chinese, the Mandarin word for "secret agent" or "spy" is *jiandie*, although *pengyou*, which means "friend," is also commonly used. For "double agent," *shuangmian*, two characters representing two faces are added. Thus, *shuangmian jiandie* would describe a double-faced spy.

Toward that end, she was encouraged by J.J. to advertise to China her contacts with the FBI and in particular her friendship with him. She was authorized to approach the MSS in Beijing, pretending to be loyal to China. No sensitive information was supposed to be given to her by the FBI, since she was not an employee and would have had a difficult time explaining her access to bureau secrets. But the Chinese, who have been spying for at least twenty-five hundred years, since Sun Tzu wrote the book on espionage, would have quickly understood that she had been recruited by the FBI and dangled to the MSS. And anyone who had a relationship with the FBI was of great interest to the MSS.

On her visits to China, PARLOR MAID was also encouraged by J.J. to boast to the MSS and other officials about her growing status in the Chinese American community, since that, too, made her an attractive source for the Chinese intelligence service.

PARLOR MAID was usually accompanied on her trips to China by her husband and their young son. On her very first trip to Beijing, according to Kam Leung, "she knocked on the door of the MSS. She was tasked to do this."

"We went to China at least once a year, sometimes more," he said. "We went to China at least twenty years, some years two or three times."

The presence of her husband and son, Kam said, "provided the excuse to visit wherever Katrina asked to go. She would say, 'Our family have never been to Xi'an,' so they would say, 'Sure, go to Xi'an.'

"Or she would say, 'My son would love to go to Harbin, to the cold country.'" Three times, PARLOR MAID traveled to Harbin, in far northeast China near the Russian border, where the temperature was well below zero, claiming that their son "loved the Ice Lantern Festival." In fact, there was another motive; she was currying favor with the head of the MSS, who came from that city in Heilongjiang Province, as did a large number of other Chinese intelligence officers.

"I was the cameraman," her husband said. "I used a Nikon and an Olympus, eventually a Sony digicam." Kam bought the cameras and the FBI reimbursed Katrina for them. He would make a double set of prints and give one to his wife to pass on to J.J.

Some of PARLOR MAID's reports made it to the White House under presidents Ronald Reagan, Bill Clinton, and both George H. W. Bush and George W. Bush, according to intelligence officials. The high-level CIA medal that J.J. received for PARLOR MAID is evidence of how valuable her work, and his, was regarded. Until later, when it all unraveled.

As Katrina Leung was ingratiating herself with the top leaders in Beijing, she simultaneously became an increasingly prominent member of the Chinese American community in Southern California. She was active in Republican political circles as well, contributing $10,000 to Los Angeles mayor Richard J. Riordan and $4,200 to Bill Simon Jr., who defeated Riordan in the Republican primary for governor of California in 2002 but lost to Gray Davis. According to campaign finance records, the Leungs contributed some $27,000 to the Republican Party during the 1990s. Katrina Leung also contributed to at least one prominent Democrat, her friend Judy Chu, who represented heavily Chinese American Monterey Park in the state assembly.

Her entrée into the wider world of Los Angeles society was through Caroline Leonetti Ahmanson, a onetime hostess on Art Linkletter's television variety show *House Party* and the widow of Howard Fieldstead Ahmanson, a billionaire savings and loan tycoon. Caroline Ahmanson, who died in 2005, was a well-known patron of the arts in Los Angeles — the Ahmanson Theatre bears the family name — and was also active in promoting improved relations between China and the United States. She was chairwoman of the Los Angeles–Guangzhou Sister City Association, and chose Katrina Leung as president. Caroline Ahmanson was close to Zhu Rongji, the premier of China for five years until 2003, and she visited the mainland several times, accompanied by Katrina.

"Without Caroline, Katrina is just another Chinatown hustler," Kam Leung said of his wife. "Caroline introduced her into the mainstream of society."

Los Angeles businessman Peter Woo, founder and president of the toy manufacturing company Megatoys, saw evidence of Katrina Leung's clout in China firsthand. In 1996, as part of a delegation of some forty community leaders, he accompanied her and Mayor Riordan on a trip to Beijing and other cities in China to promote business for the port of Los Angeles.

"She was the one who put the trip together. She was in command. There were a couple of dinners with Chinese government officials. She emceed these events. There was a banquet at the Great Hall of the People, she was emcee of that banquet. Katrina and Mayor Riordan saw Jiang Zemin in his office. She bragged about it, she can see so-and-so any time she wants. Our impression was that she was very well connected with the Chinese government." Or as one high city official in Los Angeles put it, "When you need to get something done with China, you go to Katrina Leung."

Katrina, Woo recalled, would often show up at functions with her FBI friends. "She sometimes invited J.J. and his colleagues to dinners. There were rumors she was a spy for China. You see her with FBI agents and she introduced them to us to show there was no problem with the US government. Showing up with the FBI legitimized her status."

And working for the FBI also meant that Katrina Leung enjoyed an affluent lifestyle. Of the more than $1.7 million in expenses and salary she received from the FBI, more than half, $951,000, was paid to her *after* the FBI learned in 1991 that she had passed unauthorized information to Mao Guohua, her Chinese spymaster.

In addition, because of her known connections to the leaders in Beijing, she was approached by Nortel, a major Canadian telecom company, which paid her $1.2 million as its representative in a deal to allow Nortel and its DMS-100 digital switching systems into China.

As the FBI later discovered, the Chinese government also paid her $100,000, so that her known income from the FBI, Nortel, and the PRC amounted to more than $3 million.

With the money rolling in, the Leungs' lifestyle improved accordingly. They purchased a house for $1.4 million in San Marino, an upscale section of Los Angeles, with a garage, a swimming pool, a pond, a pool house, and four cream-colored stone lions guarding the driveway. They also owned a Chinese-language bookstore in Monterey Park and two apartment houses, and had funds in sixteen foreign bank accounts.

It was in the house in San Marino that most of the trysts between J.J. and Katrina took place. It was also at the San Marino residence that J.J. would brief PARLOR MAID on her assignments, and learn the information she brought back from her trips to China.

Where was Kam Leung during J.J.'s visits? When the FBI man came to the house, he said, "I stayed away. I didn't want a tap on the shoulder in Beijing if I knew intelligence secrets. I could have been interrogated and imprisoned. I didn't want to know what they were discussing.

"For over twenty years, J.J. would come to our house any time he wanted. Three days a week, sometimes five days a week. He would call first and say, 'Can I work?' All our relatives know they cannot come to our house without calling ahead."

J.J. had become so confident of PARLOR MAID and their partnership that he began taking classified documents to her home. TOP SE-CRET and other classified materials were stored in the FBI's Los Angeles office under tight security in a secure compartmented information facility, or SCIF (pronounced "skiff"). Usually, agents would read the documents in the SCIF. Sometimes they would check out documents to be reviewed in their offices and then returned.

Not the privileged J.J., who would stuff the documents into his briefcase and take them along to the house in San Marino. He was the only agent who, at least once, kept TOP SECRET documents overnight.

Having free run of the house in San Marino was marvelously convenient for the lovers. But it was also convenient for the MSS. J.J. would leave his briefcase open; the file folder pockets in the briefcase often contained documents with the text facing out. She could see the documents she wanted.

While the FBI man was dozing, or outside smoking, or in the bathroom, perhaps showering after they had sex, PARLOR MAID took classified documents from his briefcase and surreptitiously made copies of them on her photocopier or fax machine. Sometimes she took notes on the contents and later threw out the copies of the documents in the trash.

At other times she scribbled notes about what was in the documents without copying them. She also made notes of information that J.J. shared with her. How she could have managed all this without her lover's knowledge is somewhat baffling, but there is no evidence that J.J. realized his primo source was betraying him. Over the years, PARLOR MAID passed information to the MSS that she had stolen this way.

Even more remarkably, Katrina Leung continued to pilfer documents from J.J.'s briefcase for many years after 1991, when it had become clear to the FBI from the tape that as Luo she was reporting to the MSS.

What with J.J. dropping by so often, inevitably the Smiths and the Leungs grew close. "J.J.'s family and my family were good friends all these years," Kam said. "In 1992 we went to Hawaii together, island hopping."

And was he aware of his wife's affairs with not one but two FBI agents? He replied: "Gail [Smith] didn't know, William Cleveland's wife didn't know. And I didn't know."

## Chapter 5

# DESTROY AFTER READING

**T**HEY MADE AN unlikely cast of characters for a spy drama: Chien Ning, a mystery woman and prominent Chinese geophysicist; Hanson Huang, the Hong Kong–born, Harvard-educated lawyer and friend of Katrina Leung; and Jerry Chih-li Chen, who ran a TV repair shop in Oakland, across the bay from San Francisco.

All were key players in the espionage case that the FBI code-named TIGER TRAP. At the center of it all was Gwo-bao Min, the aerospace engineer with a Q clearance who worked at the Lawrence Livermore nuclear weapons lab — the man who would give Bill Cleveland such a start when the FBI agent encountered him in a hotel lobby in remote Shenyang.

Cleveland was the case agent, the lead FBI investigator on TIGER TRAP. He pursued the case with the help of Al Heiman, another bureau special agent in the Bay Area, and J.J. Smith in Los Angeles.

William V. Cleveland Jr. had become a leading figure in the FBI's Chinese counterintelligence program from a very different background than J.J. Smith's. He grew up in Arlington, in Northern Virginia, the son of an assistant director of the FBI under J. Edgar Hoover.

He graduated from William & Mary College and after two years in the Army joined the FBI in 1969. He was sent to the Defense Language Institute in Monterey, California, to learn Mandarin, then assigned to the China squad in the FBI office in Berkeley, and later in Oakland.

Over time, Cleveland's reputation as an expert on Chinese espionage and respect for him within the FBI grew exponentially. "He was the best I ever knew," said Ken Schiffer, a former FBI Chinese counterintelligence veteran. "I thought the world of him. He was my hero." Another former colleague put it this way: "Bill Cleveland was a god."

For all but one of his twenty-four years in the bureau, Cleveland remained in the San Francisco area. The California lifestyle suited him. Always trim, he stayed in shape by jogging every morning, in later years switching to riding a bicycle.

Cleveland was active in his church, seldom missing a Sunday, but some of his colleagues found him sanctimonious and his religious demeanor off-putting. "In Berkeley," said one, "he was holier than thou, you couldn't swear around him. One day a lot of people were crowded around a window. Somebody was getting a blowjob in a car in plain view and everybody was watching with interest and Cleveland was pounding on the window yelling, 'Stop that!'"

Inevitably, Cleveland's work brought him in contact with J.J. Smith in Los Angeles, and, of course, with PARLOR MAID. The two men were close; J.J. considered Cleveland a mentor and a friend. It was Cleveland, a rabid Oakland Athletics fan, who taught J.J.'s son Kelly to play baseball.

In 1978 Cleveland and the San Francisco China squad began investigating several Chinese and Taiwanese nationals. Their leader, the FBI concluded, was the geophysicist Chien Ning, who the bureau believed had been sent to the United States by the MSS.

With a reported bankroll of $250,000, Chien had been given four tasks by the Chinese intelligence service, the FBI surmised: First, she started a glossy Chinese-language magazine, *Science and Technology Review,* for which Chinese American scientists contributed articles on subjects of interest to China. Half a dozen issues were published in the United States; after that the publication moved to China.

The magazine was no marginal operation. It clearly had the backing of the Chinese government at the highest level. For the first time, the postal service in China and a network of official bookstores allowed the unrestricted sale of a foreign magazine. Published in Berkeley and printed in Hong Kong, the magazine's first issue, in January 1980, had 104 pages, a print run of two hundred thousand copies, and an interview with two Nobel laureates. It also had a congratulatory message from Dr. Frank Press, the science adviser to President Jimmy Carter and like Chien a geophysicist. In China, a lead article in the *People's Daily* promoted the magazine, and a large number of senior Chinese government officials sent handwritten notes of congratulation to the magazine's Beijing office.

As Chien's second project, through a commercial front set up as Kentex International, libraries at the University of California at Berkeley, Stanford University, and other universities were combed for PhD theses and scientific books on a variety of technical subjects. The papers and books were copied and the copies shipped to Beijing.

In addition, Chien was tasked with opening a bookstore that would sell PRC publications and other books on Asia and Chinese language and culture. The FBI believed she may have helped to found Eastwind Books & Arts, at Stockton and Columbus streets in San Francisco. Finally, she was to open an import-export company.

All of this seemed fairly innocuous. But the FBI's suspicions about Chien's role were fueled when Gwo-bao Min, the Livermore scientist, turned up moonlighting as the advertising and sales manager of her magazine, *Science and Technology Review.*

The bureau's antennae went up because Min was an engineer at one of the nation's most sensitive and secret installations, the laboratory founded in large part by Edward Teller, the father of the H-bomb, who became its director. It was at Livermore that the hydrogen bomb, the most destructive weapon in the world, was created.

In the late 1970s, Min worked at Livermore on designing a system to shoot down enemy nuclear missiles. Min's project was a precursor to the Strategic Defense Initiative, the so-called Star Wars program launched in 1983 by President Ronald Reagan.

As part of his research, Min had run tests on full-size mockups of the Minuteman II warhead. With his Q clearance, he also had access to the design of every US nuclear missile as well as those on the drawing boards. He was, in short, privy to every secret of the country's nuclear weapons program.

Cleveland then opened the TIGER TRAP file on Min. The FBI also tapped his phones, under a Foreign Intelligence Surveillance Act (FISA) warrant.

Min's background appeared to be unremarkable. Born in Taiwan, he had received an engineering degree from Taiwan University and served two years in Taiwan's navy. After coming to the United States in 1963, he received an engineering degree from West Virginia University and, in 1970, a doctorate in aerospace engineering from the University of Michigan.

He decided to remain in the United States, became an American citizen, worked in private industry for a few years, and joined the Livermore lab in 1975. With his wife, who was born in China, he bought a house in Danville, California, a half-hour commute from the lab, and quietly pursued his hobby, collecting and studying gemstones.

Although he had a solid position at Livermore, Min seemingly felt that he was underpaid and his work not fully appreciated. He harbored ambitions to go into business trading with China. He decided to travel to Beijing in the summer of 1979 to further his prospects.

Jerry Chih-li Chen, the television-repair-shop owner in Oakland, helped Min with the paperwork for his visa application. Chen, who was born in China but grew up in Taiwan, had been active in the Diaoyutai Islands movement as a graduate student. His work brought official recognition; he was one of a group of only five students who were invited to Beijing to meet Premier Chou En-lai.

On a trip back to China, Chien Ning asked Hanson Huang, who was then in Beijing working for the Ministry of Foreign Trade, to look over Min's visa application. Huang immediately recognized Min as someone with the knowledge, and access to secrets, that could help China's nuclear weapons program.

In the month before Min left for China, investigators found, he had checked out an increasing number of classified documents from the Livermore lab's technical library. He also gained access to the lab's top-secret weapons vault, which contained mockups of every nuclear warhead designed by Livermore's scientists.

After Min arrived in Beijing in June, Chien introduced him to Hanson Huang. Min was asked to give a number of lectures in China, and did. Through Huang, he also agreed to answer questions from a small group of Chinese government scientists.

Min met with them, but since he was not a nuclear physicist, he could not answer all of their questions about weapons design. He was given several questions to take back to the States with him.

When Min returned from his trip, he told his fellow lab employees that he had gone to China to give lectures on gems. Since he was known as an amateur gemologist, his version of what happened was not questioned by his colleagues.

If Chien Ning was a female spymaster acting for the MSS, as the FBI believed, there was little on the surface to suggest that. Yet there was an element of mystery and intrigue in her background: she seemed to be all over the place, as a businesswoman buying rusted merchant ships for scrap metal, a scientist, a university professor, a magazine publisher. And she was somehow there at every twist and turn in the early stages of the TIGER TRAP story.

In an interview with the author in 2009, Chien denied that she had come to San Francisco on behalf of the MSS. "I mean, there was reason to suspect me of that," she said, "but that's not true. I'm an intellectual, I don't have the mentality to do that."

Chien was living in Northern California when she was located and interviewed. She said she traveled to China twice a year on average. Had the MSS given her the $250,000 to set up the four projects? "They gave me no money," she said.

At the same time, she acknowledged that she knew Gwo-bao Min. "I introduced Min to Hanson [Huang]," she said. "Min came to see me and Hanson was there. In Beijing."

And had she founded the Eastwind bookstore in San Francisco? "No, I helped them," she replied.

Another mystery. Doroteo Ng, one of the owners of the bookstore, when asked about Chien, said, "I don't remember that name. I don't remember this person." He said that the bookstore was founded in 1978 by "some twenty people," most of them community activists, to foster cultural understanding. Had China contributed any money to start the bookstore? "No money from the PRC, not a penny," he said.

Chien had come to America and founded the magazine, she said, "to bridge the two countries. To help the Chinese people be exposed to Western economy. Conservatives were in power, and I wanted to help China understand the market economy."

Chien Ning was born in Nanjing (then Nanking); most of her family moved to Taiwan in 1946 when she was in her midteens. Chien returned to China and said she scored number one on the national college entrance exam. She earned a degree in physics from Qinghua University, then studied geophysics. A decade later, she was caught up in the short-lived Hundred Flowers Movement, launched in 1957 by Mao Zedong and ostensibly designed to encourage "constructive" criticism of the government by intellectuals. Many of those who spoke out were severely punished when Mao cracked down on the movement.

"I was in a prison labor camp for many years because my family was in Taiwan and they thought I was a CIA agent," she said. "Anyone with a relationship with Taiwan was suspect."

Chien said she spent five years in the prison camp, from 1957 to 1962. "The camp was on the border with Siberia in the far northeast, near Lake Xingkai. It was very cold." Over time, hundreds of thousands of intellectuals and "rightists" were sent to the Lake Xingkai prison camp, where conditions were notoriously harsh. Chien built and repaired tractors in the camp.

At one point in her remarkable career, Chien led several exploration teams to remote areas of China to catalog the nation's mineral resources. She was credited with discovering the huge Baotou iron mines in inner Mongolia.

In August 1979, two months after Chien introduced Gwo-bao Min to Hanson Huang in Beijing, Huang flew to San Francisco and met twice with the Livermore engineer, once in Min's car, a second time at his home in Danville. At the second meeting, Min provided information in response to the questions posed through Huang by the Chinese scientists. Huang flew to Washington, D.C., and went to the Chinese embassy with the data he had obtained from Min.

At the embassy he wrote out a report, which was sent to China by diplomatic pouch. Huang had now effectively become Min's case agent.

Hanson Huang was born in Hong Kong in 1951. His Chinese name is Huang Yien. (His given name, Yien, means "faithful.") He and his younger brother, Henry, were given English names, a not uncommon practice in Hong Kong, then British territory.

Henry Huang, a molecular microbiologist at Washington University in St. Louis, was estranged from his brother, whose pro-PRC views he did not share. "Our family was very poor," Henry Huang said. "Our father died when we were young children; my mother was a news reporter at a newspaper, and then a TV station, but we were not well-to-do."

Of his brother, Hanson, Henry said, "He was always somebody with a cause. He was buying into communism, socialism, in a very naive way."

Hanson and his brother attended the Diocesan Boys School in Hong Kong, then both came to the United States to continue their education. Hanson enrolled in Harvard College in the fall of 1970, and graduated three years later magna cum laude with a bachelor's degree in history. He went on to Harvard Law School and received his law degree in 1976.

From Harvard Law, Hanson Huang joined Baker & McKenzie in Chicago, the city where his path first crossed with Katrina Leung, if they had not met earlier in the Daoyutai Islands protests. By 1979 he had moved to Beijing. In 1981, back in the United States, Huang briefly joined the Manhattan law firm of Webster & Sheffield, where John V. Lindsay, a former Republican congressman and two-term mayor of New York, was a partner. The law firm was hoping that Huang would help it expand its operations in Asia, but he resigned abruptly that same year and returned to China.

After Huang's meetings with Gwo-bao Min in San Francisco, and following his trip to the Chinese embassy in Washington, he flew back to Beijing. His contacts there were presumably not satisfied with the information Min had provided, because Huang was given five additional questions and instructed to put them in a letter to Min. One question contained SECRET RESTRICTED DATA, a U.S. classification category reserved for nuclear information.* Some of the questions could only be answered with classified information. Huang wrote the letter in the office of K. C. Meng, who was the Beijing director of Chien Ning's science magazine.

In case the letter should be seen by anyone, an innocuous show-and-tell letter was also prepared. The letter with the substantive questions included a warning to Min. "The other letter can be shown to others," it said. "This letter should be destroyed after reading."

---

* The Department of Energy defines SECRET RESTRICTED DATA as information "revealing the theory of operation or design of the components of a thermonuclear or fission bomb."

# Chapter 6

# "HOLY SHIT, MR. GROVE!"

**D**AN GROVE LOVED the sights and smells, the bustle of Hong Kong. A tall, affable man, he was one of the FBI's most experienced Asia hands. He was born in the Pennsylvania hard coal country, graduated from Penn State, and joined the bureau in 1955.

Fluent in Mandarin, Grove worked Chinese cases in San Francisco in the early 1960s, then spent a year on the China desk at headquarters before going out East to Hong Kong in 1966 as an FBI legal attaché. (FBI agents posted overseas are called legal attachés, or legats, pronounced "*lee*-gats"). Given a choice, Grove would have stayed in Hong Kong forever. But after six years, he was called back to the States and assigned to the FBI office in Berkeley. As a counterintelligence agent, Grove routinely sought out individuals with ties to China, and to this end he obtained a list of students who had attended the All-China Games in Beijing and began interviewing them.

"I met a nice boy from Taiwan and asked him to come in, and he came down to the office. He was very forthcoming and told me all about his trip. He was in the rifle competition in Beijing, he had been in the military in Taiwan." The young man was a PhD student at Berkeley. His name was Tommy Tang.

"They're going to be after you," Grove told him. "They'll be in touch. There's no such thing as a free lunch."

Grove's prediction proved accurate. "We knew who had recruited him, and other students. Jerry Chen." The proprietor of the shop in Oakland, it seemed, was doing more than repairing televisions.

A month later Tommy Tang returned to see Grove. "He said, 'These people want me to work in a bookshop collecting technical books to send to China.' He was busy with school work. He said, 'I don't know if I have the time.'"

Grove considered the problem. "I said, 'If I pay you, will you do it?' He said, 'I will.'" After Tang agreed to collect the books, he showed them to Grove, so the FBI agent knew what materials were going to China. Soon afterward, Tang told Grove that Jerry Chen had called him and asked him to go to Beijing for the book project. Tang agreed to go. Which is why he was in Beijing at the precise moment when Hanson Huang was casting about for a secure way to deliver his letters to Gwo-bao Min. What better courier than a reliable student who would be passing through Hong Kong en route to Berkeley?

Grove recalled what happened next. "He [Tang] was gone a week or a couple of weeks when I got a call on my home phone. 'Holy shit, Mr. Grove! You'll never guess what I have.'

"He said, 'I got a letter for this guy at the Lawrence Livermore lab and I opened it and they want more information on missile guidance systems.'

"The letter was addressed to Gwo-bao Min," Grove said. "It was a typical Chinese airmail letter where you undo the flaps to open it. He did, and I said, 'You probably ruined it.' He had opened it before he called me. He probably tore the flaps when he opened it. He bought another envelope and copied the letter; it was in Chinese script."

The student told Grove that his copying the letter would not matter because the recipient would not know who originally wrote it. "He rewrote it in Hong Kong," Grove said. "He mailed the letter in Hong Kong as instructed by the Chinese. The kid brought the original letter back to me."

Grove did not recall seeing the for-show, innocuous letter that also made its way to Min. But thanks to Dan Grove, and a bit of lucky timing, the FBI now had Hanson Huang's substantive letter. The bureau did not have to wait long to see how Min would react.

After reading the letter, Min decided to deliver the answers in person to Beijing. He did not tell the lab, as required, that he planned to travel to China. His wife called his office at Livermore and said he was sick and would not be coming to work.

Bill Cleveland then orchestrated an elaborate ruse in an effort to trap Min. As the engineer walked through the terminal at San Francisco International Airport, the public-address system blared an unusual announcement, reminding passengers that it was illegal to transport certain items. The long list of prohibited materials included firearms, explosives, and nuclear weapons information.

As Min got in line to board his plane to Hong Kong, several FBI agents were, unknown to him, in the queue immediately ahead of and behind him. The passengers were told that all carryon luggage would be subject to a search by US Customs. Min's briefcase and the bags of his fellow "passengers" were taken to a room out of view.

Inside his briefcase, the FBI found two index cards. On one card, in Min's handwriting, were the same five questions that Hanson Huang had posed in his letter. On the other card was the answer to the first question, about a method to measure the yield of hydrogen bombs when they were tested in the atmosphere. Since there were no written answers to the other queries, the FBI judged that Min already knew the answers without committing them to paper. But Min was not an expert on atmospheric testing; the FBI later discovered he had copied the answer to the first question about measuring the yield of hydrogen bombs from a classified document.

The measurement technique was based on "Teller light," named for Edward Teller, a blue fluorescence caused by the interaction of gamma rays and air that can be detected in the microsecond just before a high-altitude nuclear explosion of a fission bomb, the component that in turn triggers a hydrogen bomb.

In the early years of nuclear testing in the atmosphere, the scientists at Los Alamos had no sure way to measure the power of the weapons they had created. One key measurement they sought was the rate of increase of neutrons in a fission bomb, or "neutron flux" — the speed of the chain reaction as the weapon became supercritical. Teller calculated that if the intensity of the fleeting blue light could be captured, it would match the neutron flux. He was right; by measuring the light, it was possible to calculate the yield, the total energy released by a bomb.

One of the other questions on the index card appeared at first glance to be a general physics question. Its significance became clear only later.

Standing by at the airport, and well out of view of Gwo-bao Min, was a large group of physicists, nuclear weapons scientists, government lawyers, FBI officials, and classification experts. They were there to examine any documents or notes found in Min's carryon.

While the airport search was in progress in San Francisco, back at FBI headquarters in Washington, Paul Moore and a smaller group of scientists from the Department of Energy gathered in the office of Edward J. O'Malley, the assistant FBI director for counterintelligence, to hear the result. "If the FBI found the wrong things in his baggage he would be arrested," said Moore.

The larger contingent at the airport, after examining the index cards, decided there was not enough incriminating evidence to arrest Min. Word was relayed to the group waiting at FBI headquarters.*

Despite the elaborate deception arranged by the FBI at the San Francisco airport, Min became suspicious of the search of his carryon. Before boarding his plane he tore up the two index cards and gave them to his wife. She went into the ladies' room, followed by a woman who was part of the FBI's Special Surveillance Group, known as the G's.

The G's are a team of surveillance specialists, all civil servants, but not FBI agents, selected to look like ordinary citizens and blend in to their surroundings. A young mother with a baby in a stroller, college students out jogging, bearded bikers, white-haired grannies toting shopping bags, street repair crews in yellow hardhats, beer-belly good

---

* In espionage cases, the FBI in most circumstances needs approval by the Justice Department to arrest a suspect. The agents who discovered the two index cards in Min's carryon bag were operating under bizarre and apocalyptic instructions from the department. They were to arrest the Livermore engineer if they found nuclear information that would enable China to destroy the planet and "end the world as we know it."

old boys in pickup trucks, young lovers kissing in the park—all may be G's on the job. All are trained in surveillance, photography, and communications.

Min's wife did not dispose of the pieces of the index cards in the ladies' room. The FBI later recovered the torn pieces from the Mins' trash, in a plastic garbage bag that contained dog poop. A highly dedicated FBI agent reconstructed the cards.*

Min never reached Hong Kong or China, his original destinations. He flew to Taiwan, turned around, and came home. "When Min arrived back," Paul Moore said, "he went from the gate to the nearest departure gate to see if there were any more 'random' searches at the airport. He had become suspicious; when he looked down the concourse at the departure gate, that was plainly what was going on."

On the wiretap of Min's telephone, the FBI overheard him say that he had passed information to someone who was supposed to deliver it to an address in Hong Kong but got lost. Min also told Jerry Chen that he had been searched at the airport.

Now the FBI was faced with a delicate decision. Min had already passed information to Hanson Huang and was trying to answer more questions from Beijing, including about the technique to measure the yield of hydrogen bombs tested in the atmosphere. Could he be allowed to continue working at the lab?

The bureau decided to leave him in place while the investigation continued. But Min's access to secrets was discreetly reduced. In Washington, the secretary of energy had to sign off, every six months, on approval for Min to remain at Livermore.

By early 1981 scientists and engineers at the lab, including Min, were already working on what became the Star Wars program to intercept nuclear missiles. Officials decided that leaving Min on the job had become too risky.

The time had come, Cleveland decided, to confront Gwo-bao Min. Espionage is a peculiar crime. Unless suspects confess or, as rarely hap-

---

* The FBI does not give medals, but agents who perform hazardous or extraordinary work may receive an "incentive" reward in cash. The agent who reconstructed the index cards received a cash reward.

pens, are caught in the act, they may go unpunished. A bank robber may be caught fleeing in a getaway car, an embezzler may be ensnared by an audit. But spies are a different breed, they move in a secret world, often exercising clandestine skills to avoid detection.

Sometimes a confrontation works. When FBI counterintelligence agents question a suspected spy and reveal how much they know, in some cases even presenting him with surveillance photos, the suspect may feel it is useless to deny the evidence amassed against him. Or the suspect may harbor a hope that his FBI interrogators will offer to turn him into a double agent, working against the other side. At times skilled interviewers, using various ploys, are able to elicit a confession.

Min was told by lab officials that serious questions had been raised about him by the FBI. As a result, they warned, he could keep his job only if he resolved those issues. He was placed on leave and agreed to talk to the bureau.

In the first of several days of interviews, Min was asked about the index cards found in his carryon bag and contended that they were just notes he had taken at lectures at the lab. For six hours, he denied knowing Chien Ning or Hanson Huang, then admitted he did but said he knew nothing about any letters from Huang.

The next day, Min said he had, after all, received a letter from Huang. He agreed to return a third day and produced the show-and-tell innocuous letter. Cleveland asked Min to let the FBI's forensic experts examine the letter, and he consented.

On the fourth day, Min agreed to take a lie detector test. Cleveland then pulled a rabbit out of his hat and produced a copy of the real, substantive letter that Dan Grove had intercepted with the help of Tommy Tang, the Berkeley student.

The FBI agents did not want to reveal to Min, however, how they had managed to acquire the letter. They devised a plausible explanation. Chinese characters are frequently written on a pad with preprinted boxes that make it easier to keep the lines straight. Each character, representing a picture of an object or sounds and meaning, fits inside a box. If the substantive letter to Min was written first, as would seem likely, and then ripped off the pad, it might leave an impression on the sheet below on which the for-show letter was written.

Cleveland told Min that the FBI had retrieved the new letter from the impressions left on the innocuous letter that Min had offered to the agents the day before.

Min examined the substantive letter closely. Apparently he believed the FBI's invention.

"I wish to congratulate you," he said. "You have done your job very well."

Cleveland now thought he had Min on the verge of a confession. But it was not to be. The Livermore engineer said he wanted to talk to his wife before answering further questions. He agreed to meet the FBI agents the next day at a motel, but then telephoned to say he had changed his mind.

The lab's officials then told Min that since he had not resolved the issues raised by the FBI, he could not remain at Livermore. Min was allowed to resign.

The tiger had escaped the trap. But the FBI had forced Min out of the nuclear weapons lab and prevented any additional compromise of secrets to China.

Some who knew Gwo-bao Min argued that he may not have set out to spy for China, but had traveled to Beijing in the hope of making business contacts and once there was pressured to talk about his work at Livermore. And it certainly could have occurred to him that answering the questions he was asked might help him in his efforts to do business with China.

There was, perhaps, another factor. In Chinese culture, when people receive favors, they are expected to reciprocate, a deeply rooted tradition known as *guanxi*. Min was treated well in Beijing, as though he was an important and respected visitor. In more than one instance, China has successfully extracted information from visiting American scientists who felt they had to be polite to their hosts and ended up revealing more than they should have.

But Min seemed to know in advance what would be expected of him in Beijing. There was no other reason for him to have checked out so many classified documents from the Livermore technical library in the weeks before his trip.

The bureau had maneuvered Min out of the lab, but Cleveland and the FBI continued to pursue the case for a decade more. Now Hanson Huang offered the best hope of a break in the case. In March 1981, one month after Min was forced out at Livermore, Huang flew to New York and then booked a flight back to Hong Kong through Seattle. At the airline counter at JFK, apparently sensing he was being watched, he switched his plans at the last minute to catch his Hong Kong flight in Los Angeles.

At LAX, the airliner was about to take off with Huang as a passenger when a customs agent boarded the plane and asked Huang to come with him. He was escorted to a hotel where the FBI was waiting. Huang told them little but agreed to meet them again on his next trip to the United States. He met the agents in New York in May and again in August but refused to talk further about his relationship with Min. The Immigration and Naturalization Service then barred him from the country.

The FBI nevertheless felt it had gathered enough evidence to prosecute Min for espionage. Harry J. Godfrey, Cleveland's supervisor on the TIGER TRAP case, several times pressed John L. Martin, the chief of the Justice Department's internal security section, to move on the case. Martin refused.

Unless a spy is caught in the act, the FBI cannot make arrests in sensitive national security cases without the approval of the Justice Department. And that meant Martin. Unknown outside the closed world of intelligence, Martin was the man who ruled whether espionage cases would make the front pages and the nightly news or perhaps never become public.

Without a confession by Min, Martin insisted to both Godfrey and Cleveland, he would not go to a grand jury. In Martin's long career, seventy-six spies had been prosecuted, and all but one convicted. FBI counterintelligence agents were often frustrated by his cautious approach, however, complaining that he was more interested in protecting his reputation than in catching spies. Martin's decision had blocked any legal action against Min, but it did not prevent the bureau from continuing its investigation.

Late in 1981, Hanson Huang was asked by Chinese officials to brief them on his contacts with the FBI. Then, early in 1982, Huang disappeared from his hotel room in Beijing. A year later he was convicted of espionage against China and sentenced to fifteen years in prison. It was then that PARLOR MAID managed to visit him.

With the TIGER TRAP investigation on a hold button, although not closed, counterintelligence officials at FBI headquarters decided to launch a broader probe of whether China was advancing its nuclear weapons program by eliciting information from visiting US scientists. The new case, as an offshoot of TIGER TRAP, was given the code name TIGER SPRINGE. (A rarely used word, "springe" refers to a snare made of a noose under tension that springs when triggered.)

Dozens of scientists and senior officials in Washington were questioned in the TIGER SPRINGE investigation. Once more, Bill Cleveland and his partner, Al Heiman, conducted many of the interviews. State Department officials, ambassadors to China, and at least two White House national security advisers were questioned, Zbigniew Brzezinski, President Jimmy Carter's National Security Council chief, and Robert McFarlane, who held that post under President Ronald Reagan.

What the FBI wanted to know from Brzezinski and McFarlane was whether any US scientists or officials had been authorized to share nuclear weapons secrets with China. Both said there had been no such authorization. Cleveland and FBI headquarters officials wanted to be sure that there had been no high-level secret or tacit policy granting permission to share scientific information with Beijing; otherwise, if Gwo-bao Min or other scientists were prosecuted for leaking secrets, they would have a ready-made defense.

The FBI saw another virtue in TIGER SPRINGE. By casting a wide net, it would demonstrate that the bureau's counterintelligence agents were not interested solely in questioning people who were ethnic Chinese.

One of those interviewed at length by the FBI was George A. Keyworth, a senior scientist at Los Alamos who later served as President Reagan's science adviser from 1981 to 1985. On a trip to China in 1980,

Keyworth met with Chinese scientists at a university. For years afterward, he was bedeviled by gossip in the intelligence world that he had revealed classified information about the neutron bomb to the Chinese.

In an interview with the author, Keyworth said that this had never happened. "Someone asked me a question about deuterium and tritium." The question, he said, was related to laser fusion experiments and the neutron bomb, which releases greater radiation than standard nuclear weapons.

There was no mystery, Keyworth told the Chinese scientists. The isotopes were so unstable that mere impact would ignite them. "I said, anybody who has finished a couple of years of physics knows it is the simplest way to achieve fusion. Put it in a ball and throw it on the floor and it will go off."

Some officials believed that the Los Alamos physicist had crossed a line, but they were hardly in a position to dismiss or prosecute him for the supposed infraction. "There were good reasons there was no action on Keyworth," said Ken Schiffer, a veteran FBI counterintelligence agent. "He didn't make the trip in a vacuum. It was informal, he was not tasked. But he was made aware of certain gaps in US intelligence, a new facility that China was using in their weapons program and if he could learn anything about that it would be beneficial."

Before his trip, CIA officials briefed Keyworth on what to look for in China. Robert Vrooman, the CIA's man at Los Alamos, and later chief of counterintelligence at the laboratory, was his principal contact. "I met with other agency people too, but mostly Bob," Keyworth said. "They wanted to know about a lab down near Chengdu. We thought it was a nuclear weapons facility. I was able to validate it."

More broadly, the intelligence agencies wanted to know the state of China's nuclear weapons program. Ironically, Keyworth got into hot water when, at a CIA debriefing after his trip, he brought up what he had told the Chinese scientists about putting isotopes in a ball, as an example of how adroitly he had handled their questions. "The whole point was when this came up in my debriefing, I was trying to explain how it was possible to circumvent their question by giving a basic answer." Keyworth explained all this to the FBI's satisfaction in several interviews with the bureau during the TIGER SPRINGE investigation.

The Chinese had invited Keyworth to come back the next year to visit their nuclear weapons test site. But in 1981 Reagan appointed him the White House science adviser, and in that sensitive post, it was made clear to Keyworth, he would have to abandon any thought of returning to China.

On December 3, 1982, almost two years after Gwo-bao Min was forced out of Livermore, the telephone rang in his house in Danville, California. The FBI had maintained the wiretap on Min's phone, and it heard the caller identify himself and say that he was a nuclear weapons designer at the Los Alamos National Laboratory in New Mexico.

According to a report of a polygraph exam that was later administered to the caller, he had learned that Min "was having problems with some men in China," was aware that he was from Taiwan, and had called just "out of curiosity." He offered to find out who had "squealed" on Gwo-bao Min.

The caller's name was Wen Ho Lee. The Los Alamos scientist had surfaced in the TIGER TRAP case seventeen years before he would become a celebrated spy suspect himself, in an unrelated FBI investigation.

Wen Ho Lee claimed that he had learned about Min's problems from a story in a Chinese-language newspaper. He called Min out of more than curiosity, however. Both Lee and Min were born in Taiwan, and Lee had been in contact with nuclear researchers in Taiwan for several years and had done consulting work for them. Attorney General Janet Reno testified at a closed Senate hearing in 1999 that Wen Ho Lee told the FBI "that he contacted [Min] because Lee thought [Min] was in trouble for doing the same sort of thing that Lee had been doing for Taiwan."*

According to a detailed TOP SECRET review of the Wen Ho Lee case in 2000 by a Justice Department team, the FBI was worried that

---

* Min's name was deleted from Reno's Senate testimony and for clarity has been inserted above in brackets.

"Lee might be acting on behalf of a Taiwan intelligence service." Bill Cleveland was summoned to Albuquerque to brief the FBI field office on TIGER TRAP.

At the same time, after Lee's 1982 phone call to Min, the FBI opened a full counterintelligence investigation of Wen Ho Lee. The Albuquerque office asked the FBI Behavioral Sciences Unit to prepare a personality profile to establish whether Lee might be "involved in clandestine intelligence activities."

Not realizing that he had been overheard on the wiretap, Lee lied to the FBI and although asked several times, said that he "had never attempted to contact" Min. Lee, the review team concluded, "provided truthful answers only when confronted with irrefutable evidence (i.e. the FBI's awareness of his phone call . . .) or when faced with a polygraph."

Then there was an astonishing development. Although Lee was under active investigation as a possible spy, in December 1983 the FBI asked him to go to San Francisco and help the bureau on the TIGER TRAP case. Lee was instructed to go to Min's home and try to lure him into revealing what secrets he had passed to the Chinese. Before he left, at the FBI's behest, Lee placed four telephone calls to Min, with the bureau's agents listening in.

When Wen Ho Lee showed up at Min's home, he was rebuffed by the former Livermore engineer. The door was not exactly slammed in Lee's face; he spent about half an hour with Min. But he did not succeed in the mission he had been given by the FBI.

The Justice Department review team was troubled, however, to discover that the FBI had enlisted Lee's help "in the direct contact of the subject of an espionage investigation."

Early in 1984, Lee passed a polygraph examination in which he was asked about his telephone call to Min. On the polygraph test, he denied working for any foreign intelligence agency. Although Lee had lied by denying his phone call to Min until he was confronted with the wiretap evidence, on March 12 the FBI closed its investigation of Wen Ho Lee.

〜

With Gwo-bao Min forced out of Livermore, and Chien Ning's maga-zine operation moved back to Beijing, Chien left San Francisco and with her husband moved to Pasadena. She became an American citi-zen, taught seismology at the University of Southern California, and also engaged in a number of business ventures.

Federico C. Sayre, an activist attorney in Santa Ana — he once rep-resented César Chávez, the charismatic leader of the United Farm Workers union — knew Chien and hoped through their friendship to become a middleman between the Chinese government and US inves-tors hoping to do business in China. "We were interested in building hotels and restaurants," Sayre said.

In 1984 Chien arranged for Sayre and his law partner, Jay D. Gould, to travel to China and lecture in the law department at Beijing Univer-sity. "She was a very kind of mysterious person," Sayre said. "I've seen planes wait for her. She seemed to have a lot of power for someone who was not in the government. She said she was not in the government. She spoke English well, very free with her criticism of Communism and the Communist government, although not when they [Chinese officials] were in earshot."

Three years later, Chien was involved in procuring old tankers and cargo ships for export to China, where they would be broken up for scrap iron, which the Chinese used in steel production. Her partner in that venture was Eugene Allen of Pacific Link International, a trade and brokerage firm in Los Angeles.

Chien confirmed that in the ship-procurement business she was acting for the Chinese government. "The Chinese Ministry of Materi-als asked my help to get scrap metals," she said.

The FBI, meanwhile, was still on the trail of Hanson Huang, hoping the Harvard lawyer might yet help the bureau close in on Min. Huang was released from a Chinese prison in 1985, after serving two years, but was placed under house arrest for a time and was not allowed to leave China for another seven years.

During the 1980s, Katrina Leung traveled to San Francisco often to work with Bill Cleveland on the TIGER TRAP case. Cleveland had en-listed Leung's help because of her friendship with Hanson Huang. And it was during those sojourns to Northern California that Cleveland

and PARLOR MAID began their romance. "According to Cleveland, Leung initiated their relationship," a Justice Department review said. The affair went on from 1988 to 1993 and was revived in 1997 and 1999, after Cleveland had left the FBI.

Min had surrendered his US passport when he was confronted by the FBI. Chien Ning said she had tried to help him retrieve his passport. He got it back in 1984 and began traveling extensively to China, making eight trips in two years. He also launched an import-export firm, Grand Monde Trading, and a consulting firm, Min's Consulting Associates.

Counterintelligence agents are famously patient. In 1992, thirteen years after Cleveland had opened the TIGER TRAP case, Hanson Huang returned to his native Hong Kong, which gave the FBI another chance to contact him.

Huang wanted to be allowed to travel to the United States again, but he worried that he might be arrested if he did. He said he would meet the FBI in London to seek a deal that would give him immunity from prosecution. Cleveland and J.J. Smith flew to London in February with a Justice Department lawyer and a Livermore scientist.

Huang asked for immunity not only for himself but for Min and everyone else in the case. The FBI agents said no deal, unless Huang really opened up and revealed exactly what had happened during Min's trip to Beijing in 1979 and in his meetings afterward with Huang in California. Huang did talk about those events but offered up little that was new.

The group met with Huang for three days. In the end, he was told there would be no immunity for him or anyone else in the case.

TIGER TRAP had run its course. The London meeting was the FBI's last hope. But the FBI could and did take comfort in knowing that Min was no longer in a position to pass nuclear weapons secrets to China.

Until now, the full story of this extraordinary espionage case has been wrapped in secrecy. The key roles of Hanson Huang and Chien Ning have never previously been revealed. And the TIGER TRAP case remains classified in the government's intelligence archives.

Even today, references to Gwo-bao Min in government documents are omitted, blacked out, or veiled. But a careful reading between the lines tells the story. An FBI document filed in the PARLOR MAID case, for example, nowhere mentions Bill Cleveland, TIGER TRAP, or his quarry:

"The San Francisco FBI SSA [special supervisory agent] was the case agent for a code named FBI counterintelligence investigation which concerned a ... subject who had obtained Top Secret information regarding United States nuclear weapons technology. This subject had conveyed the information to the PRC."

Translated from cryptic bureau-speak, the meaning is clear. Bill Cleveland was the San Francisco FBI case agent, TIGER TRAP was the code-named counterintelligence investigation, and Gwo-bao Min was the "subject" who the FBI said gave the TOP SECRET information on nuclear weapons to China.

But the bland language of the FBI affidavit masked the most startling and disturbing secret of the TIGER TRAP case.

# Chapter 7

# RIDING THE TIGER: CHINA
# AND THE NEUTRON BOMB

HRISTOPHER COX, A CONSERVATIVE Republican from
Orange County, California, served in the House of Representatives for seventeen years until 2005, when President George W. Bush named him chairman of the Securities and Exchange Commission. Although he instituted a number of reforms at the SEC, targeting insider trading and backdating of stock options, for example, he had the misfortune of presiding over the agency during the Wall Street meltdown and recession in 2008. Even John McCain, the Republican presidential candidate, called for his resignation.

In the intelligence world, however, Cox was known not for his controversial role at the SEC but for a report documenting Chinese espionage against the United States. Cox was the chairman of the bipartisan House Select Committee on US National Security and Military/Commercial Concerns with the People's Republic of China. The report's jaw-breaking title was so long that it became known informally simply as "the Cox Report." The committee issued an unclassified version of its nine-hundred-page report on May 25, 1999.

The central conclusion of the Cox Report was that China "has stolen classified design information on the United States' most advanced thermonuclear weapons," enabling the PRC to develop and test strategic nuclear missiles "sooner than would otherwise have been possible." The report also warned that China had penetrated America's nuclear weapons laboratories.

The Cox Report created a firestorm. Critics argued that its conclusions were exaggerated, that the report was a political assault on the Clinton White House, and that China could have developed its nuclear weapons on its own, without using information stolen from the United States. Despite its flaws, the Cox Report served to alert the public to the reality that China was actively engaged in espionage against the United States and that the Los Alamos and Livermore labs were prime targets with woefully lax security.

Widely misunderstood in the debate over the Cox Report was the fact that at its core, the committee findings involved two separate questions. All nations spy, and there can be no doubt, from many examples, that China spies on the United States and has obtained secret information through espionage, among other means. Whether it has been able to use the information it acquired by espionage to speed its own nuclear weapons program is less demonstrable. But those are two distinct questions.

One of the most intriguing sections of the Cox Report is titled "Investigation of Theft of Design Information for the Neutron Bomb."

The neutron bomb, technically known as an enhanced radiation weapon, or ERW, is a thermonuclear weapon that is designed to release a much greater amount of lethal radiation than a conventional hydrogen bomb. The warhead releases intense waves of neutron and gamma radiation, with a minimal blast effect. In the popular imagination, the neutron bomb is understood to be a weapon that kills people but leaves buildings standing.

While that description is partly true, it is greatly exaggerated. Even a neutron bomb in the one-kiloton range would cause substantial destruction to buildings, although over a smaller area than that caused by a conventional nuclear explosion. The atomic bomb dropped on Hiroshima in World War II was fifteen kilotons. It killed approximately 140,000 people and destroyed most of the city.

Because neutron and gamma radiation can penetrate armor, the

ERW was designed primarily as a tactical battlefield weapon against tanks and infantry. During the years of the Sino-Soviet split, a period of tense political relations between China and the USSR that spanned more than two decades after the late 1950s, China sought to develop a neutron bomb to deter a potential ground assault by Soviet tanks. Similarly, during the Cold War, the United States saw the neutron bomb as a way to stop a Soviet army invasion of Western Europe and yet leave cities intact.

The principal neutron bomb developed by the United States was designed for the W-70 warhead, produced at the Lawrence Livermore National Laboratory for the Army's short-range, tactical Lance missile. President Kennedy initially decided against building the neutron bomb, but approved production after the Soviet Union broke a voluntary moratorium on nuclear testing in the atmosphere in 1961. President Carter deferred production of the neutron bomb in 1978 after mass protests in Europe against US plans to deploy the weapon there.

President Reagan ordered production of the bomb resumed in 1981. The W-70 was never deployed, and President George H. W. Bush retired the weapon in 1992, after the end of the Cold War. The last W-70 warhead was dismantled four years later.

In 1999, however, the Cox Report made news about the neutron bomb. "In the late 1970s," the report stated, "the PRC stole design information on the U.S. W-70 warhead from Lawrence Livermore Laboratory. The U.S. Government first learned of this theft several months after it took place."

According to the report, "the FBI developed a suspect in the . . . theft. The suspect worked at Lawrence Livermore National Laboratory, and had access to classified information including designs for a number of U.S. thermonuclear weapons in the U.S. stockpile at that time.

"In addition to design information about the W-70, this suspect may have provided to the PRC additional classified information about other U.S. weapons that could have significantly accelerated the PRC's nuclear weapons program.

"The Clinton administration has determined that further information about these thefts cannot be publicly disclosed."

Without identifying Gwo-bao Min by name, the Cox Report was describing the TIGER TRAP case. How China may have acquired the design details of the neutron bomb was the critical secret hidden in the government's TIGER TRAP files, the secret that "cannot be publicly disclosed."

The Cox Report did not provide any details that led it to assert that design information about the neutron bomb had been stolen from Livermore. But among the five questions in the letter to Gwo-bao Min from Hanson Huang, and copied onto the index cards Min had in his carryon bag at San Francisco International Airport, was what seemed at first to be a general physics question. On further analysis, however, government scientists concluded that the question could only relate to the neutron bomb, to which Min had access at Livermore.

Since Min had not confessed to passing nuclear weapons secrets to China, the Justice Department had turned down the FBI's repeated requests to arrest him. But the Cox Committee was not under the same restraints as a law enforcement agency. It was thus able to go a step further and assert that China "stole design information" on the neutron bomb from Livermore.

The FBI and the Livermore scientists feared that Min may have given China more than information about the neutron bomb. Another one of the five questions, when later analyzed by government physicists, appeared to relate to a critical secret that enabled the United States to develop a small, miniaturized hydrogen bomb by using two-point detonation of the fission bomb that served as the trigger. Detonating the fission bomb at only two points instead of surrounding it with explosives was the key to a breakthrough by US scientists in developing a smaller, lighter warhead.

Min seemed to suggest, in the conversation overheard by the FBI, that his answers to the questions did not reach Beijing. He had claimed that the cutout or intermediary to whom he gave the "information" got lost and could not find the accommodation address in Hong Kong.

Whether or not that story was credible, Min had other contacts with the Chinese. From the way the five questions were written, it was clear that they were in the nature of follow-up inquiries to data that Min had already discussed in China. Min provided additional information in the second of two meetings in San Francisco with Hanson Huang, who then flew to Washington and in the Chinese embassy wrote up a report on the meetings that was pouched to officials in Beijing.

In 1988 China tested a neutron bomb, according to the Cox Report. China did not announce that at the time, however. A decade later, in July 1999, China confirmed that it had successfully developed a neutron bomb. It made the announcement in a thirty-six-page angry rebuttal to the Cox Report.

The rebuttal was released at a news conference in Beijing in which Zhao Qizheng, a senior official, blasted the Cox Report as misleading and racist. The Cox Report, Zhao said, implies that "Chinese can't be as smart as Americans, so they must have stolen the technology."

Titled "Facts Speak Louder Than Words and Lies Will Collapse on Themselves," the Chinese response attacked the Cox Report as a "concoction" full of "groundless accusations" that were "utterly absurd" and a "vicious slander" that had "aroused the strong indignation of the Chinese people."

The rebuttal made only a brief reference to the neutron bomb. "The neutron bomb seems quite mysterious to ordinary people. In fact, it is a special kind of H-bomb. Since China has already possessed atom bomb and H-bomb technologies, it is quite logical and natural for it to master the neutron bomb technology through its own efforts."

The document did not reveal whether China had tested the neutron bomb, when it had developed the weapon, or whether it had produced or deployed it. But it said that China had overcome technical problems to develop its nuclear weapons and "the neutron bomb technology" by "relying on its own forces, on its large number of talented scientists full of creative spirit."

To emphasize that China had the neutron bomb, the New China News Agency put out a dispatch that same day headlined, "China Masters Neutron Bomb Technology." The story said Beijing had begun work on the bomb in the 1970s. "China has already mastered the neutron bomb design technology," the story declared.

The Cox Report asserted that in 1996 the intelligence community learned that China "had successfully stolen" more secret information about the neutron bomb from a US weapons lab. It offered no further details about the second alleged theft or whether the source of the leak had been uncovered by the FBI. But there was a TOP SECRET investigation, apparently code-named SILENT CHORUS, of the second reported theft.

One published account, cited by the Congressional Research Service, quoted unnamed American officials who speculated that China may have sought more US information about the neutron bomb because the Chinese test in 1988 was not successful.

In January 1999 the classified version of the Cox Report circulated among White House and government officials, and the Clinton administration knew it would have to react when the report became public. In February, George Tenet, then the director of the CIA, appointed Robert D. Walpole, a senior agency manager and former State Department official, to head an interagency task force to conduct a damage assessment on Chinese acquisition of US nuclear weapons secrets.

Despite the uproar over the Cox Report, in the end the damage assessment agreed with a number of the report's central conclusions:

> China obtained by espionage classified US nuclear weapons information that probably accelerated its program to develop future nuclear weapons. . . .
> China also obtained information on a variety of US weapon design concepts and weaponization features, including those of the neutron bomb.

Like the Cox Report, the damage assessment — or at least the version made public — never mentioned by name the case it was referring to, the case that had begun two decades earlier, code-named TIGER TRAP.

# Chapter 8

# THE WALK-IN

E ARLY IN 1995, an event took place that jolted American intelligence agencies and touched off years of controversy inside their closed and secret world.

A middle-aged Chinese man appeared at a CIA station in Southeast Asia with a large cache of documents. Among them was a blockbuster, a Chinese government memo, classified SECRET, that described, in chilling and specific detail, the miniaturized W-88 thermonuclear warhead that sits atop the ballistic missiles on US Trident submarines. The W-88 is the crown jewel, the most advanced weapon in the nation's arsenal.

The man who brought the documents was a classic walk-in, the designation in the intelligence business for someone who shows up and volunteers information. In this case, the walk-in presented a document that displayed the classified measurements of America's most secret nuclear weapon. He might just as well have walked in with a bomb in a suitcase.

The walk-in, whose identity has never been revealed by US intelligence, was cautious. He did not, in his initial contact, bring the documents. But he told the CIA he had what he described as a duffle bag full of Chinese classified secrets that he wanted to sell. The next time he came, he brought the papers with him. He said he had gotten them out of China by shipping them to himself abroad — by DHL.

The walk-in then told the CIA officers who questioned him at length a story so bizarre that it just might have been true. He said he worked in China's nuclear weapons program and had access to a library storage facility that housed sensitive classified information. The library was in a government institute.

He said he entered the storage area at night, rifled the files, collected the documents, and put them in the duffle bag. But the next problem was how to get the duffle bag out of the building and past security. He hit on an unusual solution. He threw the duffle bag out of a second-story window.

But the duffle bag broke, and papers scattered all over the ground. The man lost his nerve and, fearful of being caught, hid in the storage area and waited for a chance to get away undetected. At one point he heard footsteps approaching, but he was not seen and eventually the footsteps went away.

Relieved, he lit a cigarette. Bad move. Someone came into the room and saw the smoke rising. He was caught. He explained coolly that he had been working late, fallen asleep in the library, and decided to have a smoke. But he was leaving now.

As the walk-in related the story, he then ran downstairs, out of the facility, and found the papers that had scattered when the duffle bag broke. He scrambled and recovered them, stuffing them all back into the bag.

His story might have been dismissed as improbable but for the fact that one of the documents in his possession accurately described the measurements of the W-88. The stark fact, which could not be ignored, was that China had somehow acquired highly secret data about America's most sophisticated nuclear warhead.

The documents were flown to CIA headquarters in Langley, Virginia, where teams of translators began poring over the trove. There were so many documents to translate that the CIA had to hire contractors to supplement its own staff.

The effort went on for years. As the documents were translated, the work began of sifting through and analyzing the mass of data.

Initially, the CIA did not share its hoard of documents with the FBI and other US intelligence agencies, under the rationale that the agency first needed to translate and study the material. Not until several months later, in the fall of 1995, was the Department of Energy given the W-88 document, and an interagency group, including the FBI, DOE, and scientists from the national weapons labs, was brought in to assess the documents.

The CIA, it appeared at first glance, had struck gold. Intelligence operators always hope to keep a walk-in as an "agent in place," so that he or she can continue to supply information. A spy who becomes a defector and loses access to more secrets is much less valuable.

Under the CIA's rules, a prospect cannot be recruited as a full-fledged agent until vetted. The CIA station that proposes the recruitment must also receive provisional operational authority from Langley headquarters. Traces were run on the walk-in, and it was determined that he had no previous contact with the CIA and no known connection to the MSS or the MID, the Chinese military intelligence arm of the People's Liberation Army.

CIA headquarters officials then gave provisional operational approval to enroll the walk-in and keep him on the job as an agency asset. With provisional status, he was one step away from being recruited.

The walk-in was closely questioned on how he had obtained the documents. He claimed that he had access to the library containing the documents because he worked in the Chinese nuclear weapons program, and he stuck to his story about collecting the information in a duffle bag and throwing it out the window. He also said that his official status allowed him to travel. Although he wanted money in return for the documents, at the same time he alleged that his motive was ideological.

Not only did the walk-in provide the key document with astonishing and highly classified details about the W-88, he also turned over data describing five other thermonuclear warheads designed for ballistic missiles in the US arsenal.

The five other warheads were the W-78, for the Minuteman III intercontinental ballistic missile (ICBM); the W-76, like the W-88 designed for a submarine-launched ballistic missile (SLBM) on the Trident sub; the W-87, designed for the Peacekeeper (MX) ICBM; the W-62, for the Minuteman III ICBM; and the W-56, for the Minuteman II ICBM. The first two and the W-88 were designed at Los Alamos National Laboratory in New Mexico; the others were created at the Lawrence Livermore National Laboratory. All were deployed.

In the walk-in's documents the warheads were shown on a matrix, or grid. The warheads were listed down the left side and the headings across the top described the yield, size, and weight of each warhead, along with a drawing of the outer dimensions. The data, the scientists determined, was accurate.

The CIA's analysts concentrated on the W-88 document. The information about the outside dimensions of the other warheads was generally available from public sources. But in the case of the W-88, the walk-in's document gave precise measurements of the components inside the warhead, information that was secret and highly classified.

Thermonuclear weapons consist of two parts, the core, or "the pit," known as the primary, a fission bomb containing either plutonium-239 or highly enriched uranium. The bomb, the size of a grapefruit, is triggered by conventional explosives, creating an implosion and a chain reaction. That in turn triggers the secondary, the much more powerful thermonuclear, or fusion, bomb. It is called a fusion bomb, or H-bomb, because during detonation, the thermonuclear fuel lithium deuteride is compressed and two isotopes of hydrogen, deuterium and tritium, fuse to rival the energy of the sun.

Alarmingly, the Chinese secret document, which bore a 1988 date, gave the exact diameter of the W-88's primary, 115mm, or about four and a half inches. Even more significantly, the document disclosed that the W-88's primary was "two-point aspherical" — a highly sensitive and, it was thought, carefully guarded US secret — which meant that it was shaped more like a football or a pear than a grapefruit, with implosion points at each end. Instead of packing a series of explosives all around a perfectly round primary, the explosives could be set off at only two points. And Beijing knew it.

It got worse. The Chinese document accurately gave the radius of the round secondary as 172mm, or just under 7 inches, and it disclosed that, unlike other nukes, the primary of the W-88 was at the tapered tip of the warhead, forward of the secondary, another secret that was supposed to be closely held.

Finally, the document accurately reported the overall length of the warhead as 1522mm, or 5 feet. There were other documents in the walk-in's cache, hundreds that dealt with other foreign missile and defense systems, including those of Russia and France. But it was the W-88 that was, from the outset, the focus of the CIA's interest.

The W-88 warhead is the payload of the Trident II (D5) sub-based missile carried by the Ohio-class submarines, which are usually called Trident subs, after the name of the missiles they carry. Each Trident sub is armed with twenty-four missiles. The nuclear warheads are multiple independently targetable reentry vehicles (MIRVs), which means that several W-88s are released by the missile as individual targets come within range.

The importance of the W-88 is that it is small. Miniaturized nuclear bombs, unlike the huge early versions, fit into warheads that can be launched from a single missile at multiple targets. The United States was able to produce small hydrogen bombs by the late 1950s and early 1960s. US intelligence concluded that China did not test its first miniature nuclear warhead, similar to the W-88, until September 1992.

The precise number of warheads carried by each MIRVed Trident missile is secret, but is thought to be four. As many as eight, perhaps even ten, reentry vehicles, each with a W-88 warhead, could fit atop the Trident II missile, which has a range of forty-six hundred miles.

The current Trident II missiles cost $30.9 million each, are forty-four feet long, and weigh 130,000 pounds. The missile is launched underwater by gas that expands in the launch tube; when it is far enough away from the sub, the first stage ignites, an "aerospike" telescopes out to reduce drag, and the boost stage starts. In two minutes, the third-stage motor ignites, and the missile travels at the speed of twenty thousand feet per second toward its targets.

There was a fundamental reason that the W-88 document produced by the walk-in caused so much consternation inside the US intelligence community. The United States relies on a triad of nuclear weapons to deter an attack: land-based ICBMs, Air Force bombers, and nuclear-armed submarines. In the Strangelovian world of nuclear deterrence theory and mutual assured destruction (MAD), land-based missiles might be destroyed in an enemy first strike, bombers can be shot down, but submarines are relatively invulnerable. The Navy boasts that the Trident subs give the United States "its most survivable and enduring nuclear strike capability." And now the Trident's payload, the W-88, had been compromised.

The Trident subs, known as "boomers," are huge — 560-feet-long nuclear-powered ships that can travel at speeds up to twenty-five miles an hour underwater. With their crews of 155, the subs can spend two and a half months at sea. Of the eighteen Ohio-class subs, fourteen carry the Trident II missiles and W-88 warheads. Each sub has twenty-four missiles, and each W-88 has an estimated yield of 475 kilotons.

Writing in an official Navy publication, retired captain Edward L. Beach, a highly decorated World War II sub veteran and author of the best-selling 1955 novel *Run Silent, Run Deep*, described the enormous power of the Trident subs. "A single broadside from such a submarine — all 24 missiles fired at the same time — can destroy any nation on the face of the earth. No nation — and this includes our own — could even hope to function, or even continue to exist, in the face of such a salvo."

To the intelligence agencies and the US military, China's acquisition of the design details of the W-88 meant that there had been a horrendous leak somewhere along the line. But how, when, and where was unknown. The walk-in was seen as the key; perhaps he could unravel the mystery and help the counterintelligence operators trace the leak back to its source.

But a problem soon developed. Before the walk-in could move from provisional status to that of a recruited agent, he had to be polygraphed. The CIA sets great store by the polygraph, even though the results of lie detector tests are notoriously inaccurate. Aldrich Ames, the CIA traitor who revealed agency secrets to Moscow and caused the death of ten agents — Russians working for the CIA — passed a polygraph test after consulting the KGB for advice. He was told to get a good night's sleep, come in rested and refreshed, be relaxed, calm, and cooperative, and try to establish a rapport with the examiner. It worked.

When the walk-in was "fluttered" — given a polygraph test — the CIA concluded he was lying. "When asked, 'Are you being run by another intelligence service?' his answer went off the charts," said one CIA officer. "Eventually the guy was practically admitting it."

The CIA decided, from the lie detector test and interrogations, that the walk-in was "a dangle," a dispatched agent under the control of Chinese intelligence. In the summer of 1996, despite the astonishing accuracy of the W-88 document, the CIA circulated an internal memo to its officers warning that some of the Chinese material was disinformation provided by a source being run by Beijing. The walk-in was not recruited.

Aside from the walk-in's failure to pass the lie detector test, the CIA concluded he was a plant because some of the documents contained information that appeared to be wrong. "At first," the CIA officer said, "he [the walk-in] said he stole the stuff, then the agency discovered there was bogus stuff mixed in, so that meant he was given material by Chinese intelligence."

There were additional reasons to be skeptical, another intelligence official asserted. "He wanted to give us more information inside China, during Chinese New Year, when nobody was on the streets. That sounded like a setup for the arrest of a [CIA] officer trying to clear a drop inside China. We didn't like the way this whole thing looked."

The FBI, however, did not agree with the CIA's analysis. "There was a woman at CIA who always says no to a source," one FBI agent said. "She's notorious for saying no. She must have a big 'No' stamp. She pulled out her stamp and used it on the walk-in documents. She is the one who said it's a provocation, the walk-in was sent."

The bureau gave the walk-in a separate polygraph, and the FBI's China specialists decided he was exactly who he said he was. By 1999, if not earlier, the walk-in had left China and settled in California. Later, he moved to another state, where the FBI was able to locate and interview him.

To question the walk-in, the FBI sent Special Agent Doug Gregory, whom the bureau considered its most skilled interviewer, and Dave

Lambert, an FBI counterintelligence agent who had worked on the Aldrich Ames and Robert Hanssen spy cases. They came away convinced that both the walk-in and his material were legitimate.

The FBI, thus reassured, continued to deal with the walk-in. The split between the two agencies, historic rivals in the intelligence world, caused a major row. To this day, both sides have stuck to their positions.

The CIA, despite its disavowal of the walk-in, was able to validate the 1988 date of the W-88 document. Whether or not the walk-in was a directed agent, his information on the W-88 was accurate.

Although the walk-in's document made it clear that China had somehow learned the measurements of the W-88, the Chinese would need more to replicate and support the miniaturized warhead. According to one intelligence official, "If the Chinese have the W-88, the next thing they would be looking for are the computer programs to maintain these systems. There is a high possibility of failure unless you understand these weapons. They would need computer codes that simulate what would happen to the warhead with age. It has to be constantly tested over time with computer simulations. To certify that the weapons actually work."

Was China in fact able to use the data its spies acquired to build a miniaturized warhead and replicate the W-88? That was one of the key questions that the CIA faced. "The agency wrestled with this in its classified damage assessment," an intelligence official said. "An earlier 1997 study by CIA only agreed that whatever they got saved them time, maybe two to fifteen years, and saved them resources.

"Chinese underground testing hit a peak in 1994–95 of a device somewhat similar to the W-88. You can't really tell, but you can bracket the yield, an analyst can put multiple sources together, and with the yield from seismographic information they can guess what was tested. Also you pick up a lot of SIGINT [signals intelligence]. They're chattering when a test takes place."

In May 1999 the bipartisan House committee headed by Christopher Cox issued its controversial report on Chinese espionage. The Cox Report expressed no doubts that China had taken advantage of stolen secrets. "The People's Republic of China (PRC) has stolen classified information on all of the United States' most advanced thermonuclear warheads, and several of the associated reentry vehicles," the report asserted. "These thefts are the result of an intelligence collection program spanning two decades, and continuing to the present.

"The stolen U.S. secrets have helped the PRC fabricate and successfully test modern strategic thermonuclear weapons. The stolen information includes classified information on seven U.S. thermonuclear warheads, including every currently deployed thermonuclear warhead in the U.S. intercontinental ballistic missile arsenal."

The report also judged that China was "capable of producing small thermonuclear warheads based on the stolen U.S. design information, including the stolen W-88 information."

A number of US scientists took issue with the report and have argued that China could produce small nuclear warheads on its own, without bothering to copy American designs. However, the report included statistics that tended to support the theory that China did in fact benefit from the US technology it had somehow obtained.

The report noted that "the PRC had conducted only 45 nuclear tests in the more than 30 years from 1964 to 1996 (when the PRC signed the Comprehensive Test Ban Treaty), which would have been insufficient for the PRC to have developed advanced thermonuclear warheads on its own. This compares to the approximately 1,030 tests by the United States, 715 tests by the Soviet Union, and 210 by France."

The damage assessment by the intelligence community, while not agreeing with every aspect of the Cox Report, supported many of its major conclusions. The "Key Findings," an unclassified summary released in April 1999, found that China acquired US nuclear weapons information "by espionage" that "probably accelerated its program to develop future nuclear weapons" by allowing the Chinese to avoid dead ends in its research and development.

The summary also found that "China obtained at least basic design information on several modern US nuclear reentry vehicles, including the Trident II (W88)." China, it added, "also obtained information on a variety of US weapon design concepts and weaponization features, including those of the neutron bomb."

The "Key Findings" obliquely reflected the argument within the interagency group over whether China had been able to use the information its spies obtained. Chinese espionage, the assessment noted, had not resulted "in any apparent modernization of their deployed strategic force or any new nuclear weapons deployment." Finally, the summary concluded that China had the capacity to develop MIRVs but had not done so.

But the damage assessment, at least the portion made public, ducked another mystery. The FBI stood by its conclusion that the walk-in was who he claimed he was. If the CIA was correct that the walk-in was under the control of Chinese intelligence, why had China allowed him to deliver the W-88 document and hundreds of others?

The CIA was unable to arrive at an answer to the puzzle, but theories abounded within the intelligence agencies. One idea was that China may have been trying to rattle Washington by revealing it had acquired US nuclear secrets. In that view, the walk-in was sent to confuse or demoralize US intelligence by playing a game of "gotcha." Others speculated that the W-88 document was included by sheer accident, or to disguise the actual date when the information was acquired. Another theory held that the walk-in was part of an operation to intimidate Taiwan, which Beijing regards as part of China.

There were other theories, including one that the W-88 document was designed to support the credibility of the Chinese agent who brought it, in order to set the stage for a major deception of US intelligence. Often, a dispatched agent will hand over legitimate information to build his credibility, and then provide false information.

In the end, the experts could come up with no satisfactory answer. Whether the walk-in was sent or not, and aside from the debate about that between the CIA and the FBI, the central question remained of how China had obtained the information about the warhead in the first place. But one counterintelligence official at the Department of Energy was convinced that the W-88 details had come from Los Alamos, where the weapon was designed.

He had zeroed in on a suspect, a scientist at the lab. The official was sure he was the spy.

# Chapter 9

# KINDRED SPIRIT: WEN HO LEE

NOTRA TRULOCK GREW UP outside Indianapolis, the son of
a fireman who became a gunsmith, and a mother who started
her own doll-making business. He was a self-described mediocre
student at Indiana University.

The Vietnam War was on; when he graduated in 1970 he was drafted
into the Army, which sent him to the Defense Language Institute in
Monterey to learn Russian. The Army Security Agency posted him
to Germany, to the Bavarian Alps, where he spent eighteen months
listening to Soviet radio traffic. After he got out, he joined the National
Security Agency in 1975, then worked for a think tank in Denver. In
1990 he took a job at the Los Alamos National Laboratory. Four years
later, he was promoted to director of intelligence at the Department of
Energy in Washington.

Counterintelligence at the department was "little more than a joke,"
Trulock said. Although he had no background in CI, Trulock was determined to do something about the problems at DOE, particularly
to improve what he perceived as lax security at the nuclear weapons
labs. He was swimming against the current; scientists believe in the
free exchange of ideas and are inherently resistant to security restric-

tions, polygraphs, and the counterintelligence mindset. There was, and probably always will be, tension between the physicists who design the nation's nuclear weapons, and "the cops" who are responsible for keeping secrets from falling into the wrong hands.

In 1992 an event took place that led in time to a prolonged mole hunt at DOE, presided over by Trulock. On September 25, China tested a nuclear weapon underground. US analysts concluded that Beijing had succeeded in exploding a miniaturized bomb. Over the next few years, other Chinese tests followed. In the spring of 1995 two scientists at Los Alamos, after analyzing the test data, told Trulock that China, in achieving a small warhead in a very short time, probably gained its success through espionage.

By July, under the code name KINDRED SPIRIT, an interagency working group with experts from the nuclear labs, the CIA, and the Defense Intelligence Agency was studying the question of whether China had developed a miniaturized warhead through spying. The group's cautious conclusions were never sent to the FBI, however. That same month, the FBI opened a file under the same code name, KINDRED SPIRIT, on the possible loss of nuclear secrets to China.

A month later, the CIA shared with the Energy Department the startling document with details of the W-88 warhead obtained from the walk-in who claimed to work in China's nuclear weapons program. Up to then, the suspicion of Chinese espionage had been based on an analysis of China's nuclear tests. The document provided by the walk-in dramatically changed all that. Now the focus of the inquiry shifted to the W-88. In September, DOE opened a formal investigation of how China had obtained precise classified details of America's most advanced weapon, the Trident warhead.

Trulock eagerly embraced the idea that American labs had been penetrated by China and nuclear secrets stolen. Someone in China had obtained the measurements of the W-88. Trulock was convinced the spy must be at Los Alamos, where the weapon had been designed in 1984, although data about the warhead had been widely circulated within the government.

With the assistance of an FBI agent who was dispatched to Los Alamos, a list of a dozen suspects was drawn up and sent to the bureau by

Trulock. Wen Ho Lee was on the list, along with his wife, Sylvia, who had also been employed at Los Alamos. Lee worked in X Division, where the nuclear bombs are designed, the most secret part of the Los Alamos lab, and he had specific knowledge about the W-88.

Trulock, who quit as an officer of his college fraternity and moved out when it refused to pledge a black student, vehemently denied that Wen Ho Lee was singled out because he was Chinese. "We came up with a list of about a dozen people," he said. "There were Americans of Chinese origin and not of Chinese origin on the list."*

But a memo written by Dan Bruno, the chief of counterintelligence investigations at DOE — who reported to Trulock — explicitly recommended that Chinese Americans who worked with the W-88 be targeted by the investigation.

"A crucial element of this inquiry is the identification of personnel who worked on the various aspects of the design," the memo stated. "An initial consideration will be to identify those US citizens, of Chinese heritage, who worked directly or peripherally with the design development. . . . This is a logical starting point based upon the Intelligence Community's evaluation that the PRC targets and utilizes ethnic Chinese for espionage rather than persons of non-Chinese origin."

In the same vein, one of the more bizarre documents churned up in the Wen Ho Lee investigation is a memo in DOE files dated November 15, 1995, of a meeting about China's nuclear weapons program. It states that Charles Curtis, the deputy secretary of energy, "noted that there are seven Chinese restaurants in Los Alamos."

The question of whether Wen Ho Lee was singled out because he was Chinese was examined in a TOP SECRET Justice Department review completed in 2000 by Randy Bellows, a federal prosecutor. The exhaustive review, which was extremely critical of both DOE and the FBI, found "no evidence of racial bias" by DOE or "that the selection of Wen Ho Lee was based upon an investigation of Chinese Americans to the exclusion of any other group of potential suspects."

At the same time, the Bellows review found that DOE's final report

---

* According to a secret Justice Department report on the Wen Ho Lee case, there were six "ethnic Chinese" on the list of twelve suspects, including the two Lees.

to the FBI was edited at DOE to convert it from "a broad identification of potential suspects to a virtual indictment of the Lees." The forty-four-page DOE report found that Wen Ho Lee "was the only individual identified during this inquiry who had the opportunity, motivation and legitimate access" to the design of the W-88.

"Wen Ho Lee should never have been the *only* suspect," the Bellows review asserted, finding that "the message communicated to the FBI was that the FBI need look no further within DOE for a suspect. Wen Ho Lee was its man."

In short, Wen Ho Lee quickly became DOE's and Trulock's prime suspect. The widely held public perception that Lee was singled out because he was a Chinese American is a controversy that may never be fully resolved. Even those who investigated Lee are ambiguous in dealing with the question. For example, Robert Vrooman, a former CIA officer who was chief of counterintelligence at Los Alamos, said in a sworn court declaration in August 2000 that the scientist was singled out "because Lee is ethnic Chinese." But a month later, appearing on the PBS television show *The NewsHour with Jim Lehrer,* he told interviewer Gwen Ifill that the cause was not "ethnic profiling or racism. It was really just the lack of intellectual rigor in the original investigation. . . . Once they found Lee, and he was ethnic Chinese, they didn't go on and look at the entire population."

There were, however, several good reasons that Wen Ho Lee came up so rapidly on the radar screen. He had previously been investigated twice by the FBI for suspicious behavior.

In 1982 he was scrutinized at length by the FBI after he made the telephone call to Gwo-bao Min, the TIGER TRAP suspect, offering to find out who had "squealed" on Min. He had lied when asked about that, denying he had contacted the Livermore scientist, admitting the truth only when confronted with the transcript of the wiretap on Min's phone.

There was some question about how he learned that Min had been forced out of Livermore. In his memoir, *My Country Versus Me,* Wen Ho Lee wrote that he read "in a popular Chinese-language magazine" that "a Taiwanese nuclear scientist was fired from Lawrence Livermore." The publication, he said, had named Min. But Min's name did not surface, at least in any English-language publication, until after his identity was disclosed in a court document in the prosecution of Wen Ho Lee. The FBI suspected that Lee had learned about Min from another scientist.

On December 23, 1998, Lee was given a lie detector test administered by the security firm Wackenhut, an Energy Department contractor. He answered no when asked if he had ever committed espionage against the United States. In the pretest interview he acknowledged that, many years before, he had learned that "Ko Pau Ming," whom he knew was from Taiwan, "was having trouble with some men in China" and "out of curiosity" had telephoned him.* The Wackenhut report was declassified by the government in the subsequent prosecution of Wen Ho Lee. Min was later identified by name in a story by reporter Dan Stober in the *San Jose Mercury News.*

Early in 1994 the FBI opened a second investigation of Wen Ho Lee after an incident known in counterintelligence circles as "the hug." It began when Lee showed up uninvited at a meeting in Los Alamos of senior officials with a high-level visiting delegation of scientists from China.

The delegation was led by Hu Side, China's leading nuclear weapons designer. During a break in the meeting, Lee went up to Hu and was warmly embraced by the top Chinese weapons scientist. Some of the American participants in the meeting were immediately suspicious. How did Wen Ho Lee, a relatively low-level employee at Los Alamos, know Hu, and how did he merit a hug?

An FBI memorandum about the 1994 meeting cites an unidentified source who quoted Hu as saying of Wen Ho Lee, "We know him very well. He came to Beijing and helped us a lot."

Lee had been to China twice to attend scientific meetings, in 1986 and 1988. In his trip report after the 1988 meeting, Lee failed to mention that he had been visited at his hotel room by Hu Side, who was accompanied by another scientist, Zheng Shao Tong. Nor did he re-

---

* Wen Ho Lee told the polygrapher that he had called Gwo-bao Min. The Wackenhut employee who administered the lie detector test apparently did not bother to confirm the correct spelling and simply rendered the name phonetically in his report as "Ko Pau Ming."

port that Zheng had asked whether the United States used two-point detonation on the W-88. Lee was aware that the answer was highly classified. He later claimed that he told Zheng "he did not know the answer" and did not want to discuss the matter.

Two-point detonation was, of course, the key to the design of the W-88, the way that US scientists had solved the problem of how to build a miniaturized warhead. And Hu Side was credited with developing the small warhead that Beijing tested four years later, in 1992.

Robert Vrooman, the Los Alamos counterintelligence chief, interviewed Wen Ho Lee after his 1988 trip to China. According to Vrooman, Lee not only omitted any mention of his hotel room meeting with Hu Side, "He answered no to a direct question," when specifically asked if any approach of that kind had occurred.

As a result of "the hug," the FBI investigated Wen Ho Lee for a year and a half, until November 1995. Six months later, on May 30, 1996, at the request of DOE, the FBI opened a full-fledged investigation of Wen Ho and Sylvia Lee. This time the probe, still code-named KIN-DRED SPIRIT, was not about a suspicious hug. It was about whether Wen Ho Lee had given the design secrets of the W-88 to Beijing.

The walk-in, whether under Chinese control or not, had produced a document that proved China had acquired details of America's most deadly and sophisticated warhead. That should have led immediately to a massive investigation by the FBI, the CIA, and DOE, to try to determine the source of the leak. Astonishingly, that did not happen for three years. In 1999, months after Wen Ho Lee was fired from the Los Alamos lab, a broader investigation was finally begun by the FBI.

Because of the narrow findings of the DOE formal inquiry, which pointed only to Wen Ho Lee, the FBI for three years was not investigating how and where China might have stolen the design details of the warhead. Instead, it was investigating Wen Ho Lee and his wife. In the words of the Bellows Report, "the FBI investigated the wrong crime."

Wen Ho Lee was born on December 21, 1939, into a poor farm family in Nantou, Taiwan, one of ten children who grew up in a three-room adobe mud house, surviving on the vegetables the family grew, and the chickens, ducks, geese, and pigs they raised. With his brothers and sisters, he caught fish and frogs each day for dinner. As a child during World War II, Lee lived through the Japanese occupation of Taiwan. After graduating from Cheng Kung University he served in Taiwan's air force for a year of compulsory military service. He came to the United States as a student in 1964, enrolled in Texas A&M, and earned a master's degree and then a PhD in engineering. He met his wife, Sylvia, in 1969 at the Rose Bowl parade in Pasadena; she had been born on the mainland but, like Wen Ho Lee, grew up on Taiwan. They were married soon afterward, and had two children.

In 1974 he became a US citizen, and four years later he was hired to work at Los Alamos on hydrodynamics codes of nuclear weapons. When metals liquefy in a nuclear explosion, they behave like fluids. Using computer models, scientists can write codes that simulate what happens in a real nuclear detonation. At Los Alamos, Lee worked on computer simulations of both primary fission components and the secondary hydrogen bombs. And he ran codes to test the W-88.

Sylvia Lee also was hired by the lab, as a secretary and then a data-entry clerk, and she soon volunteered as a sort of unofficial greeter for visiting scientists from China. She also reported to the FBI and the CIA on what she gleaned from those contacts.

Behind the scenes, the investigation of Wen Ho Lee created a dilemma for both the FBI and DOE. If he was a spy and remained in X Division, it was feared he might do more damage. But if he was pulled out, he might become suspicious that the government was closing in.

In 1996 DOE came up with an elaborate scheme to limit Wen Ho Lee's access to the vault at Los Alamos containing X Division's most sensitive secrets, but to do it in a way that would not alarm him. The lab would install an electronic device that would read palms to allow entry to the vault; then several employees, including Wen Ho Lee, would be told they no longer had access under the new system. The lab chief thought the palm reader had been installed, but it never was.

In July 1997 the Justice Department turned down an FBI request for a wiretap on Lee's telephone, saying the bureau lacked enough evidence to apply to the special Foreign Intelligence Surveillance Court for a warrant. John F. Lewis Jr., then the FBI assistant director in charge of the national security division, met with Attorney General Janet Reno and pressed again for the wiretap, which was denied once more.

In the spring of 1998 Edward J. Curran, a former counterspy for the FBI and the CIA, was brought in to the Energy Department to head its Office of Counterintelligence. A tall, athletic father of four, Curran had been named chief of the CIA's counterespionage group after the Aldrich Ames debacle. At DOE, he was appalled to find Wen Ho Lee still in X Division at Los Alamos.

In August the FBI ran a "false flag" sting against Lee. An FBI agent who was a Chinese American telephoned Lee, claiming he was "a representative of the 'concerned department' from Beijing." He identified himself with a false name, Wang Ming-Li. But like so much about the Wen Ho Lee case, the sting was badly handled. The agent posing as an MSS officer spoke only Cantonese, even though officials in Beijing speak Mandarin.

The original plan was to use a Chinese American agent who spoke both Mandarin and the Shanghai dialect, because the FBI suspected that Wen Ho Lee might have had some link to the Shanghai State Security Bureau, the MSS arm in that city. Because the FBI agent sent to Santa Fe spoke only Cantonese, he had no credibility as an intelligence officer from Beijing.

In a series of telephone calls, the undercover FBI agent explained to Wen Ho Lee that he had come to New Mexico to make sure that all was well with Lee in the wake of the conviction in California of another Chinese American scientist, Peter Lee, for passing defense information to China. He asked to set up a meeting with Wen Ho Lee. Lee was skeptical of the caller's pitch, and said he was required to report any meeting with a foreign official. He said he preferred to talk on the phone.

The undercover FBI agent pressed to meet Wen Ho Lee in person, saying there were other sensitive matters besides the Peter Lee case that he wanted to discuss. Wen Ho Lee then agreed to meet the agent at the Hilton hotel in Santa Fe. But ten minutes later, Lee called back to say he had changed his mind.

The next day, the FBI man posing as a Chinese intelligence agent called again to say he would be leaving Santa Fe and gave Lee a pager number that he said belonged to a trusted American friend and could be used if Lee wanted to get in touch with him. Lee did not report the phone calls, but told his wife, Sylvia, who told a friend, who told DOE security. When Lee was then questioned about the calls by DOE counterintelligence, he acknowledged the phone calls but did not mention that he had accepted the beeper number.

Two days before Christmas, with Curran still determined to pull Lee from X Division, he was finally transferred to T Division, which performs unclassified work, where he remained until Bill Richardson, the secretary of energy, dismissed him altogether.

Richardson, a seven-term congressman and a veteran diplomat, had stepped into a political minefield. Washington was in an uproar. President Clinton was facing impeachment for lying about his affair with Monica Lewinsky; charges that China had contributed money to try to influence Clinton's 1996 presidential election campaign continued to bubble up in the press; and Richardson knew that the Wen Ho Lee case was rapidly coming to a head. The Cox Committee, with Trulock as its key witness, was gearing up to issue its sensational report on Chinese espionage, and Republicans in Congress smelled blood.

Richardson now saw his chances of becoming the nation's first Hispanic vice presidential candidate evaporating. Despite his Anglo name, his mother was Mexican, and he had high hopes that his Latino credentials and diplomatic and legislative record might help catapult him onto the Democratic ticket in 2000. But Richardson was seasoned enough to know that the turmoil at the Energy Department, damaging reports of flawed security at the labs, and the Chinese spy scandal, although not of his making, meant his political ambitions would have to be put on hold.

Wen Ho Lee, meanwhile, was blissfully unaware that the FBI had been intensively investigating him for three years, or that he was the prime suspect in how China had acquired design details of the W-88. Life was good in White Rock, the Los Alamos County community where the Lees had bought their house. Wen Ho Lee liked to cook for his friends and garden, and he continued to indulge his lifelong passion for fishing. As a respected nuclear scientist, he had traveled far from his dirt-poor roots a world away in Taiwan.

All of that came crashing down on Saturday, March 6, 1999, with the publication of a front-page story in the *New York Times.* The story,

later the subject of much controversy, reported that China had succeeded in building small nuclear warheads, a "breakthrough" that officials said was speeded "by the theft of American nuclear secrets from
Los Alamos National Laboratory in New Mexico." The story, by James
Risen and Jeff Gerth, quoted Notra Trulock at length. It did not directly name Wen Ho Lee, but described "the main suspect" as "a Los
Alamos computer scientist who is Chinese-American."

It was apparent that Trulock had leaked the story to the *Times,* a fact
he later publicly confirmed on CBS's *60 Minutes,* in an interview with
Lesley Stahl.

On the afternoon of Sunday, March 7, as the story reverberated
throughout Washington, Wen Ho Lee was closeted in the El Dorado
hotel in Santa Fe with two FBI agents, Carol Covert and John Hudenko.
They shoved the *Times* story at him and warned, "It's not good, Wen
Ho . . . it's very bad . . . There's a person at the laboratory that's committed espionage and that points to you!"

"But do they have any proof, evidence?" Lee asked.

In response, the agents pressed him, over and over again, about
what had happened in the hotel room in Beijing in 1988 when Hu Side
had visited him and he had been questioned about the detonation
points of nuclear weapons. "Tell us what went on in that room," Covert
demanded.

She warned, "You are going to be an unemployed nuclear scientist.
You are going to be a nuclear scientist without a clearance. Where is a
nuclear scientist without a clearance gonna get a job?"

He would not be able to get a job, Lee conceded. He could just retire.

"If you retire . . . and we come knocking on your door, we have to
arrest you for espionage! When somebody comes knocking on your
door, Wen Ho . . ."

"No, no, no," Lee protested.

". . . they're not going to give you anything other than your Advice
of Rights and a pair of handcuffs! That's all you're going to get. What
are you going to tell your friends . . . your family . . . your wife and son?
What's going to happen to your son in college . . . when he hears the
news? . . . [A story] on the front page of the paper would say 'Wen Ho

Lee arrested for espionage.' They're [reporters] going to find your son
. . . and they are going to say, you know your father is a spy?"

"But I'm telling you," Lee said, "I did not do anything like that."

Then the interrogation, hardly a walk in the park up to that point,
turned really brutal.

> COVERT: Do you know who the Rosenbergs are?
>
> LEE: I heard them, yeah, I heard them mention.
>
> COVERT: The Rosenbergs are the only people that never cooper-
> ated with the federal government in an espionage case. You
> know what happened to them? They electrocuted them, Wen
> Ho.
>
> LEE: Yeah, I heard.
>
> COVERT: The Rosenbergs professed their innocence. The
> Rosenbergs weren't concerned either . . . The Rosenbergs are
> dead.

Wen Ho Lee, exhausted by now, stood his ground, insisting he had
done nothing wrong. Always polite, he actually thanked the agents
when the interrogation came to a close. When he finally left the FBI
office, he was shaking.

On Monday morning, his name leaked out to the news media. At
11 A.M., he was called in and, on orders from Secretary Richardson,
fired from Los Alamos for failing to report his encounter with Hu Side
and other security infractions. After twenty years, his career at the
laboratory was over.

When the Cox Report came out two months later, in May, it described how the 1995 "walk-in" to the CIA brought out the document
containing design information on the W-88 and data about the other
thermonuclear warheads. The report did not mention that Wen Ho
Lee was DOE's prime suspect in the loss of the W-88 data, the real
reason he was dismissed.

But the report did discuss two instances in which there had been
leaks of information about the neutron bomb. Wen Ho Lee fell under
suspicion in one of those cases as well. Referring to the TIGER TRAP

case without using that code name or identifying Gwo-bao Min, the report said that in the late 1970s "the PRC had stolen classified U.S. information about the neutron bomb."

The Cox Report also contained a cryptic reference to a second neutron bomb leak to China, discovered in 1996. DOE sleuths suspected that Wen Ho Lee might be linked to that second loss.

Behind the brief reference in the Cox Report to an alleged second loss of neutron bomb data was a series of events backstage at DOE. China had tested a neutron bomb in 1988, but analysts at Los Alamos thought that if Beijing had used data acquired from the TIGER TRAP operation it may have encountered some of the same problems that the United States had experienced in developing a neutron warhead.

Yet China by the mid-1990s had managed somehow to solve those problems. Some of the scientists at Los Alamos said this sounded like the Chinese had learned of the "pill boosting" solution to making a neutron bomb, a secret process that US scientists had explored. There had been a secret conference at Los Alamos in 1992 reporting how the United States had solved the problem of designing the neutron bomb. Pill boosting was discussed at the conference. DOE investigators decided that the report from the conference must somehow have been passed to China. Once again, DOE suspected Wen Ho Lee.

Had Wen Ho Lee attended the conference? The frustrated counterintelligence agents at DOE were not sure, because scientists with Los Alamos badges could enter and leave the conference freely. Scientists with Livermore badges were checked in and their names recorded, so it was known which of them attended, but that was not the case for their colleagues at Los Alamos.

Beyond that, there was a dispute over whether the additional information about the neutron bomb had been acquired by China. Other scientists thought the original tip about a second theft of neutron bomb data was actually about a neutron generator, which is not secret. A neutron generator, colloquially known by bomb designers as a "zipper," is a device for producing high-energy neutrons with a particle accelerator. Although miniature neutron generators, produced by the Sandia National Laboratories, a DOE facility in Albuquerque, New Mexico, are used in all US nuclear weapons, neutron generators also have a wide application in medicine, geology, and basic laboratory physics experiments.

In the aftermath of his dismissal from Los Alamos, Wen Ho Lee hired Mark Holscher, then with the high-powered Los Angeles law firm of O'Melveny & Myers, to represent him. The FBI had accused him of espionage and the news media was camped outside his house; he needed a lawyer. As a federal prosecutor, Holscher had made his reputation prosecuting Heidi Fleiss, the Hollywood Madam. He was joined on the defense team by John Cline, a shrewd expert on the Classified Information Procedures Act (CIPA), a law that permits those parts of cases that might reveal government secrets to be heard by a judge in camera. It was enacted in an effort, only partly successful, to prevent defense attorneys from engaging in "graymail" by threatening to expose government secrets if prosecutors brought a case to trial.

But the more the government examined the case against Wen Ho Lee, the more prosecutors realized they could not charge him with espionage. There was, in fact, not a shred of evidence that Lee had passed information about the W-88, the neutron bomb, or any other secret to China. In searching his office at the lab, however, investigators discovered that he had downloaded computer files, the codes simulating nuclear explosions, from the classified computer to the open, "green" computer network. Moreover, he had then copied the codes onto tapes, and no one was sure how many tapes existed and what had become of them.

Operation KINDRED SPIRIT now metamorphosed into operation SEA CHANGE. If Lee could not be prosecuted for spying, he could be charged with mishandling nuclear secrets. The Justice Department began preparing a case against Lee for downloading the codes.

Ironically, DOE knew about Lee's massive downloading of classified files six years before the government indicted him for it. The computer office at Los Alamos had set up a system that it called Network Anomaly Detection and Intrusion Recording (with the inevitable acronym of NADIR) to ferret out unusual computer usage by the lab's scientists. The detection system flagged Wen Ho Lee's downloading in 1993. But the DOE official who knew about Lee's suspicious downloads failed to act and did not tell the DOE counterintelligence staff or the FBI.

In August 1999 Notra Trulock was forced out of DOE. To help deal with the counterintelligence crisis, Richardson had brought in Lawrence Sanchez, a veteran CIA officer who had been detailed to New York when Richardson was the US ambassador to the United Nations. He installed Sanchez above Trulock as chief of a newly created Office of Intelligence.

In the restructuring, Trulock was marginalized. He had touched off the chaos over Wen Ho Lee, leaked the original story to the *New York Times,* and spilled secrets to the Cox Committee. "I feel like a pariah in this department," Trulock said, accurately, a few days before he resigned. Still, given the political firestorm that had broken over DOE, Richardson found it prudent to give Trulock a hearty handshake and an award of $10,000.

That same month, Wen Ho Lee went on *60 Minutes,* and the government lost its case before it ever started. Lee's appearance with a sympathetic Mike Wallace turned the tide of public opinion in Lee's favor, and the prosecutors never regained their footing.

"The truth is I'm innocent," Lee said on the CBS television broadcast. "I have not done anything wrong with — what they try to accuse me."

Had he never passed United States nuclear secrets to China? Wallace asked.

"No I have never done that. . . . I devote the best time of my life to this country, to make the country stronger . . . so we can protect the American people."

Wallace then asked why Lee had downloaded the files. "To protect my code," he replied. "To protect my file."

Lee was asked why he thought he had become a target.

"My best explanation of this is they think I'm a, you know, Chinese people — I was born in Taiwan. I think that's part of the reason. And the second reason, they want to find out some scapegoat."

Lee's explanation on *60 Minutes* of why he had illegally downloaded the codes was enigmatic. In later statements, he elaborated. He said he had once lost his work when the lab converted to a new computer system and did not want it to happen again. Government investigators theorized that it was more likely he wanted the material in case he ever left Los Alamos to look for a new job.

Four months later, on December 10, 1999, a federal grand jury in Albuquerque handed down a fifty-nine-count indictment charging Lee with mishandling classified information. If convicted he faced a sentence of life in prison. He was arrested by the FBI at his home, handcuffed, and taken to the Santa Fe County jail. Three days later, he was denied bail after Stephen Younger, the associate director of nuclear weapons programs at Los Alamos, warned ominously that the codes Wen Ho Lee had downloaded could, in the wrong hands, "change the global strategic balance."

Lee spent the next nine months in solitary confinement. Under the harsh special administrative measures, or SAM, ordered by the attorney general, he was placed in handcuffs, waist shackles, and leg irons during the one hour a week he was allowed outside his cell.

Lee's defense lawyers pressed unsuccessfully to have him released from the onerous prison conditions. But as the months dragged by, the government's case suffered a series of setbacks. Two lead prosecutors left. One quit to run for Congress, another was replaced because of reports he had an affair with a woman on his staff. Robert A. Messemer, an FBI supervisory special agent, admitted in court that he had given erroneous testimony about Lee.

John Cline was promising to force the government to produce highly classified evidence if the case went to trial. FBI director Louis J. Freeh worried that if Lee was convicted, the government would never find out why he had downloaded the nuclear weapons codes and transferred them to tapes, seven of which were missing.

Alberta Lee, Wen Ho Lee's daughter, was tireless and effective in appearing at rallies and on television on her father's behalf, asserting that he was innocent and a victim of racial profiling because of his Chinese heritage. In August, James A. Parker, the federal district judge presiding over the case, said he was not persuaded that Lee should be kept in jail, and ordered him released. The government blocked his release. By September, however, prosecutors, their case unraveling, were ready to give up. They offered Lee a plea bargain.

The terms were worked out among the lawyers for the two sides; the government would drop fifty-eight of the fifty-nine counts in the indictment. In return, Lee would plead guilty to one count of mishandling defense data, a felony, and would tell the government why he had downloaded the secrets and what he did with his tapes.

Then Judge Parker stunned the hushed courtroom in Albuquerque with his words. "I believe you were terribly wronged by being held in custody pretrial in the Santa Fe County Detention Center under demeaning, unnecessarily punitive conditions. I am truly sorry that I was led by our executive branch of government to order your detention last December. Dr. Lee I tell you with great sadness that I feel I was led astray last December by the executive branch of our government. . . . They did not embarrass me alone. They have embarrassed our entire nation and each of us who is a citizen of it.

"I might say that I am also sad and troubled because I do not know the real reasons why the executive branch has done all of this. . . .

"Although, as I indicated, I have no authority to speak on behalf of the executive branch, the president, the vice president, the attorney general, or the secretary of the Department of Energy, as a member of the third branch of the United States Government, the judiciary, the United States Courts, I sincerely apologize to you, Dr. Lee, for the unfair manner you were held in custody by the executive branch."

Wen Ho Lee was free. He walked out into the bright New Mexico sunlight, accompanied by his lawyers and Alberta, to face the television cameras. "For the next few days, I'm going fishing," he said.

The prosecution was derided because the government had thrown fifty-nine counts at Lee and was able to convict him of only one. But the unusual length of the indictment was a result of the fact that each count listed a separate file that Lee had "removed" or altered and copied.

The plea agreement was almost derailed when at the last minute Lee mentioned to the lawyers that he had not only downloaded the codes and copied them onto tapes, he had also made copies of the tapes. He claimed he had thrown the tapes into a dumpster near his office in the lab. The FBI later assigned a hapless team of agents to dig through the city dump looking for the tapes, but they were never found.

In the aftermath of the case, Brian Sun, an astute Los Angeles lawyer who later represented J.J. Smith in the PARLOR MAID case, brought an invasion-of-privacy suit on behalf of Wen Ho Lee against the government for leaking Lee's name to the press. In 2006 the suit was settled for $1,645,000, with five news organizations agreeing to pay almost half that amount.

The news outlets were not named in the suit, but joined in the settlement to avoid having their reporters punished and possibly jailed for refusing to name their sources. The reporters had been held in contempt of court and ordered to pay fines of $500 a day, but the fines were suspended while they appealed.

And so the saga was over, with no real winners. The case was a fiasco, and a tragedy. The evidence suggests that Wen Ho Lee may have been singled out, at least in part, because he was a Chinese American. That should never have happened. There were certainly other significant factors that led to the focus on Lee; his actions had led to two previous FBI investigations.

Although critics blamed Trulock for the Wen Ho Lee debacle, he did alert Congress and the public to the fact that China had somehow obtained details of the nation's most sophisticated nuclear weapon. And responsibility for mishandling the Wen Ho Lee case was shared among a wide spectrum of officials at DOE, the Department of Justice, the federal prosecutors in Albuquerque, and the FBI.

As an Asian American casualty of government misconduct, Wen Ho Lee was a deeply flawed hero. He pleaded guilty to a felony, mishandling defense information. He lied to the FBI, denying that he had called the TIGER TRAP scientist until confronted with the wiretap evidence. He downloaded thousands of classified nuclear weapons files to an insecure, unclassified computer system and then onto tapes, for his own, still unclear, reasons. Several of those tapes were never found. He concealed his contact in China with Hu Side, China's top nuclear weapons designer, the scientist who built that country's small nuclear warhead.

He had very smart lawyers and a shrewd sense of public relations—his appearance on *60 Minutes* was a brilliant move, although he never convincingly explained to Mike Wallace exactly why he had downloaded all those files. But he was jailed and held under excessively harsh conditions, and the government bungled the case against him at every turn. He was portrayed to the public as a dangerous spy yet never charged with espionage or found guilty of espionage.

Almost forgotten amid the furor over the Wen Ho Lee case was the still-unanswered question that started it all — the mystery of who stole the design of the W-88 warhead and gave it to China.

# Chapter 10

# SEGO PALM

ROBERT M. "BEAR" BRYANT was raised on a farm in Springfield, Missouri, went to law school at the University of Arkansas, and then joined the FBI. He rose through the ranks to head the national security division, and in 1997 was named the bureau's second in command, as deputy director.

By September 1999, Bryant was unhappy with the Wen Ho Lee investigation, which was dragging on and seemed no closer than ever to discovering how China had acquired the dimensions of the W-88 warhead. In fact, there was so much controversy over the botched probe of Wen Ho Lee that the larger question seemed in danger of being lost in the shuffle.

Bryant reached his decision. The FBI needed to launch a separate, major investigation of how China had gained access to the secret of the nation's most advanced nuclear weapon.

He knew whom to call. Steve Dillard, the special agent in charge in Jackson, Mississippi, had worked for Bryant in Kansas City, Salt Lake, and at headquarters. He had run the section in charge of foreign counterintelligence and espionage and over the years had earned Bryant's complete trust.

A thin, bespectacled, soft-spoken man, Dillard was pleased to be back in his native Mississippi. He grew up in New Albany (pop. 7,607), in the hill country in the northeast corner of the state, and had a master's degree in sociology and criminology, as well as a law degree. In manner and appearance, he could easily be mistaken for a college professor rather than the counterspy and FBI veteran he was.

Dillard recalled how his Mississippi idyll ended. "I got a phone call out of the blue from Bob Bryant. He said the FBI was taking a hit in congressional hearings and in the national media." Bryant bluntly laid out his concerns and asked Dillard to fly back to Washington and take a look at the origin and status of the Wen Ho Lee investigation.

"I asked that a copy of the Albuquerque field office case file be shipped in to FBI headquarters," Dillard said. "I came in to headquarters on a Monday morning and over the next three days, read both the headquarters and the Albuquerque files."

On a secure phone, Dillard made several calls to the field office in Albuquerque and to CIA headquarters. On Thursday afternoon, he reported his conclusions to Bryant, who had him brief FBI director Louis Freeh the next morning. In the afternoon, Dillard and Freeh met with the attorney general, Janet Reno.

Early the following week Reno, Freeh, and Dillard sat down with Secretary Richardson at the Department of Energy. The FBI would continue its investigation of Wen Ho Lee, they told Richardson, but it also would open an "overall investigation" of the documents obtained in 1995 from the walk-in, including the one displaying the measurements of the W-88, "to examine other potential areas of compromise."

Dillard was given carte blanche to assemble as big a staff as he needed. The new, broader investigation of the W-88 compromise was given a secret code name: SEGO PALM, named after a plant, *Cycas revoluta*, native to southern Japan that is poisonous to humans and animals.

Soon, Dillard put together a task force of three hundred people in eleven government agencies. He worked from FBI headquarters, but also enlisted several agents at the Washington field office. One, Dave Lambert, served as case agent at the field office for the new investigation. Lambert was one of the two FBI men who later interviewed the walk-in and judged him authentic, not a plant as the CIA contended.

Most members of the task force were from the Defense Department. There were researchers, and agents from a little-known Pentagon unit, the Counterintelligence Field Activity. A large group of translators worked on the walk-in documents, mostly from the FBI and the CIA, although some were from the NSA and the Defense Intelligence Agency (DIA).

The investigation was, to say the least, challenging. How China had accomplished its coup of obtaining the W-88 data, the source or sources of the documents or information that had ended up in Beijing, the individuals who might have passed the secrets, exactly when that had occurred — all were unknowns, the answers locked in the minds and files of Chinese intelligence half a world away across the Pacific.

Bryant and Dillard recognized that there was no assurance the new investigation would discover the answers. Even so, Dillard was startled by what he had found even as he was assembling the huge task force.

The administrative inquiry by DOE's intelligence branch, Dillard said, reported that the information in the walk-in document "had to have come from X Division within Los Alamos, and Wen Ho Lee was the only person in X Division who could have compromised the information. It was completely wrong."

The internal evidence in the W-88 document made that clear, Dillard said. "In any nuclear weapon, you have the physics package and the delivery system," he continued. "The physics package is the configuration and parts of the two-stage bomb itself. The delivery systems are the mechanisms we use to deliver the bomb to the target — the ICBMs, the submarine-launched ballistic missiles, and the strategic bombers. This document had a small amount of information about the physics package, but it had even more stuff dealing with the delivery system. That meant that DOD, the Defense Department, not DOE, was the proprietor of the majority of the information in the document."

Although that did not exclude Los Alamos and the Energy Department as the source of the leak, it suggested that the Pentagon was a more likely place to look. The information in the W-88 document,

Dillard said, was not only "all over" the Defense Department and DOE, "it was in Trident submarine manuals, and some of it had even been shared with the Brits."

Under an agreement reached in 1982, Britain was allowed to equip its submarines with Trident II missiles. "It had been public knowledge for nearly a half century that the US and the Brits had a cooperative and shared arrangement for their nuclear weapons programs. We've even had our scientists from DOE's national laboratories detailed to the British nuclear weapons facilities at Aldermaston and Burghfield."

Dillard was not saying that the walk-in's information had leaked from Britain. His point was that the Energy Department's analysts "failed to perceive that the material could have been compromised through various components of the US government, including the Defense Department, possibly even through a foreign government."

After China tested its small warhead in 1992, the Energy Department pulled together about two dozen scientists in its KINDRED SPIRIT advisory group. That in turn led to the DOE administrative inquiry that produced the forty-four-page report to the FBI stating that Wen Ho Lee was "the only individual" who could have leaked the information about the W-88. The administrative inquiry had supposedly drawn upon the findings of the KINDRED SPIRIT advisory group. Dillard resolved to dig deeper; he decided that the FBI would talk to the advisory group.

"I couldn't believe that two dozen of our weapons scientists could be so wrong. By that time, the original members of the group had scattered around all over the country. I had our agents locate and interview every single member of the original group. Only about four or five of that group said that it had to have originated in Los Alamos and X Division. The rest of them, along with me and my FBI and Justice Department colleagues, thought that idea was baseless."

According to Dillard, "about twenty members of the advisory group said they could not identify the source of the information in the walk-in document. But what DOE sent to the FBI was the administrative inquiry which pinpointed not only X Division, but specifically Wen Ho Lee."

The Bellows Report, the exhaustive review of the Wen Ho Lee case, agreed that DOE had sent the FBI on a wild-goose chase. But it was equally critical of the FBI for unquestioningly accepting DOE's conclusion and focusing all of its resources on Wen Ho Lee. It faulted "the FBI's own lack of investigative interest in looking beyond Wen Ho Lee."

But for Dillard, that was ancient history. He had now been assigned to the investigation that should have taken place three years earlier. And the trail was cold.

The Chinese, he realized, could have obtained the information about the W-88 not only from Los Alamos, where the warhead was designed, or from elsewhere in DOE, but from a much broader spectrum of agencies within the government — from the Pentagon, the armed services, hundreds of defense contractors, even the British. Pinpointing the source of the leak was proving nearly impossible.

Nor did the rivalry between the CIA and the FBI help matters. When the bureau wanted to interview the walk-in, the CIA said he was inaccessible. Dillard thought otherwise, and the FBI found him, living in the United States.

Doug Gregory and Dave Lambert, the two agents who interviewed the walk-in, concluded he had not been sent by Chinese intelligence. Unlike the CIA's view, their assessment was that he was not controlled. However, the walk-in was unable to shed any light on the source of the W-88 document.

Dillard did not confine his investigation to the W-88, although that was the major focus. Although only a few documents in the walk-in's trove dealt with nuclear weapons, there were others of counterintelligence interest, including classified US documents containing data from the Army, the Navy, and the Air Force.

In a vault in the basement of the CIA, languishing in dust-covered boxes, Dillard was astonished to find thousands of documents that had never been translated when they were brought out by the walk-in four years earlier. Now they would have to be examined by the task force.

It was slow and painstaking work. The titles of the documents were translated first. Dillard assigned priority to those that looked the most interesting. These were summarized, and if they had intelligence value, some of the full texts were translated. But there was nothing in the other material that gave any clue to the origin of the W-88 document.

Dillard was hoping to find a document, somewhere inside the defense and nuclear weapons establishment, that might match up to the details in the Chinese document. Then it might be possible to zero in on a US agency or even one of its components in the search for the source.

But there was a problem. Some US documents contained data about the fission and hydrogen bombs inside the warhead. Other documents dealt with the delivery vehicle itself. But few combined the two. The fact that the Chinese W-88 document contained data about both the physics package — the bombs — and the outer shell or nose cone made it likely, Dillard concluded, that the information obtained by China had come from more than one document.

While SEGO PALM was under way at FBI headquarters in 1999, others were also trying to solve the mystery of the W-88 leak and the documents obtained from the walk-in. At Los Alamos, Robert Vrooman, who headed counterintelligence at the lab for a decade, wrote a memo reporting that four scientists at the lab believed that the documents originated with a defense contractor in Colorado Springs that manufactured subcomponents for much of the US nuclear arsenal.

Dillard also looked at defense contractors in California, Florida, Texas, Nevada, and elsewhere. In trying to pinpoint the source of the W-88 document, the FBI sought help from the Navy, and the Naval Criminal Investigative Service, as well as the Pentagon and DOE.

Dillard's task force also had to look at several other locations. The warhead was designed at Los Alamos, but DOE's Sandia National Laboratories in Albuquerque did the engineering of the W-88, and many nonnuclear elements are manufactured at DOE's Kansas City site. Tritium, a key component of hydrogen bombs, comes from DOE's Savannah River plant near Aiken, South Carolina. The warhead itself was assembled at Pantex, the DOE plant, northeast of Amarillo, Texas.

At Los Alamos, meanwhile, Ken Schiffer, a Chinese counterintelligence specialist at the FBI for twenty-nine years, had retired and in 1998 became director of internal security at the laboratory. Schiffer, too, asked three nuclear weapons scientists at Los Alamos to analyze the W-88 document for clues as to its origin.

Schiffer had an unusual background. He grew up near Sheridan, Wyoming, where his father raised horses and cattle and later bought a ranch in Kaycee, Butch Cassidy and the Sundance Kid territory. Schiffer, who joined the bureau after graduating from the University of Colorado, had entered and won prizes in rodeos and continued competing during his FBI career. Possibly he forgot he was not on a bronco in February 1970 when he wrecked an FBI Plymouth Fury III.

As punishment he received a letter of censure from J. Edgar Hoover — "It is clear that you did not give proper attention to your driving" — and in addition was ordered to Chinese-language school. Apparently the FBI chief suspected there were spies in the nation's Chinatowns, because Schiffer was required to learn Toishan, a Cantonese dialect spoken by many of the older immigrants who came to the United States and opened Chinese restaurants.

Schiffer, who framed Hoover's letter and put it on the wall of his home, much to his wife's dismay, might never have become a Chinese counterintelligence agent had he not wrecked the Plymouth. In the 1980s he ran the China squad at the Washington field office, then worked at headquarters, and later supervised counterintelligence in San Diego.

The Los Alamos scientists reported to Schiffer that the walk-in's document on the W-88 appeared to match a 1986 "interface" document from an earlier stage in the development of the warhead. The term is used to describe a progress report on a project. When the Pentagon wants a new nuclear weapon, an interface document is generated and sent to DOE and the labs, which design the weapon.

Schiffer relayed the scientists' conclusions to the FBI, but their findings did not bring the bureau closer to determining how the Chinese had acquired the details of the warhead. And because the document had circulated back and forth throughout the labs and the Pentagon, even if China had acquired it, there was no way to tell at what point in the loop it might have been intercepted.

One cause of contention among the intelligence experts who analyzed the walk-in's documents was a very slight discrepancy between the measurements of the W-88 in the Chinese document and the true size of the warhead. The Chinese data was said to be one millimeter off.

Ken Schiffer said the discrepancy could be explained by the fact that the walk-in document was based on dimensions in the 1986 document. "This was an early stage that changed later on."

Ray Wickman, who headed the FBI's China squad and later worked in counterintelligence at DOE, offered a different reason for the minuscule variance in the Chinese data from the actual dimensions of the warhead. "The US document had measurements in inches. The Chinese document had dimensions in millimeters. If you translated the US document into millimeters and rounded off the number and then translated it back to inches there could be a slight discrepancy."

About six months into the SEGO PALM investigation, Dillard decided to call in the Jasons. A secretive, elite group of the nation's top scientists, Jason — the organization uses the singular rather than the plural form of the name — probably has about fifty members, only some of whose identities are known. Twice a year, the group prepares studies for the Pentagon and the intelligence community. Most of its reports are classified.

Dillard asked the Jasons and Richard L. Garwin, a brilliant nuclear physicist and government adviser, to review the W-88 document. A number of other nuclear scientists were brought in to help.

The CIA was prevailed on to give the Jasons a TOP SECRET briefing on the document and its provenance. The briefing was held in a SCIF at the headquarters of the Mitre Corporation, in McLean, Virginia, which administers Jason. In a SCIF, a vault supposedly secure from eavesdroppers, no laptops or other electronic devices are allowed. The scientists, at least for a while, were deprived of their BlackBerrys and cell phones.

The Jasons endorsed SEGO PALM's methodology, and provided some additional recommendations. But even the brainy scientists could only guess at where or how the information about the W-88 warhead might have found its way to China.

At DOE, Richardson's new director of intelligence, Larry Sanchez, was also looking into the loss of the W-88 design details. Sanchez was not a typical cubicle-dwelling government official. He grew up in Washington, DC, where his mother was vice counsel of the Brazilian embassy. After working as a charter boat captain and scuba instructor, he joined the CIA in 1984 and served overseas in several posts in East Asia in the agency's clandestine service. Dark-haired and muscular, he was a competitive weightlifter who jumped out of airplanes for relaxation; he reported to work at DOE with a gold bead in his pierced left ear, awarded the year before, after he'd completed five hundred jumps.

Sanchez quickly discovered that dissemination lists of more than half a dozen DOE classified manuals, each several pages long and containing the same information as in the Chinese document, had been distributed inside DOE, as well as to the Defense Department, the armed services, and some five hundred government agencies and private contractors.

Officials conducting the intelligence community's damage assessment in 1999 thought that the document turned over by the walk-in closely paralleled a US Navy document that was circulated widely within the government. In Los Alamos alone fifty copies were found. The Navy document was a memo from the undersecretary of defense for research and engineering to the chief of naval operations. It appeared to have been written in the Navy's Strategic Systems Project Office in the early 1980s.

With so many different theories floating around, Dillard had his hands full, juggling a mountain of information, much of it conflicting. And then tragedy struck. At 9:37 A.M. on September 11, 2001, some of the investigators on Dillard's task force were among those lost when American Airlines Flight 77, hijacked by terrorists, struck the west wall of the Pentagon, killing 125 people and all 64 people aboard the aircraft.

The work went on, and a Pentagon unit, part of the SEGO PALM investigation, did find precise evidence of the origin of at least one of the walk-in's documents. According to Dillard, "We found one original document from a defense contractor with the same schematic diagrams, the same information, the same names, and it matched exactly with one of the walk-in documents written in Chinese. But this was not the W-88, it was a classified portion of one of the delivery systems."

In the end, Dillard judged that the Chinese had most likely put together the data about the W-88 and the other weapons systems little by little over a long period of time. "When you look at all of the materials we examined, we concluded that the compromises were likely to have been made by either multiple personnel or multiple means over a several-year period from the '70s to the early '90s." China had obtained the information, Dillard said, "by spies, or through technical means, or through negligent acts."

After two and a half years running SEGO PALM, Dillard early in 2002 was nominated by FBI director Robert S. Mueller III to head the Office of Counterintelligence at DOE. The office had been created in the wake of the Wen Ho Lee case. Dillard remained a senior FBI official, detailed to his new position at the Energy Department.

Mike Donner, a veteran FBI counterintelligence agent, took over the SEGO PALM investigation. Donner, who had worked on the Aldrich Ames spy case, was well informed on both the W-88 conundrum and the history of the Wen Ho Lee affair. He had helped to put together the Bellows Report on the case two years earlier.

Donner ran SEGO PALM for another two years. During that period, the FBI pursued another investigation, an offshoot code-named FALLOUT. SEGO PALM examined the walk-in's documents for clues about their origin. FALLOUT was looking at suspects who might have leaked the W-88 details. None was pinpointed or prosecuted.

SEGO PALM and FALLOUT were unable to resolve the mystery of how China obtained the design of America's most advanced nuclear weapon or who had leaked the information. While the Wen Ho Lee disaster garnered all the headlines, the FBI, unknown to the public, worked in secrecy for four and a half years, enlisting three hundred people and ten other agencies, in a massive effort to find the leak and solve the enigma of the man who walked into the CIA with a duffle bag full of secrets. In the end, the answer stayed hidden where it had begun, in China.

# Chapter 11

# TROUBLE IN PARADISE

S PECIAL AGENT J.J. SMITH was sitting on top of the world. With Katrina Leung as his golden informant on China, he continued to enjoy a unique status in the FBI's Los Angeles field office and at headquarters in Washington. An extrovert, confident — some would say brash — he was not easily fazed by the unexpected. But even J.J. froze, at least momentarily, when he heard the news that PARLOR MAID brought back from Beijing in March 1991.

This time, she reported on an extraordinary meeting she had with Jiang Zemin, the general secretary of the Communist Party, destined to become China's president; Jia Chunwang, the head of the MSS and the nation's top spy; and Mao Guohua, the head of the MSS's American department.

A month later, J.J. would learn, from the National Security Agency intercept, that Mao was Leung's MSS handler and that, using the code name Luo, she was spilling FBI secrets to him. But PARLOR MAID gave no hint of that when Smith debriefed her at her home in San Marino.

It was the subject of the meeting in Beijing that rocked J.J. Jiang

Zemin and the other Chinese officials wanted Leung to become a major contributor to the Republican Party. President George H. W. Bush was up for reelection the following year.

According to PARLOR MAID, as J.J. wrote in an FBI memo classified SECRET, "Secretary Jiang asked, 'What are President BUSH's chances of being reelected?'" Leung, mistakenly as it turned out, ventured that his chances were "excellent"; Bush was defeated by his Democratic opponent, Bill Clinton.

"JIANG said, of course we care because we don't know if a new president would be as friendly as BUSH." The party chief, according to Katrina, added that "we take every opportunity to support people we like. . . . It would be nice to have friends like you (pro-China) to be involved in U.S. politics. Every little thing adds up."

Jiang warmed to his subject. "You could be involved at various levels. If your involvement makes you a friend of the Republican Party at the local, state or congressional level then we have one less enemy. I am sure we will give you the support you need."

Uh-oh. Smith realized that this conversation in Beijing, with Chinese officials at the highest level, was about influencing the American presidential election. It was sensitive, politically explosive information, not the sort that counterintelligence agents normally gather and report to FBI headquarters.

The early-morning meeting had taken place on March 4 at Zhongnanhai, the leadership compound adjacent to the Forbidden City in Beijing.* Mao Guohua asked Leung, "How can you actively participate in this election?" Leung then offered the Chinese leaders a short course in US Politics 101. "Most people start at the state level. A person could participate as a 'major member' if you donate about $10,000 to the Republican Party. Then you are in the inner circle."

She explained what would happen next. "Then you can become

---

* Zhongnanhai, guarded and closed to the public, is the central headquarters for the Communist Party and the government. The name is commonly used to refer to China's center of power, much as in the United States "the White House" means the president and the administration.

inner circle at the national level of the party. Of course once you are invited to the inner circle you are automatically invited and expected to donate lots of money at various fund raisers.

"These fund raising parties would include parties for the President, Senators, Congressmen and other state politicians. All of these people would look you up. Even people from out of state. And they would have their hand open for donations."

Mao asked, "When will this process start?" A year before the election takes place, Katrina replied. "MAO asked, if we want you to be involved you should start early, right?" Leung said yes.

There was a discussion as well of President Bush's campaign staff, in which the Chinese officials displayed a keen interest. Mao briefed Jiang Zemin on what he had learned from Leung about the Bush campaign, that "a man named Yeutter will head it replacing a man named ATWATER who is very ill."

Two months earlier, Clayton K. Yeutter, a Nebraska corn farmer and Bush's agriculture secretary, had replaced Lee Atwater as the Republican National Committee chairman. Atwater, the master of attack politics, entered the hospital the day after Leung's meeting in Beijing and died of a brain tumor three weeks later at age forty. It was Atwater who had orchestrated Bush's election in 1988, crushing the Democratic candidate, Michael Dukakis, with the aid of the famous Willie Horton television commercial.

When the meeting broke up after an hour, Mao accompanied Leung to her hotel, where they talked four hours more, according to Smith's report. "MAO said I have the approval for you to make contributions to the Republican Party. If you are correct about $10,000 making you a major member of the Republican Party, we want you to join as a major member."

She replied, "$10,000 will get me in but I will need a lot of money to sustain the effort over a long period of time." MAO responded, "I know. $10,000 is nothing to the Republican Party or to us. We do not expect you to manipulate anyone with $10,000."

Mao then explained, "One of the reasons we want you to go ahead is that it would enhance your image and heighten your profile so that you might be in a better position to handle other things. I clearly understand that once you start this process it is a never ending series of donations. If $10,000 is a reasonable amount to get you in and if it takes a reasonable amount of money to continue then we will support you."

Leung and Mao then fenced about the money. She said, "Define your terms. What is reasonable to you? Give me a budget and I'll work with it."

Mao ducked. "I have this approved in principle," he said. "I have no details."

That evening, Minister Jia Chunwang, the MSS chief, showed up at the hotel and hosted a dinner meeting in room 17, the presidential suite. Jia "had a serious upper respiratory infection" and, solicitous of their important asset, "insisted on sitting at least 5 feet away from the source [Leung] and he covered his mouth with a napkin when he talked." Coughing away, the top spy ordered only hot water to drink.

Here, the meeting among spies took a farcical turn. Leung "insisted he try an old Chinese student flu remedy, boiled Coca Cola with lemon." Never mind me, the MSS chief responded, "you should take better care of MAO, he is too skinny." It was true, Mao replied, he had an ulcer. Leung said "me too" and then Leung and her MSS handler "compared symptoms."

As the officials at the hotel discussed their ailments with Leung, China was preparing to celebrate Lei Feng Day, named for the national hero, a twenty-two-year-old soldier in the People's Liberation Army who was killed in 1962 when a truck he was directing backed up and hit a telephone pole, which fell on him. He was later glorified by Mao Zedong's propagandists as a symbol of patriotic youth, loyalty to China, and selfless devotion to others. "Be like Lei Feng" was the slogan drilled into Chinese schoolchildren.

Leung remarked, "You probably think I am too young to remember Lei but I do and I remember the song that was written about him." She then proceeded to sing a few bars of the lyrics. "JIA thereafter sang the song in its entirety to everyone's amusement," the FBI report said.

*"Emulate the fine example of Lei Feng, ever frugal and simple,"* the spy chief trilled. *"Emulate the fine example of Lei Feng, who kept Chairman Mao's teachings ever in his heart."* And so on.

Then the group got back to business. "Minister JIA said, I am sure MAO told you that once you establish a budget to join the Republican Party, we will give you the money. Don't worry there is no special tasking from us. I think it would do you a great deal of good to have a higher profile which gives you more protection. If anything good comes your way for China so much the better."

Jia's instructions were very much in the "thousand grains of sand" mold. Become an active Republican, donate money, and let's see what happens. The entire discussion was a precursor to the much more active, and controversial, role of Chinese donors in President Clinton's 1996 election campaign, in which Katrina Leung would serve as a major FBI source.

Leung in fact did become a substantial contributor to the Republican Party. As noted, she gave $10,000 to Los Angeles mayor Richard J. Riordan, who lost the Republican primary for governor of California in 2002. And after the Beijing meeting, Leung and her husband contributed about $27,000 to the Republican Party during the 1990s.

It was only a month after Leung's meeting with Jiang Zemin, Jia, and Mao Guohua that Bill Cleveland contacted J.J. to warn that PARLOR MAID, using the code name Luo, had been caught on tape reporting FBI secrets to Mao.

It was a mark of Leung's growing importance that she had acquired the code name Luo from none other than Zhu Qizhen, a ranking official in China's foreign ministry. As vice minister, he had run the North American department, and he was ambassador to the United States from 1989 to 1993. Zhu himself had assigned Leung the code name Luo Zhongshan.

But there had been danger signals about PARLOR MAID well before the NSA tape provided incontrovertible evidence that Leung was reporting to the MSS. Late in 1987, PARLOR MAID asked an official in the Chinese consulate in San Francisco to call her from a pay phone. The implication was that she assumed or knew that the consulate was bugged by the FBI and had something to tell him that she did not want the bureau to overhear.

If the consulate was wiretapped, the FBI may have heard Leung make her request that she be called from a pay phone. Or perhaps the

FBI learned about her request from a recruitment in place, or RIP, that the bureau had inside the San Francisco consulate. In any case, the bureau opened an investigation. But the inquiry was quickly closed when it was discovered that Leung was J.J.'s asset.

In June 1990, almost a year before J.J. Smith and Bill Cleveland learned about Leung's intercepted conversation with Mao Guohua, the FBI received the information that PARLOR MAID had tipped off the Chinese to the FBI's bugging of China's consulate in Los Angeles. Soon after, the FBI's supersophisticated listening devices abruptly went silent.

When headquarters questioned J.J. about the compromise, he contended that PARLOR MAID could not have informed the Chinese of the electronic eavesdropping of the Los Angeles consulate, because J.J. himself did not know about it. FBI headquarters accepted his explanation and let the matter drop. But it was not then known that Leung, during her trysts with J.J., had been quietly helping herself to secret FBI documents from his briefcase.

J.J. was so well regarded at the time that FBI headquarters decided he could personally handle any concerns about Leung's reliability. So the pay phone incident, the report that she had blown the bugging of the Los Angeles consulate, and the intercept of her conversation with Mao were all left in J.J.'s hands.

Which was fine with him. An episode in the mid-1980s illustrated how confident J.J. was that he could handle whatever came along. J.J. Smith was the lead case agent in the FBI investigation of one of its own, Richard Miller, an overweight, klutzy FBI man in Los Angeles who became romantically entangled with Svetlana Ogorodnikova, a sultry thirty-four-year-old KGB agent, and as a token of his affection gave her classified documents. She was sentenced to eighteen years; Miller, the first FBI agent to be convicted of espionage, was sentenced to twenty years. At the very time that J.J. was investigating Miller, he blithely continued his affair with his own mistress, Katrina Leung.

Despite the red flags raised about Leung, the FBI was reassured by the fact that she had passed two polygraph exams, and because a Chinese defector confirmed much of her reporting. The CIA, as well, was pleased with the information she was supplying to J.J. This was especially true in 1989, when she traveled to China soon after the Tiananmen Square crackdown. When she returned, she provided the FBI with information about political rivalry inside the Chinese leadership at a time when almost no information of that kind was coming out of China.

But not everyone in the FBI and the CIA was enthusiastic over PARLOR MAID. In the late 1980s Leung had brought back a videotape she made in China. Bill Cleveland played the videotape for the China squad in the San Francisco field office.

He did not identify PARLOR MAID as the source of the video, but the squad knew it had come from J.J.'s premier source in Los Angeles. Leung had gone to the headquarters of the MSS in the West Garden section of Beijing. The videotape showed the entrance and then a courtyard inside the spy headquarters.

How could she do that without getting caught? some of the counterintelligence agents on the squad wondered. And CIA officers in the agency's San Francisco base expressed doubts about the amazing access that J.J.'s source seemed to have and the intelligence she brought back from China. It was, one of the CIA officers remarked, "too good to be true."

Another red flag went up in March 1992 after the London interview with Hanson Huang, the Harvard-educated lawyer who was a key player in the TIGER TRAP espionage case. After Smith and Cleveland had interviewed Huang in the British capital, J.J. took five days of leave for a sightseeing trip around England.

Unknown to anyone in the Los Angeles FBI office, Katrina Leung had flown to London to join J.J. on the tour of Britain. Dorothy E. "Dot" Kelly, who had become J.J.'s supervisor a few months earlier, admired him greatly. To Kelly, J.J. could do no wrong. The two often lunched together. She decided to surprise him by meeting him at LAX on his return.

Kelly was startled to see both J.J. and PARLOR MAID, whom she knew, going through customs. They had obviously been on the same flight. Kelly greeted J.J. and gave him a ride home. All the while in the car, J.J. worried that his supervisor had spotted Katrina Leung and would question him about it or peach to FBI headquarters. To J.J.'s relief, she did neither.

The inspector general's report of the incident found that the supervisor "was overly dependent on Smith, reluctant to confront him, and inappropriately deferential to him." As one FBI agent in Los Angeles said, "I've seen Dot bring J.J. coffee at squad meetings."

Another danger signal arose in 1992. According to the Justice Department review, an FBI source reported that a woman named "Katrina" was a double agent "working in the FBI." Headquarters ordered J.J. to interview the source. J.J. brushed off the tip, saying the source was "a liar and a misogynist," and explaining that the information accurately described his officially approved relationship with Leung as an FBI asset.

Three years later, another incident came perilously close to derailing PARLOR MAID. A supervisor at FBI headquarters had become wary of Leung's reporting and all that money the bureau was paying her. He suspected that she had been turned and doubled back against the United States.

The supervisor assigned an FBI analyst to do an in-depth review of Leung's file. The analyst discovered that Leung had not been polygraphed in ten years, and drafted a message to Los Angeles ordering that she be given a lie detector test.

But the supervisor thought that headquarters could not compel the field to act unless required by the rules. He softened the language of the message simply to suggest that Los Angeles consider polygraphing PARLOR MAID. Since it was only a suggestion, J.J. was able to ignore it.

The ponderous FBI bureaucracy overlooked the series of red flags that might have unmasked PARLOR MAID more than a decade before she was finally caught. For example, the headquarters supervisor who believed Leung had been doubled back against the United States was transferred before the review of her file was completed.

The constant turnover of FBI managers meant that no one was really looking at J.J. and Leung. Between 1990 and 1996, when the series of danger signals came in rapid succession, there were four different supervisors at headquarters and three different supervisors of the

China squad in Los Angeles, all responsible for PARLOR MAID. As a result, J.J. was the only FBI agent who knew the complete history of the PARLOR MAID operation. And because of his standing and Leung's accepted value as a prime bureau asset, nothing came of the various clues that raised questions about her.

In October 1996 Dot Kelly left Los Angeles and J.J. succeeded her as the supervisor of the China squad. Normally, a counterintelligence agent who becomes a manager would not continue to handle a source. But such was J.J.'s prestige that an exception was made in his case. He was permitted to continue to run PARLOR MAID.

For the next three years, J.J. supervised the field office's work in CAMPCON, the FBI investigation of alleged Chinese involvement in the 1996 presidential campaign of Bill Clinton. Leung became a principal source for J.J. in the campaign-contribution inquiry.

That same year, Johnny Chung, a California businessman, met in Hong Kong with General Ji Shengde, the head of Chinese military intelligence. The general, using an alias, appeared from the shadows at the kitchen entrance of an abalone restaurant. The spy chief, Chung later testified to a House committee, sent him $300,000 and said he hoped that the money would be given to help elect President Clinton. Some $35,000 of the total did find its way into the campaign. "We really like your President," General Ji said, according to Chung.

It was explosive testimony and put Johnny Chung at the center of the congressional and Justice Department investigations into Chinese influence in the Clinton presidential campaign. It was J.J. Smith who questioned Chung for the FBI.

J.J. then guarded Chung when he received mysterious death threats from a California man who suggested that Chung would live considerably longer if he refrained from talking any more. Among other issues that the FBI was later forced to reexamine was whether Katrina Leung may have fed misinformation to the bureau in its CAMPCON investigation of China's role in the Clinton campaign.

Johnny Chung pleaded guilty in 1998 to bank fraud and other charges in connection with illegal campaign contributions. He was sentenced to five years' probation and three thousand hours of community service. General Ji fared less well; caught in an embezzlement and bribery scandal reported to involve millions of dollars in guns, luxury cars, and tanker loads of crude oil smuggled into China through the southeastern port of Xiamen, he was initially sentenced to death in 2000, but his punishment was eventually reduced to fifteen years.

Katrina Leung vigorously and publicly defended her friend Ted Sioeng, another figure involved in the campaign-contribution investigations. The Chinese consulate in Los Angeles had issued the $3,000 check to a hotel owned by Sioeng that, when disclosed by *Newsweek,* nearly blew the cover on the fact that the FBI had bugged the consulate's copying machines. In the 1980s Sioeng, a millionaire Indonesian businessman, won a contract from the Chinese government to sell overseas China's most popular cigarette, Hongtashan, marketed abroad as the Red Pagoda Mountain brand. Sioeng through his daughter donated $250,000 to the Democratic National Committee, channeling the funds to John Huang, another key figure in the CAMPCON investigation.

Sioeng moved to Los Angeles, where he was an influential figure in the Asian community and worked with Leung on a number of local events. He also owned a pro-Beijing Chinese-language newspaper in Monterey Park, the largest Chinese American neighborhood in Los Angeles. A striking figure, with bushy silver muttonchop sideburns, Sioeng sat next to Vice President Al Gore at the notorious Buddhist temple Democratic fundraiser in Hacienda Heights, California, in April 1996.

Both Attorney General Janet Reno and FBI director Louis Freeh told Senate investigators that there was credible intelligence, reportedly gleaned from electronic intercepts, linking Sioeng to an effort by the Chinese government to influence US elections through campaign contributions. Sioeng denied that he or his family had ever acted as agents of the Chinese government. Leung, in an interview with the *Los Angeles Times* in 1997, called the reports about Sioeng "nonsense."

"If China needed a good agent, why would it turn to someone who doesn't know the United States and doesn't speak English well?" she asked. In retrospect, her comment was ironic. At the very time she derided reports that Sioeng was a Chinese agent, she herself was passing FBI secrets to the MSS.

In the late 1990s the FBI discovered that some of its operations had been compromised and several assets originally recruited by the bureau had been seized and interrogated in China. Typically, the FBI does not operate assets abroad; that is primarily the job of the CIA, known by FBI counterintelligence agents as "the cousins." When the FBI recruits an intelligence asset, a student or businessperson, for example, if the recruit returns to China he or she normally would be handed off to the CIA. After the compromises and problems inside China were discovered, a special counterintelligence task force was formed to investigate what happened. The task force was to look at Leung's file as part of its review.

Then, in the spring of 2000, an informant run by the San Francisco field office who was a double agent for the FBI and Chinese intelligence reported that Leung was working for a PRC spy service and had a source inside the FBI. Although the source inside the FBI was obviously J.J., the section chief at headquarters told him about the report. The informant also claimed that Leung had revealed to the Chinese that he, the informant, was an FBI source.

FBI headquarters ordered the task force to investigate the informant's claims, but the inquiry moved slowly and eventually fizzled out, reaching no conclusions. Then, later in 2000, the same informant reported that Leung was "in bed with" the FBI's LA division. While it was literally true, J.J.'s superiors at headquarters did not take it that way.

In November 2000 J.J. Smith retired. There was a big turnout of FBI and other intelligence agents, including some from the CIA, at the retirement party, which was held at the upscale Riviera Country Club. But few eyebrows were raised when Katrina Leung, an outsider, showed up, along with J.J.'s wife and son. And hardly anybody seemed to notice when PARLOR MAID set up a video camera on a tripod in the back of the room, recording all the speeches and the faces in the crowd.

In December, J.J. received a final accolade. CIA director George

Tenet awarded him the National Intelligence Medal of Achievement, capping his thirty-year career in the FBI.

Despite his medal and the retirement celebration, J.J. had a sense of foreboding. The PARLOR MAID operation was a dicey business. Dealing as she was with the most powerful leaders of China and its intelligence service, sooner or later there was bound to be trouble. Like a skilled player in a game of Whac-a-Mole, J.J. had managed to knock down the danger signals and questions that kept popping up. But he was out of the bureau now and no longer in control of the operation. It might only be a matter of time before his luck ran out.

# Chapter 12

# ETHEREAL THRONE: THE SPY WHO NEVER WAS

I T HAD BEGUN innocently enough. His laptop was acting up, so Jeffrey V. Wang, an engineer at Raytheon, in El Segundo, California, called the company's tech support. It was August 1999.

The tech who came looked in the computer, fiddled around, and solved the problem. Wang, then a thirty-seven-year-old engineer with the defense contractor, thought no more about it. But soon afterward, he received a telephone call from a woman in Raytheon's security department.

Would Wang mind coming by? There were concerns about something on his laptop and an Air Force investigator would like to talk to him to clear it up.

Wang didn't mind. He worked in Raytheon's airborne radar division on sensitive projects, including the F-15 and F-18 fighter jets and the B-2 stealth bomber. He had both a regular security clearance and a "special access" clearance for even spookier subjects. He knew that the Air Force was always looking over the contractor's shoulder to make sure security was tight.

That was not surprising — Raytheon's Space and Airborne Systems in El Segundo developed not only airborne radars but a variety of sophisticated weapons — electronic warfare systems, scanned array radars, space and missile technology, and intelligence, surveillance, and reconnaissance systems.

Wang met with the Air Force investigator, who flashed his ID and asked Wang to take a polygraph. The lie detector test was supposed to be administered at the Air Force base in El Segundo. But then there was a change: Wang was instructed to go instead to the FBI office on Wilshire Boulevard in Los Angeles. Still unconcerned, Wang was wired up to the polygraph machine. It was turned on and he was asked five questions.

The polygrapher examined the printed readout.

"You're not telling the truth about foreign contacts," Wang was told.

An American, born in Honolulu, Wang could not imagine what the FBI man was talking about. He could not think of any foreign contacts.

The polygraph done, Wang was questioned by Special Agent Gil Cordova. A tall, heavyset man, a bureau veteran, Cordova had been a counterintelligence agent for fourteen years. He worked out of the FBI office in Long Beach, but had come to Los Angeles to interview Wang.

"Be a man," Cordova admonished Wang. He then told him a story. "Once, when I was young, I threw a baseball through a window. At first I denied it. Then I stood up like a man and admitted it."

Wang was unimpressed. Baseballs through a window? It seemed like Interrogation 101. About now, it also dawned on him that the trouble with his laptop had perhaps not been accidental, after all. He suspected the computer had been tampered with; the security issue had been a ruse designed to maneuver him to the FBI office in Los Angeles for questioning. For reasons he could not fathom, he had somehow fallen under suspicion.

It seemed like a script written by Kafka. Wang was upset, and then he remembered: he had a friend in the FBI, in that very building. Denise Woo was a special agent in Los Angeles and a childhood friend of Wang's wife, Diane.

Diane Misumi had been born in Los Angeles of a Japanese American mother and father, both second-generation Americans. During World War II, in the panic after Pearl Harbor, when tens of thousands of Japanese Americans were interned, Diane's mother, Grace, and Denise Woo's mother, Sarah, were both sent off to the "relocation centers." Woo's mother was a Japanese American, and her father was half Chinese.

The two families were close; they had gone on camping trips together, and Jeff Wang's older brother and Denise's younger brother were the same age and good friends from school. From the FBI office, Jeff called his wife, who telephoned Denise Woo.

Jeff had been called in by the FBI, would it be OK if Denise talked to him and tried to help? Denise was sympathetic, and after hearing back from his wife, Jeff called Woo.

She listened to what had happened and asked Wang, "Was there anything that could have triggered the polygraph result?" Nothing Wang could think of. Denise said she would come and see him, since she was in the building.

Unknown to Jeff Wang and his wife, he had been under investigation by the FBI for more than a year. The FBI had given the case the code name ETHEREAL THRONE. J.J. Smith, as the supervisor of the Chinese counterintelligence squad, was in charge. He had assigned Cordova and two other agents, Serena Alston and Brad Gilbert, to the case.

Jeff Wang did not know any of that, or that Special Agent Denise Woo had also been ordered to work on the case almost a year earlier, precisely because of her friendship with Wang and his family. Wang had reported to the FBI at noon and it was now 6 P.M. and he was still sitting in the bureau's office on Wilshire. Cordova told him that the FBI wanted to search his house. Since Wang had nothing to hide, he called Diane, and she agreed to the search. Jeff signed a release allowing the bureau to conduct the search.

Denise Woo showed up and offered to accompany Wang to his house. He was relieved that his friend would be present, and Woo followed in her car.

At the house, Woo and another FBI agent sat in the living room with Jeff and Diane. It was getting on toward bedtime for the Wangs' two young children, Daniel, three, and Kiane, a baby girl, just one.

At 9:30 P.M. more than a dozen FBI agents, led by J.J. Smith, arrived at the house. Jeff had not expected such a large group. The agents seized the Wangs' home computer. Diane protested, to no avail, because she had her own private files in the computer. As a practicing clinical psychologist, she specialized in treating children. The computer held confidential reports on the children who were her patients.

The agents searched the house from top to bottom. They took CDs and notebooks and floppy disks, and opened letters that were lying on the mail table. Three agents searched through toy boxes in the three-year-old's room, as three others rummaged through the one-year-old's toys.

Daniel was upset because his favorite Tonka truck game was in the computer. For days afterward, he asked his father, "When are those bad people going to bring my game back?" But the computer, with the Tonka truck game and Diane's confidential files, remained in the possession of the FBI.

As the search progressed, J.J. asked to talk to Jeff privately. They went into the master bedroom, and J.J. introduced himself. China's in turmoil, Smith said, it's the mother country. People are turning one another in. If people are naming you, you should name them.

Jeff was thinking, but didn't say it, "I don't know what the hell you're talking about."

Think of who you know who has contacts with China, J.J. urged him.

Wang was more mystified than ever. His father had come from China before the Communist takeover in 1949 to study in New York on a scholarship. He became a radiologist and settled in Hawaii. Jeff's mother was a second- or third-generation Chinese American who grew up in New York. Jeff had graduated from the University of California at Berkeley, and got a master's degree at UCLA in electrical engineering. He was hired in 1983 by Hughes Aircraft, which merged with Raytheon in 1997, and he had worked for the two companies for sixteen years.

He did not speak a word of Chinese, and felt no personal tie to China, which he had never visited. "Most of my friends are Japanese Americans," Wang told J.J.

He was baffled by what was happening. First the Air Force was investigating him, now the FBI. He had been told to stand up like a man and confess, but confess what? People in China were naming him, J.J. had implied, and he was supposed to name them. Name who? It was surreal.

Was it something to do with his family, Jeff asked? No, J.J. said. "That's not it." Whatever Jeff could think of, he got the same answer: "That's not it." The conversation was going nowhere.

Although it had not been said in so many words, it was clear to Wang that the FBI suspected he was a spy for China. While the search of his house was going on, Denise Woo also talked to Jeff. She encouraged him to think of anyone who might have accused him of passing secrets to China. Did he have any enemies?

Jeff racked his brain, digging back in his memory more than twenty years to high school, trying to think of coworkers, acquaintances, anyone who might have made such a horrendous accusation. He came up with a few names for Woo, but was not convinced that any of them were behind the terrible difficulty in which he now found himself.

The team of FBI agents continued to search the house. They combed through the Wangs' cars, and the attic, everywhere. It was 2 A.M. when they finally left, fourteen hours after Jeff had walked into the FBI office on Wilshire to take a polygraph test.

The nightmare for Jeff Wang and his wife had only begun. The cloud of suspicion hanging over his head cost him his job at Raytheon. The contractor would not continue to employ an engineer under FBI investigation who worked on radar for the Air Force's most sophisticated fighter jets and the stealth bomber. Jeff was suspended from his job and lost his special access clearance. Without it, he was going to have a difficult time finding work in the aerospace industry.

For Denise Woo, ETHEREAL THRONE had become a different sort of ordeal. Intensely loyal to the bureau, she had been put in an impossible position. From the start, she was skeptical that Jeff had done anything wrong. Yet she had to conceal from her longtime family friend that she had been assigned to investigate him some eleven months earlier.

Worse yet, after Wang was called in to the FBI, she was told to renew their friendship, to take advantage of it, and become close to Jeff. To spy on the spy, as it were. Denise Woo had never expected to be put in such a difficult situation when she joined the bureau in 1994. She had worked her way through college at UCLA, then graduated from business school at the University of Southern California.

When Woo joined the FBI, then in her midthirties, she was sent to Quantico, Virginia, for agent training, then assigned to the Long Beach, California, FBI resident agency to work white-collar crime. There she greatly impressed her boss, Special Agent Jack Keller, a handsome, square-jawed Irishman and bureau veteran who helped to train her in criminal investigations. US attorneys and other government officials she worked with praised Woo as a top-notch agent.

From time to time, fellow agents had suggested to Woo that because of her Asian appearance, she should work in Chinese counterintelligence. Although her mother was Japanese American and her father half Chinese, Woo, a fourth-generation Californian, did not write or speak Chinese. She was not interested in following her colleagues' advice, partly because inside the FBI there was a belief, held by some agents, that if you were not good enough for criminal work, you ended up in counterintelligence. As a result, CI was not considered the best career path.

In September 1998 Gil Cordova sent a supervisor to meet with Woo. She was pressured to take a counterintelligence assignment. The bureau, the supervisor said, was aware that Woo knew Jeffrey Wang. The FBI had strong evidence that Wang was a spy for China, the supervisor went on, but it had not been able to prove the case and needed her help. The supervisor waved the flag: this is what it means to be an American, he said, this is why you joined the bureau.

Reluctantly, Woo agreed to help the three case agents working on ETHEREAL THRONE. She provided information on Jeff's family background and her own family's long friendship with the Wangs.

Early in 1999 Woo decided that she wanted to get out of Long Beach and try something new. In June her request was approved, and she was transferred to the Los Angeles division to work on child pornography cases, tracking predators on the Internet. Which is how she happened to be in the Wilshire office the day that Jeff was called in and polygraphed there.

By that time, Woo had gleaned some of the details that had cast suspicion on Jeff. But she did not know everything.

She was not aware of the backstory that had begun in San Francisco. Dave LeSueur was an FBI counterintelligence agent in that city, on the China squad. A bit on the heavy side, LeSueur spoke slowly and always seemed to feel underappreciated. But he had two attributes in his favor. He spoke Cantonese, and perhaps because of that he had developed a number of useful informants, including two women.

But LeSueur's prize informant was a man who, over the years, had provided a good deal of valuable information to the FBI. The source did not work in the Chinese consulate in San Francisco. But he appeared to be trusted by Chinese officials, because some of the tips he provided to the bureau were far too intriguing to have been picked up by someone just hanging around bars in San Francisco's Chinatown. The FBI concluded that the source, although providing useful information to the bureau, was being run by Chinese intelligence.

Sometime in the 1990s LeSueur's informant moved to Los Angeles. The reason remains murky, but perhaps romance called, because at some point during this period he appears to have married. Although the source had relocated, he continued to be run by LeSueur.

In September 1997 the informant told a story to the FBI that triggered the ETHEREAL THRONE investigation. He claimed to have met a Chinese intelligence officer, or IO, in a hotel in the San Gabriel Valley. The officer, the FBI source claimed, spoke no English but asked him to dial a telephone number in Torrance, California.

A man answered the telephone, the FBI informant went on, and said he had been expecting the call. As instructed by the Chinese IO, he told the man to come to the hotel. As the source related the tale, the person he called came to the hotel and exchanged envelopes with the IO. Although the informant could not see what was inside the envelopes, he assumed that cash had been exchanged for secret documents.

The envelope the man brought to the hotel was big enough to hold documents, the informant said. And the envelope given in exchange looked the same as one in which he himself had been given money. That was an interesting statement, because, if true, it meant that the informant, who was on the FBI payroll, had also been paid by China.

Investigating the source's story, Serena Alston, Cordova, and Gilbert were able to obtain toll records showing that a telephone call had been placed from a room registered to the supposed Chinese intelligence agent. The number called was the home telephone of Jeff Wang.

Now the FBI had a suspect. A FISA authorization was obtained and the bureau began wiretapping Jeff's telephones. Counterintelligence is a difficult and often complicated business. The FBI had no reason to doubt the informant's story. He was a longtime bureau source who had always provided useful information.

But there were problems from the start with ETHEREAL THRONE. Often the MSS recruited people by inviting them to China. Alston and the other agents could not find any connection between Jeff and China. So they started to investigate his relatives, to see if that might turn up any leads.

Jeff's father, the FBI learned, had emigrated from the Shanghai area in the 1920s. But the bureau was unable to locate his immigration file, which would have included a list of his relatives. His father's file was either lost or destroyed.

In the meantime, with help from Denise Woo, Jeff was trying his best to figure out who might have led the FBI to suspect him as a spy. He knew nothing of the story told by the informant, about a phone call from a hotel, or an exchange of envelopes.

Jeff's father had died at age seventy-two in July 1999, a month before Jeff was called in and grilled by the FBI. He asked his mother whether she knew of anyone who might have had reason to accuse him. She was able to shed the first ray of light on the mystery.

He learned from her that relatives of his father in Los Angeles were claiming that before his father died, he had promised he would help them out financially. There was nothing in his will, however. But the relatives contended that he had told them that if they needed money he would try to assist them.

By now, Denise Woo had become convinced that Jeff Wang was innocent. She had suspected as much all along. Now she had learned that there was a family disagreement over money, which might hold the key to the puzzle. Jeff gave her the name of a few relatives who he believed might have had a grudge against him over the money his father had supposedly promised them. Woo provided the names to her FBI superiors but was told that none of those individuals was the informant who had fingered Jeff.

Meanwhile, Woo found that although the hotel toll records showed a call had been made to Jeff's number, the duration was only thirty seconds. After six rings, there would be a record of the call even if it was not answered. It was not clear whether anyone had picked up at the Wang residence, or if so, whether the person who answered or the caller said it was a wrong number.

When the FBI examined the computer the agents had taken from Jeff's house, besides Daniel's Tonka truck game they found a few work-related documents from Raytheon, but none that were classified. And there was nothing in the computer to suggest that Jeff Wang was anything but a loyal American citizen.

The FBI investigation was stalled. It had been under way for more than a year, and the bureau was no closer to proving its case. Moreover, the investigation was split between Los Angeles, where J.J. Smith was Alston's supervisor, and Long Beach, where an agent named Linas Danilevicius was Cordova's supervisor.

On the wiretap of the Wangs' house, the FBI overheard Jeff discussing the investigation, trying to figure out who had cast suspicion on him, talking to his mother about his relatives, and mentioning various aunts and uncles. By now, the FBI had learned the names of a number of relatives, even though his father's old immigration file could not be found.

Checking out their names, Alston noticed that one of Jeff's cousins, his father's niece, owned a house and that the co-owner of the house, her husband, had the same name as the FBI informant. That seemed an odd coincidence. But there was a reason for this.

Her husband, the co-owner of the house, *was* the informant.

Now the FBI had to face the fact that an informant it had relied upon for years had concealed the fact that his wife was Jeff Wang's cousin. Confronted, the informant denied, and kept denying, that he knew his wife was related to Jeff. Eventually, he admitted that Jeff was his wife's cousin, but claimed he had not known that.

The informant's entire story was falling apart. Pressed by the bureau, he admitted that he actually had met Jeff. It was, the source said, at a big family dinner. But the source said they did not talk, because Jeff did not speak Chinese and all the others did.

The gathering had taken place about a year before the informant told his story to the FBI. Jeff's parents had come to visit him and Diane and arranged for the large family dinner in Monterey Park. Jeff met his father's brother for the first time, as well as his father's nephew, niece, and other relatives. The informant was there.

By now, the picture was clear. J.J. Smith, Alston, and the FBI did not believe the informant's tale. He had used his relationship with the FBI to settle a personal score. He had invented the whole story. Later, when the San Francisco office investigated the mess, it determined that the informant was well aware all along that his wife was Jeff's cousin.

"It was a frame job," one senior FBI agent put it bluntly.

If the clouds of the bogus espionage accusation hanging over Jeff Wang were now dissipating, there was another storm gathering for Denise Woo. She had been told to become Jeff's confidante. He had been trying for months to figure out who had set him up and why. It was logical, therefore, that Woo, convinced of his innocence, would have encouraged him in that effort.

But the FBI fiercely guards the identity of its sources. And the bureau's agents, listening in on Jeff's conversations with Woo on the wiretap of his home telephone, decided that she had crossed the line, even by discussing the subject with Jeff of who his accuser might be. The fact that Jeff was speculating about what relative might have had a grudge against him did not seem to matter. Nor did it seem to make a difference that Woo's assignment by the FBI was to win Jeff's confidence, lend him a sympathetic ear, and act as his friend.

In the weeks after Wang was called in by the bureau, Woo argued with her superiors that he was innocent. She pushed, asking what evidence they had on him. She was told she had fallen prey to a version of the Stockholm syndrome, becoming too close to the person who was being investigated as a supposed spy.

In November, Woo was interviewed by the FBI. She denied that she had discussed the identity of the informant with Jeff, or given him any hints, or tipped him off that his phone was tapped. That the FBI had the Wangs' phones wired would hardly have surprised Jeff, an engineer; he and Diane assumed from the time the FBI agents had swarmed their house that their phones were tapped. A few weeks after Woo was questioned, the FBI suspended her.

In trouble now, Woo hired a lawyer, Marc S. Harris, who had worked with her on criminal cases when he was an assistant US attorney for eight years. "She was a fantastic agent," he said. "She was outstanding, extremely diligent and conscientious."

But Harris's small law firm could not handle what loomed as a long investigation of Woo. Mark Holscher, then with O'Melveny & Myers, took the case pro bono.

Federal prosecutors convened a grand jury — not to investigate how an FBI informant had lied to the bureau and framed an innocent man as a Chinese spy, but to build a case against Denise Woo, the FBI agent who tried to help clear his name.

Jeff and Diane Wang were called to testify before the grand jury. The prosecutors played a tape of a conversation between Diane and her mother. The tape confirmed the Wangs' suspicions that their phones were bugged. On the tape, Diane apparently told her mother that she would call her on another line. The government played the tape to attempt to show that the Wangs knew they were being wiretapped, and had been tipped off.

Woo remained suspended by the FBI. Early in 2003, after four years, the bureau fired her. In August 2004 Denise Woo was indicted on five felony counts for supposedly disclosing the identity of the "covert agent" to Wang, allegedly telling Jeff that his phone was wiretapped, and lying when she denied having done either of those acts. If convicted she faced a minimum sentence of ten years. On December 6, she was arraigned and freed on $50,000 bail.

The government was coming down hard on Denise Woo, even though its case against Jeff Wang had totally unraveled. The prosecution of Woo carried some hidden risks for the FBI, which was not at all anxious for the public to learn that one of its star Chinese counterintelligence informants had framed an innocent man. In the indictment of Woo, Wang was not identified. He was referred to only as "J.W."

Facing five felony counts and a possible ten years in prison, Woo, on the advice of her lawyers, decided to accept a plea bargain. On June 6, 2006, she pleaded guilty to a single misdemeanor of disclosing confidential information.

The original charges, that she had identified the FBI source, revealed the wiretap to Wang, and made false statements denying that she had done so, were dropped. Nor, in the plea bargain, did she state that she had disclosed the identity of the informant to Jeff.

The language of the plea was artful, dancing all around the subject, implying that Woo had revealed the source's name without explicitly saying so. The plea bargain asserted that Woo "discussed with and thereby disclosed to J.W. confidential information concerning the identity of an FBI confidential informant." The wording does not claim that Woo revealed the identity of the informant, only that she disclosed information "concerning the identity." That could mean almost anything, perhaps something as innocuous as encouraging Jeff's speculation that a relative, or a relative by marriage, bearing a grudge over his father's estate, was responsible for the false accusation against him.

On October 30, 2006, seven years after she was suspended by the FBI, Woo was sentenced by US District Court judge Gary Klausner to probation and a $1,000 fine. "This is a kind of bittersweet ending to a long and continuing tragic injustice," Woo said after the sentencing. "I am relieved that after years of false allegations, my family and I can finally get on with our lives."

Mark Holscher criticized the government's pursuit of Woo. "It was very unfortunate that the FBI chose to indict Denise," he said. "She loved the bureau. She was put in a horrible position of investigating a family friend. The FBI has policies and procedures in place for agents placed in undercover roles, including you don't investigate someone you know. If those policies had been followed Denise would be a decorated FBI agent today."

Had the case gone to trial, Holscher was prepared to show a link between the Woo and Wang investigations and J.J. Smith and Katrina Leung. And here, the plot, like so many aspects of counterintelligence, becomes both shadowy and complicated.

Although it was not known at the time, J.J. had briefed Katrina

Leung on the Jeff Wang investigation and consulted her on all details of the case. J.J. later told the Justice Department's inspector general that the informant's reporting about Jeff "did not make any sense."

The source who in the spring of 2000 told the FBI that Leung was an agent of China's intelligence service was the same informant who fabricated the story about Jeff Wang. The informant was angry at PARLOR MAID, accusing her of having told the MSS about his relationship with the FBI. He also claimed that Leung had told Beijing about the Jeff Wang investigation.

He was the same informant who, a few months later, said that Leung was "in bed with" the FBI's Los Angeles division. But FBI headquarters regarded this as informants pointing fingers at each other, and no further action was taken.

When the bureau finally determined that the informant had falsely accused Jeff Wang, he was dropped from the FBI payroll for lying, according to a former FBI counterintelligence agent and a current bureau official. By 2006, when Woo signed her plea, he was no longer being used as an informant.

When it was all over, Jeff Wang was able to obtain another job in the defense industry, one that required a security clearance. His name briefly surfaced in the press when he attended the sentencing of Denise Woo. But he will learn many of the details of ETHEREAL THRONE for the first time when he reads them in this book.

Brian Sun, who represented Jeff Wang early on in the FBI probe, summed up what had occurred. "A truly innocent man and his family suffered some very damaging consequences. Here's a guy at Raytheon for over fifteen years, had a great record, loses his job. It was just devastating for them to have to go through that ordeal."

Jeff and his wife have tried to pick up the pieces of their lives and move on. The FBI finally told his attorney that he was no longer "a person of interest." That was nice to know. But Jeff Wang could not understand why he never received an apology from the FBI.

## Chapter 13

# STORM CLOUDS

I N 2000 THE FBI'S national security division, then headed by
Neil J. Gallagher and his deputy, Sheila Horan, was preoccupied
with tracking down the Russian mole in US intelligence, who
turned out to be the FBI's own Robert Hanssen. But the division had
also begun to hear disturbing hints that something was very wrong
with the Chinese counterintelligence program in Los Angeles.

In July, Ken Geide had taken over as chief of the division's China
section at headquarters. Encouraged by Gallagher, Sheila Horan and
Geide began a detailed review of the Los Angeles Chinese counterintelligence program. They concentrated on PARLOR MAID, if only
because Katrina Leung had been a source for so many years.

The group examined what PARLOR MAID might have told the MSS,
and what she had gained in return. "The balance," one FBI agent said,
"did not look favorable. Storm clouds started gathering."

As Geide examined the case, he concluded that Leung was well
known to the MSS all the way back to her days in graduate school at
the University of Chicago. He wondered if she might even have been
operating for the MSS all along. If that scenario were true, then the

bureau would have to look back at every case. Because, Geide worried, it might mean that the FBI's Chinese counterintelligence program was controlled by China.

There were "anomalies," as counterintelligence agents call suspicious or unexplained problems. Late in 2000, the investigators discovered the information that had been received ten years earlier identifying PARLOR MAID as the source who had tipped off the Chinese about the FBI's highly successful electronic operation against the consulate in Los Angeles. Once the Chinese discovered the bugs, the FBI operation was toast.

"It would not have been news to the Chinese that the consulate was bugged," one FBI agent explained. "It was the sophisticated method used that was compromised."

Although the microphones went silent, it was several years before officials in the consulate suspected that their copying machines had been ingeniously tampered with to transmit documents to the FBI. It was not until the fall of 1999 that the copiers were shipped back to China to be disassembled and analyzed.

In 2001 the Chinese uncovered twenty-seven satellite-operated listening devices that the National Security Agency and the FBI had planted in the Chinese version of Air Force One while the plane was being refitted in Texas. The aircraft, a Boeing 767, was ordered for Jiang Zemin, the president of China. US contractors in San Antonio built a large bedroom, a bathroom with a shower, and a sitting area with a large-screen TV for Jiang, while a contingent from the People's Liberation Army guarded the $120 million aircraft.

The work was done by four contractors, Dee Howard Aircraft Maintenance, Gore Design Completions, Rockwell Collins, and Avitra Aviation Services. The plane was delivered to China in August 2001, and soon afterward the bugs were discovered, including some in the headboard of Jiang's bed. According to reports from China, twenty Chinese air force officers and two officials were detained and interrogated after the devices were uncovered.

The FBI looked into the possibility that Leung had also betrayed the aircraft bugs to Beijing, but was unable to link her to the episode. "Maybe she had nothing to do with it," one official concluded.*

Counterintelligence is such a convoluted, mirror-image world that some US officials speculated that the entire aircraft-bugging episode was an elaborate ploy by Chinese intelligence. Under this theory, the Chinese, knowing that the United States would surely try to bug the plane, made a show of guarding it but deliberately allowed the devices to be planted, and used American contractors instead of insisting on Chinese workers. Once back in Beijing, the aircraft would be pulled apart and the bugs analyzed to learn the state of the art of US eavesdropping technology.

In October 2001 Gallagher flew to Los Angeles to talk to Ron Iden, the assistant director in charge of the Los Angeles division, about J.J. Smith and PARLOR MAID. A month later, the FBI asked for a FISA warrant from the special court established by the Foreign Intelligence Surveillance Act to place Katrina Leung's home under electronic surveillance. The FBI already had a video camera in PARLOR MAID's living room, disguised as a motion detector, but that was installed with her knowledge, so that the FBI could secretly tape and record Chinese or other visitors.

Armed with the court warrant, the FBI secretly searched Leung's home, and tapped her phone calls, faxes, and e-mails. The bureau also placed her under physical surveillance.

The approval for the FISA warrant was granted by the secretive court in December. That same month, Sheila Horan became the acting chief of the FBI's national security division, succeeding Gallagher, who had retired.

By then, rumors of the romance between PARLOR MAID and J.J. had reached headquarters. Once the wiretap and bugs were in place in the house in San Marino, PARLOR MAID's affair with J.J. was quickly confirmed. The "special techniques" used by the FBI discovered, as the Justice Department inspector general's report put it delicately, that the relationship between J.J. and Leung was "more than friendship."

---

* After the PARLOR MAID case became public in April 2003, J.J. Smith vehemently denied that he had ever discussed the plane bugging with Leung. His lawyer, Brian Sun, said there was "absolutely not" a connection. "My client flat-out did not talk about the plane with her," he said.

Sex is not a federal crime, for which everyone can be grateful. But the electronic surveillance of the Leungs' home provided graphic evidence that there was a major problem in the bureau's Los Angeles field office. What the bureau now had to contemplate was the horrendous possibility that China had penetrated the FBI.

Early in January 2002 Horan briefed Robert Mueller on the situation. A veteran bureau agent, Horan had been sent to Africa by the FBI to take charge of the investigation into the 1998 US embassy bombings in Kenya and Tanzania that killed 224 people and wounded 4,000.

Because the FBI director had taken over just before 9/11, the terrorist attacks on New York and Washington had occupied most of his attention. When he heard what had been going on in Los Angeles, he went ballistic.

Early in January 2002 Mueller held a flurry of meetings with Horan, Geide, Iden, and Lance Woo, the China squad supervisor in the Los Angeles field office. The atmosphere was beyond tense.

The Los Angeles and headquarters officials blamed one another for the slow progress of the investigation into the Chinese counterintelligence program in Los Angeles. "Who's in charge?" Mueller demanded. No one offered an answer.

At one point, Iden left FBI headquarters for Dulles International Airport, and was on a flight en route to Los Angeles when he was reached by Mueller, who ordered him to return to headquarters for another meeting. As soon as Iden landed at LAX — there was no time for him even to run home and change his shirt — he turned around and boarded the redeye back to Washington.

Sheila Horan, an experienced career agent with twenty-nine years in the bureau, was caught in the fallout. As acting chief for national security, she was in the bull's-eye and received the full fury of Mueller's wrath.

"I'm removing you," Mueller told her.

Swept aside in the turmoil over PARLOR MAID, and with no other good options open to her, Horan transferred to an administrative post in the bureau and retired later that year. Many of her colleagues in the FBI felt she had been unfairly blamed for the debacle in Los Angeles.

After Mueller had been briefed, he ordered a full field investigation opened of J.J. Smith. He also appointed Randy Bellows, the same federal prosecutor who investigated the FBI's handling of the Wen Ho Lee case, to review the situation in Los Angeles and recommend what should be done. Bellows, who had prosecuted Robert Hanssen, the KGB mole in the FBI, moved quickly. He urged that Mueller appoint an FBI agent with the rank of inspector to take charge of the investigation.

Mueller knew what he had to do. He sent for Les Wiser.

# Chapter 14

# THE COUNTERSPY

T HE DIRECTOR WANTS to see you."

Les Wiser, the FBI's ace counterintelligence agent, the man who caught Aldrich Ames, had no idea why FBI chief Robert S. Mueller III had summoned him to his office. But Wiser's antennae were up; whatever it was could not be good news. The director would not have sent for him unless major trouble was brewing.

Even so, Wiser was not prepared for what he learned. Mueller wasted no time on preliminaries. The FBI, he told Wiser, had been penetrated by Chinese intelligence. Katrina Leung — code name PARLOR MAID — the woman the bureau had relied on as its best spy against Beijing, had actually been working for Communist China for more than a decade. It was a nightmare come true. Mueller was grim, still furious over the details, which he had learned only days earlier.

It got worse. Wiser could hardly believe what Mueller revealed next. PARLOR MAID's handlers, who had been the FBI's two top counterintelligence agents targeting China, had carried on long-running sexual affairs with Katrina Leung. The FBI agent in Los Angeles, who had recruited her twenty years earlier, was her lover. So, for several years, was the bureau's top China expert in San Francisco.

Not only that, both FBI agents *knew* that PARLOR MAID had been recruited by Chinese intelligence. They found that out in 1991, yet headquarters had agreed they could continue to run her. It was an unbelievable mess.

The bureau would have to review everything PARLOR MAID had told the FBI for years, including information that had gone straight to the White House. Leung had been considered so reliable that her information was passed up the chain of command to four US presidents — Ronald Reagan, George H. W. Bush, Bill Clinton, and George W. Bush. Now the FBI would have to assume that much of it might be false.

Then Mueller gave Wiser his marching orders.

"Go to LA and take care of this," he said.

The FBI director did not have to spell out what remained unspoken. The disaster in Los Angeles was only the latest calamity to hit the bureau. Still reeling from its failure, along with the CIA, to prevent the 9/11 terrorist attacks in 2001, and the arrest earlier that year of FBI special agent Robert Hanssen as a Russian spy, the FBI now was dealing with an explosive internal scandal that was sure to become public.

Sex! Espionage! A Chinese dragon lady! Wiser's head was spinning when he walked out of the director's office in February 2002. He had just been handed a scorpion and he wasn't wearing gloves.

It was one thing for Mueller to tell him what had been going on in Los Angeles. But how was Wiser going to prove it? He would have to gather solid evidence to break the case open, to prove that PARLOR MAID was working for Beijing, that the two FBI men had been having sex with their agent, and that they knew she had been recruited by China but continued to work with her anyhow. The task seemed impossible. It was even further complicated by the fact that both FBI agents, J.J. Smith in Los Angeles, and Bill Cleveland in San Francisco, had retired.

And Wiser knew that he would face stiff resistance within the bureau, which always closed ranks to protect its own. In trying to build a case that involved the two FBI agents, Wiser would be seen as an outsider, a headquarters stooge. He would be violating the core precept of the bureau's culture, the old J. Edgar Hoover command, "Don't embarrass the bureau."

Sure, Hoover was long gone, but the headquarters building in Washington bore his name, and the old edicts had not been entirely forgotten. Wiser was already a target of jealousy and criticism within the bureau's ranks because of his success and the publicity he received in the Ames case. It was Wiser, defying orders from his superior, who had dug out from Ames's trash barrel a yellow Post-it note that proved to be the smoking gun in the case. The note proved that Ames was an active Russian spy, and it was the evidence the FBI needed to arrest him.

Wiser had made his bones in the Ames case, when he was thirty-eight, but it was nothing compared to the challenge that awaited him in Los Angeles. He felt a little like the lone sheriff in *High Noon*. But this wasn't a Hollywood western. If he screwed up, Mueller would know just whom to blame.

Nor had he exactly volunteered for this job. In the FBI, agents usually hope in time to rise to the level of an assistant special agent in charge (ASAC) of a major field office, and then perhaps to the top job of special agent in charge, or SAC. Wiser, after nineteen years, was up for a SAC post. Now that would have to be put on hold. He would have to do as Mueller asked; he had no choice.

Even before Special Agent Wiser had put Aldrich Ames behind bars for life, he had worked in counterintelligence for most of his years in the FBI. He had earned a reputation as quick, decisive, and discreet.

Tall and thin, with graying brown hair and a wide mustache, Wiser, a former Navy lawyer, did not fit the stereotype of the laconic, square-jawed FBI agent familiar from movies and television. Wiser smiled a lot and could laugh at himself; in a serious and demanding job, he had a saving sense of humor.

To preserve security, Wiser knew he would need a new code name for Katrina Leung, and the investigation of which she was also a target. He could not afford to have any documents generated by his investigation end up in the PARLOR MAID file, where other agents might see them. For Leung, the computer came up with a randomly generated new code name: POETIC FIT.

J.J. Smith, and the investigation directed at him, were given a separate code name, RICH FOLIAGE.

With four handpicked agents from headquarters, Wiser flew to LAX. Along with some two dozen carefully selected agents from Los Angeles, Wiser moved offsite into an office building in Santa Monica, well away from the FBI field office at 11000 Wilshire Boulevard. J.J. had retired, but he sometimes dropped by the office and it would not do for him to run into Wiser's team.

Although Wiser had not wanted the assignment that Mueller gave him, if China had penetrated the FBI, and two agents had been compromised, he was determined to get to the bottom of the mess and let the chips fall where they may.

By April 2002, Wiser was armed with another FISA warrant, and the FBI began wiretapping its own former agent, J.J. Smith. Agents on Wiser's team started tailing him as well.

The FBI, meanwhile, had continued to run PARLOR MAID as an asset. A new handler, Special Agent Steve Conley, had been assigned to her when J.J. retired. Not long after Wiser arrived in Los Angeles, he discovered that the FBI office on Wilshire was still approving her payments. He considered whether stopping the money would tip off PARLOR MAID that she was under investigation, but decided it was a risk that could be taken. Wiser reasoned that with J.J. retired, Leung would simply assume the bureau had less need for her services. He ordered the payments stopped.

To explain his presence in Los Angeles, Wiser told the field office on Wilshire that he was in town to do an efficiency study. His title of inspector helped his cover.

Sooner or later FBI agents are tapped for a stint in the bureau's inspection division. They visit the field offices, poke around, and write a report on how well or badly the offices are working. Since nobody, as might be imagined, likes a visit from the inspectors, Wiser was not asked a lot of questions.

And it became quickly clear from the wiretaps and surveillance on both J.J. and Leung that their romantic relationship had not ended with Smith's retirement more than a year earlier. In March, the watchers had seen them spending time together in a hotel.

Meanwhile, the agents operating out of the secret office in Santa Monica were delving into PARLOR MAID's financial activities. The Leungs owned a Chinese bookstore on East Garvey Avenue in Monterey Park. In July, Katrina Leung filed a petition for Chapter 7 bankruptcy for the bookstore, which meant that the premises had to be closed and all business ceased immediately, unlike a Chapter 11 proceeding, where a company reorganizes and emerges to operate anew.

According to an affidavit filed in federal court by FBI special agent Sharon Lawrence, Kam Leung called his wife on July 9 to say there was a "big problem" with their bankruptcy plan. "Mr. Leung explained to his wife that she could go to jail for filing a fraudulent bankruptcy petition since her name alone would appear on the petition, and she would be the person actually lying by stating that the subject business was closed for business when, in actuality, it was still operating."

The FBI spent hundreds of man-hours watching the bookstore to see if it was indeed still open. Some of the events described in the dry, stilted language of the lengthy affidavit were unintentionally comical. The store was managed for the Leungs by Kwong Wai Li Tang and her husband, I. Kuo Tang. "On August 8, 2002," the affidavit relates, "FBI surveillance revealed the following: At approximately 8:57 A.M., Ms. Tang exited a vehicle and entered the back door of [the bookstore]. Tang carried several white plastic bags with her." Half an hour later, "At approximately 9:28 A.M.," an FBI employee entered the bookstore and found it bulging with magazines, newspapers, videos, and books.

"The FBI employee told Ms. Tang that he was looking for a present for a friend. Ms. Tang told him that the store was closed." For the next forty-five minutes, the FBI sleuths watched as "several Asian people walked in and out" of the bookstore, and "one Asian male walked out . . . with a newspaper which he apparently obtained while inside."

No doubt tumbling to the fact that they were being observed, the bookstore proprietors knew just what to do. Two weeks later, the store had a "Closed" sign on the front door. "However the rear entrance door . . . was (propped) open." For the next hour the FBI watched as "eight people, all appearing to be Asian," entered the store and later emerged happily with newspapers or shopping bags. The Leungs were doing business out the back door. The bookstore was only closed to the FBI.

There was an extra irony in this, because when PARLOR MAID's contacts in China apparently suggested that she open a bookstore, J.J. had encouraged her to do so. The FBI was always greatly interested in Chinese bookstores on the West Coast, regarding some as propaganda outlets or fronts for the MSS. Eastwind Books in San Francisco, for example, had figured on the margins of the TIGER TRAP case. So when Leung opened the bookstore in Monterey Park, Smith regarded it as another successful move by PARLOR MAID for the FBI.

At the bankruptcy hearing in August, Katrina Leung had a great deal of difficulty explaining how the minutes of a meeting approving the bankruptcy petition by the bookstore's board of directors had been signed by Xie Shanxiao, the CEO, and Peter M. Chow, a director, since the minutes also showed that she was the only one present. Somehow, the store managers "probably have, uh, faxed them," she said.

The perplexed bankruptcy judge wondered how it was possible that Xie had signed the minutes, since Leung said she had not seen him in ten years. In fact, both Xie and Chow were in China, a long way from Monterey Park.

On September 5 PARLOR MAID was interviewed about the bankruptcy by two FBI agents and claimed that her attorney had told her to forge the signatures. She was still worried about those signatures a week later, however; in a phone call to Ms. Tang, according to the FBI document, she said "she had been losing sleep over the fraudulent signatures of the directors, because she stated that 'if one forges a signature, that's a very serious crime.'"

By now, PARLOR MAID must have realized something was up. She had been taken off the bureau payroll. She surely knew from the Tangs that FBI surveillance agents were skulking around the bookstore. And why were her good friends in the bureau asking about such an inconsequential matter as the bankruptcy of a small retail store in Monterey Park? There was no point in fretting any further; whatever it was would probably blow over, and J.J., although retired, still had plenty of friends in the bureau.

In July, Katrina Leung, unaware of the fact that she was being wiretapped and followed by Wiser's team, had contacted Ron Iden, the Los Angeles FBI chief, and asked to meet with him, ostensibly about "outreach" by the bureau to the Chinese community. More likely, the FBI investigators assumed, she wanted to be able to boast to the MSS on her next trip to Beijing that she knew and had personal access to the assistant director of the FBI in charge of the Los Angeles division.

As the top bureau official in Los Angeles, Iden had been told of the investigation being run out of the Santa Monica office. Wiser asked Iden to go ahead and meet with Leung, which he did on July 22. It was arranged to have Randall Thomas, one of Wiser's key agents, secretly monitor the meeting via audio piped in from an adjoining office.

Four months later, on November 5, 2002, the FBI videotaped J.J. Smith and PARLOR MAID in a Los Angeles hotel room. Technicians placed a hidden camera in the room after the FBI on a wiretap heard the two arranging to meet. That in turn required the cooperation of the hotel, to ensure that the couple was given the right room. Randall Thomas, who participated in the operation, reported in a court document: "The electronic surveillance revealed Smith and LEUNG having sexual relations."

The videotape provided in graphic detail confirmation of the fact that almost two years after J.J. had retired, his relationship with PARLOR MAID was still ongoing. Only a week later, on November 11, the bureau learned that he was also continuing to provide her with information about FBI agents.

Wiser's team covertly searched Leung's luggage at LAX as she prepared to leave on a trip to China. They found a fax from J.J. with six photos taken at a meeting of the Society of Former Special Agents of the FBI the previous month. Two of the photos were of agents still on active duty.

Two weeks later, when PARLOR MAID returned from China, Special Agent Peter Duerst was at San Francisco International Airport, waiting backstage as her luggage came off the plane. When he searched her bags, he found a piece of paper with handwritten notes in English and Chinese. One of the notes said, "Visited Ron Iden 7/29/02 re: community outreach." On the same paper, he found names and information about the FBI agents who worked with Leung.

PARLOR MAID continued her journey, flying on the same day to LAX, where Thomas took part in a second clandestine search of her luggage. All the searches had been authorized by the Foreign Intelligence Surveillance Court. When the FBI went through her bags they noted that the six photographs of FBI agents they had seen in her luggage on the outbound flight on November 11 were gone.

Now Wiser was ready to move. On December 9 J.J. was interviewed by FBI agents in a room at the Crowne Plaza Hotel on Century Boulevard, as Wiser watched from his office in Santa Monica on a closed-circuit video feed. It was not a good day for J.J., who had retired two years earlier with the plaudits of his colleagues and a medal from CIA director George Tenet.

It was in fact a very bad day, the first of many that would follow for Smith. Over two days of interviews in the hotel room, J.J., according to the Thomas affidavit, said that "he had probably told LEUNG too much." Several times J.J. conceded that any information PARLOR MAID had obtained about FBI operations and sources must have come from him.

Interrogators are always happiest when they already know the answers to the questions they ask. Their hand is even stronger if the person being interrogated does not realize that his questioners know the truth. In this case, Wiser's team had the videotape made the previous month of J.J. and Katrina's hotel room tryst.

Asked whether he was having a sexual relationship with Leung, J.J. at first refused to answer, "and then denied having a sexual relationship." For J.J., it was to prove a costly denial.

At another point in the interview, when asked about any trips abroad, J.J. said he had traveled to Hong Kong in February 2001, soon after he retired, and had gone there again in 2002. Each trip lasted about a week, and J.J. said he had traveled alone each time and had not met with anyone in Hong Kong. Later in the interview, he again said he made the trips alone.

One of the agents then asked J.J. point-blank if Leung had gone with him to Hong Kong. Smith replied, "She's, she was there."

But J.J. insisted he had never traveled with Leung to any place overseas except Hong Kong. When the interrogators pressed him, Smith conceded he had met Leung in London and flown back to the United States with her. That was the trip he had taken in 1992, when J.J. and

Bill Cleveland had flown to London to interview Hanson Huang about TIGER TRAP. Afterward, J.J. and Leung had gone on their sightseeing trip around England, and on their return were spotted in the customs area at LAX by Dot Kelly, his supervisor, who had decided to surprise Smith by picking him up at the airport.

On December 11, after two days of intensive interrogation of J.J. Smith, it was PARLOR MAID's turn. She consented to being interviewed, and the FBI questioned her at a hotel in the San Fernando Valley. Once again, Wiser was watching via closed-circuit television. What happened then, and in several days of later interviews, was described in a court document by Randall Thomas.

Bruce Carlson, the assistant chief of the China section at FBI headquarters, had flown to Los Angeles to conduct the questioning. Carlson, tall, slim, and smooth, fluent in Mandarin, got PARLOR MAID talking far beyond what he could have imagined. In the hotel room, Leung began describing classified documents she said she had secretly taken from J.J.'s briefcase and copied.

It was a stunning admission. Why Katrina Leung confessed to taking the documents is something of a mystery. Perhaps, after twenty years as an FBI asset, of working closely with the bureau, she felt she had nothing to fear. These were FBI agents, her friends, they would understand the Byzantine ways of double agents, the subtleties of counterintelligence operations. She could talk her way out of any trouble.

Asked whether she had an "intimate" relationship with J.J., she first described their association as a "business relationship" and said she was no more than "a good family friend." She was unaware, of course, of the videotape that the FBI had made of their hotel room liaison only a month earlier. She also denied traveling overseas with J.J.

As the questioning continued, however, Leung finally admitted that she and J.J. were more than friends. She said she had first become intimate with him in the early 1980s, "Very long ago, but I cannot tell you what year."

PARLOR MAID readily agreed to meet with the FBI at her home in San Marino and show them documents she said she had removed from J.J.'s briefcase. The interview adjourned to her house.

With Carlson and another FBI officer, Special Agent Edgar Del Rosario, watching, Leung opened a locked safe in an upstairs bedroom and took out a five-page document that was an even bigger surprise. It contained excerpts of transcripts of her conversation, using the code name Luo, with Mao — Mao Guohua, her MSS handler in Beijing.

Leung now admitted that Mao was her MSS control and Luo her MSS alias, and that the code name Luo Zhongshan had been assigned to her by none other than Zhu Qizhen, the Chinese ambassador to the United States. She recounted the story she had told to J.J. Smith eleven years earlier in their kitchen confrontation. She claimed that Mao had obtained the notes about a defector that had been taken from her luggage, and because they were more detailed than what she had told him, she admitted to Mao that she was working for the FBI and agreed from that point on to tell the MSS whatever she knew of FBI operations.

The transcript the agents found in Leung's safe was, of course, the 1990 conversation intercepted by the National Security Agency in which PARLOR MAID had tipped off the MSS that Bill Cleveland was planning a trip to China under State Department cover. The intercept that led Smith and Cleveland to fly to Washington to persuade head-quarters to let J.J. continue to run PARLOR MAID.

Wiser was stunned, furious to learn of the intercept, which had now turned up in Leung's house. He had been dispatched by the director of the FBI to investigate the mess in Los Angeles, but, astonishingly, headquarters had never told him about the conversation between Luo and Mao. An essential part of his job was to find proof of whether PARLOR MAID was an agent of Chinese intelligence. But no one in Washington had seen fit to tell him of the key piece of evidence in the case, the phone conversation that clearly tied her to the MSS.

Asked how she had obtained the transcript of the intercept, Leung replied, "I think I sneaked it."

She said that J.J. "would leave his briefcase open, and that the file folder pockets in the briefcase often contained documents, with the text facing out." That way, she said, she could see the documents she wanted and "remove them and copy them without Smith's knowledge when he left his briefcase unattended."

Leung said she made copies of the documents with either a photocopier or a fax machine in her home. "Generally, she stated that she

FBI agent James J. Smith and Katrina Leung, code name PARLOR MAID, watch the 2001 inaugural parade of President George W. Bush in Washington, DC. For years Leung secretly passed FBI secrets to the MSS, the Chinese intelligence service.
© 2001 *Michael Lutzky*/The Washington Post

The FBI's William V. Cleveland Jr., like Smith a top Chinese counterintelligence agent, worked with Leung on the TIGER TRAP case. The central figure in that case, Gwo-bao Min, a scientist at the Lawrence Livermore nuclear weapons laboratory, was forced out after the FBI suspected he had leaked details of the neutron bomb to China. © 2002 *Robert C. Bain/San Jose State University*

Hanson Huang, a Harvard-trained lawyer and friend of Katrina Leung, met clandestinely with Min, the TIGER TRAP suspect, and according to the FBI passed nuclear weapons information to Beijing through the Chinese embassy in Washington.

Chien Ning, a prominent Chinese geophysicist, introduced Gwo-bao Min to Hanson Huang when the Livermore scientist visited China. The FBI believed she was sent to California to handle intelligence assignments for the MSS, which Chien denied.
South China Morning Post

Veteran FBI agent Dan Grove was able to intercept a letter from Beijing that provided key evidence in the TIGER TRAP case, revealing China's efforts to steal US nuclear secrets.

"It was a nightmare come true." FBI director Robert S. Mueller III was furious when he learned that PARLOR MAID — the double agent the bureau relied on as its best spy against Beijing — had actually been passing secrets to Communist China for more than a decade, and that the FBI's two top agents handling Chinese counterintelligence had both carried on long-running sexual affairs with her. FBI

Leslie G. Wiser Jr., the FBI's ace counterintelligence agent, was called in by Mueller to investigate the PARLOR MAID debacle. With a team of some two dozen carefully selected agents, Wiser set up a secret office in Los Angeles and broke open the case. In April 2003 both Leung and Smith were arrested by the FBI.

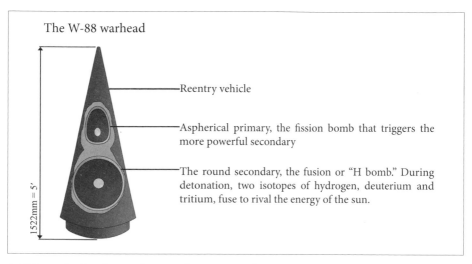

The W-88 warhead

1522mm = 5'

Reentry vehicle

Aspherical primary, the fission bomb that triggers the more powerful secondary

The round secondary, the fusion or "H bomb." During detonation, two isotopes of hydrogen, deuterium and tritium, fuse to rival the energy of the sun.

A Chinese "walk-in" turned over a document to the CIA revealing that China had somehow acquired the ultra-secret details of the W-88, America's most sophisticated nuclear warhead, which sits atop the missiles on the Navy's Trident submarines. Despite Beijing's knowledge, details about the warhead are still secret in the US. Enough information was learned about the Chinese document, however, to make this artist's rendition fairly accurate. *Ian Cunningham*

This unusual photograph of the W-88's cone-shaped reentry vehicle reveals the warhead's small size. The man in the photo is Bob Putnam of the Los Alamos National Laboratory, where the weapon was designed. *LANL*

September 13, 2000: Los Alamos scientist Wen Ho Lee leaves federal court in Albuquerque, New Mexico, with daughter Alberta and attorneys Mark C. Holscher (right) and John D. Cline after pleading guilty to one felony count of mishandling classified documents and receiving a dramatic apology from a federal judge for the harsh conditions in which he was jailed. Lee was originally suspected, but never charged, with leaking the W-88 to China. The government produced no evidence he had. Unknown to the public, however, Lee had been the subject of two previous FBI investigations for suspicious actions — contacting the TIGER TRAP suspect and concealing a meeting with China's top bomb maker. *AP Images*

A secret FBI report on President Nixon's relationship with Marianna Liu, a beautiful Hong Kong bar hostess, was given to J. Edgar Hoover, the bureau's director. This photo of Liu and Nixon was taken in 1966 at the Den, the popular nightspot where she worked.

Hong Kong Standard

For the information of and future handling by recipients, Bureau file concerning captioned matter reveals
information concerning subject was originally brought to the
attention of this Bureau by Legal Attache, Hong Kong, letter
dated 10/12/67 wherein suspicions of possible Chicom intelligence involvement of subject were inferred but not substan-
tiated by Special Branch, Hong Kong Police and a U. S. Customs
representative in Hong Kong indicated he had heard from a
former Customs representative in Hong Kong, that subject was
a regular bedmate of Vice-President Nixon when he visited
Hong Kong. The Customs representative indicated he had no
firsthand knowledge, was furnishing the information in confidence and requested no further dissemination of the information. No active investigation of the subject was conducted
by the FBI.

      The file on captioned subject has not been sent to
the Attorney General as indicated in SFairtel 7/2/76; however,
the Attorney General has been furnished full facts concerning
this matter. No information has been reported concerning
subject which warrants investigation by the FBI under the
current Attorney General's foreign counterintelligence guidelines. Any allegations concerning discrepancies or irregu-
larities with regard to subject's entrance into the U. S. is
strictly within the jurisdiction of Immigration and
Naturalization Service and/or State Department.

This secret 1976 FBI document repeats unconfirmed reports that Liu "was a regular bedmate" of former vice president Nixon during his visits to Hong Kong in the 1960s. Liu, found and interviewed by the author, denied both a romance with Nixon and British and US suspicions that she worked for Chinese intelligence.

Katrina Leung and her husband, Kam, face reporters outside the federal courthouse in Los Angeles on December 16, 2005, after she pleaded guilty to lying about her affair with FBI agent James J. Smith and failing to pay taxes on thousands of dollars the bureau paid her as a double agent. Although the government said she secretly passed FBI secrets to Chinese intelligence for years, she was not charged with espionage. *AP Images*

The Spymaster: Geng Huichang moved up in 2007 to become chief of the MSS, the Ministry of State Security, as part of a government shakeup by President Hu Jintao, who sought to consolidate his power by naming five political allies as ministers. *CNS*

Michael W. Emmick prosecuted Katrina Leung for copying FBI secrets for China. The Justice Department was stunned when federal judge Florence-Marie Cooper threw out the case against PARLOR MAID, charging government "misconduct." She singled out Emmick, but later retracted her remarks about the prosecutor, saying he was not responsible.

ETHEREAL THRONE: Jeff Wang, a defense engineer, lost his job after being falsely accused as a Chinese spy by an FBI informant who had a personal grudge against him. Denise Woo, a decorated FBI agent, was dismissed and prosecuted after she tried to clear the innocent man. She is shown here in happier times, receiving a congratulatory handshake from then FBI director Louis Freeh. *FBI*

Chinese intelligence penetrated the CIA for thirty years with Larry Wu-Tai Chin, a top translator for the agency, who was caught by the FBI when he was careless with a Beijing hotel room key. A Catholic priest in New York's Chinatown may have been sent by China's spy service to try to help Chin escape when the FBI closed in. *AP Images*

Wen Ning, code name ANUBIS, spied for the FBI while a diplomat inside the Chinese consulate in Los Angeles. He later went to prison for illegally exporting electronic parts and militarily useful technology to China.
*Courtesy of* Herald Times Reporter, *Manitowoc*

Family of spies: Chi Mak, shown here with his wife, Rebecca Chiu, secretly passed sensitive Navy documents on US weapons systems to China for more than twenty years. He was convicted and in 2008 sentenced to twenty-four years in prison. The government charged he headed a spy ring that included his wife, his brother, Tai Mak, and Tai Mak's wife and son. All five were convicted on various charges. *FBI*

"I work for Red Flower of North America." Tai Mak's phone call to his contact in Zhongshan, China, was intercepted by the FBI. About to board a flight to Hong Kong, he was arrested at Los Angeles International Airport with computer disks containing data about the Navy's Quiet Electric Drive, designed to allow submarines to run silent. He was sentenced to ten years. *FBI*

"This channel is much safer than the others." Dongfan Chung (right) is shown with Gu Weihao, an official of China's Ministry of Aviation, who assured him he could safely pass defense secrets through Chi Mak. Chung, an engineer for Boeing, collected data for China on the space shuttle and the B-1 bomber. He was convicted of economic espionage and in 2010 sentenced to fifteen years and eight months. *FBI*

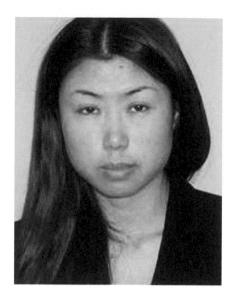

Tai Shen Kuo, a New Orleans businessman, was paid by Lin Hong, a Chinese military intelligence officer, to enlist Pentagon officials in a Chinese spy network. Caught by the FBI, which took this surveillance photo of him, Kuo pleaded guilty under the espionage laws. In 2008 he drew a sentence of almost sixteen years, later reduced to five for cooperating with prosecutors. *FBI*

Yu Xin "Katie" Kang, Tai Shen Kuo's young Chinese girlfriend, served as a cutout between Kuo and his handler in China, Lin Hong. Kuo had dominated her life since she was a teenager. Prosecutors recognized that she had been used and controlled for years by Kuo, and she received a much lighter sentence of eighteen months. *FBI*

Gregg W. Bergersen, a Defense Department official with a weakness for gambling, turned over Pentagon documents to Tai Shen Kuo, who passed them on to China. Bergersen, shown in this FBI surveillance photo, thought the data was going to Taiwan. He pleaded guilty to conspiracy to disclose national defense information and was sentenced in 2008 to just under five years. *FBI*

A second Pentagon official, James W. Fondren Jr., held a TOP SECRET clearance as deputy chief of the Washington liaison office for the US Pacific Command (PACOM). He met in China with Lin Hong, who gave him the code name FANG. Fondren, who turned over classified information to Kuo, was convicted and sentenced in 2010 to three years. *FBI* would make handwritten notes from documents she surreptitiously copied, and then discard the copies in the trash."

She also said that she sometimes made notes about documents "she surreptitiously obtained from Smith without copying the documents," and also made notes about information Smith told her. Over the years, she "admitted that she provided intelligence she gained in this manner to the MSS."

There was an even more startling revelation. PARLOR MAID admitted that China had paid her $100,000 because Chinese president Yang Shangkun "liked her." Yang, the president of China from 1988 to 1993, a veteran of the Red Army's Long March, was best known as the military leader who cracked down on the student demonstrators in Tiananmen Square on June 4, 1989, killing hundreds of students and workers.

Since J.J. Smith often consulted Leung on FBI investigations, and virtually treated her like an unofficial member of the China squad, there was no way to be sure about the volume of information she had passed to Chinese intelligence. For example, one investigation she certainly knew a lot about was the TIGER TRAP case, on which, because of her friendship with Hanson Huang, she had worked closely with both Bill Cleveland and J.J.

A few days after PARLOR MAID produced the transcript of her conversation with Mao, Peter Duerst and Carlson went to the FBI's Wilshire field office and into the SCIF, the secure vault where secret documents are kept. They found several TOP SECRET summaries of conversations between Luo and Mao that contained portions of the transcripts in the document that Leung had produced from her bedroom safe.

At first, the FBI agents wondered what led Smith to take the transcript of PARLOR MAID's conversations with Mao to her home. Surely, J.J. would need no reminder of the intercept that had revealed to him that PARLOR MAID, his top source, had been flipped by the MSS. But Smith had used the transcript as proof that Leung was working for the MSS when he confronted her in 1991 about the intercepted call to Beijing. And the document ended up in her bedroom safe.

The next day, with Leung's consent, two FBI agents searched her home and discovered a document classified SECRET that was in a way even more significant, because of its 1997 date, than the intercept of the conversation between Luo and Mao. The date was crucial, because it meant that six years after being confronted by J.J., PARLOR MAID was still extracting documents from his briefcase.

The document, dated June 12, 1997, was one of four discovered by Special Agent Stephen Lawrence in a bookcase on the second floor. It was an FBI electronic communication, or EC, written by the bureau's legat in Hong Kong.

The document reported that China was trying to purchase US electronic equipment that would enable Beijing "to intercept the same intelligence" collected by US spy satellites as the data was beamed to ground stations.

But here the story took an unusual twist. The document said the MSS had offered a $1 million reward for information on the whereabouts of two Chinese nationals, Liu Zuoqing, the manager of a company in northern China, and Zheng Dequan, his son-in-law. The pair were accused of stealing $140 million that was supposed to be used to buy the high-tech "most-up-to-date satellite retrieval systems technology manufactured by a U.S. firm."

According to the legat's report, the MSS had ordered its agents in the United States to find the fugitives; Chinese intelligence was ready to kill the two men and their families. The document also said that the spy operation to acquire the satellite technology had been ordered by the "highest level" of the Chinese government and that the revelation of the attempt to buy the technology would be "far more detrimental to [Beijing] than the loss of the money."

The sensational report was obviously based on information from a source that had reached the FBI agent in Hong Kong. And there it was, sitting in a bookcase in Katrina Leung's house in San Marino.

In the same bookcase where the FBI found the report from Hong Kong about the two Chinese fugitives, the agents also found three other documents. One was a 1994 telephone directory of the NSD-2 China squad in Los Angeles, the initials standing for the FBI's national security division. The directory included the home telephone numbers of the FBI agents on the counterintelligence squad.

Another document discovered was a 1994 legat directory, listing the names, telephone numbers, and office addresses of FBI legal attachés overseas. Finally, the bookcase held a phone list of FBI agents and members of the Special Surveillance Group, the civilians known as G's, who had worked on an espionage case code-named ROYAL TOURIST.

In that case, Peter Lee, a Taiwan-born nuclear scientist who had worked at both the Los Alamos and Livermore labs, pleaded guilty in 1997 to passing classified defense information to China and lying about it to the government. Although J.J. supervised ROYAL TOURIST, government documents do not explain why he brought the list of FBI agents to Leung's house.

The agents searching Leung's house also uncovered a journal with handwritten notes in Chinese and English. Among the words in English were "military double agent," "rocket knowledge," and "US Airforce." Bruce Carlson translated the journal and explained to a fellow agent that it was difficult to express those terms in Chinese, and easier for someone fluent in both languages to use English.

It crossed the minds of Les Wiser and his team that there might be another explanation of how PARLOR MAID had obtained the FBI's classified documents. They wondered, but did not know, if perhaps J.J. suspected or knew that Leung was taking the documents and tacitly allowed her to do so to "build" her, a term of art in counterintelligence that describes how a double agent is given information in order to appear more valuable to the opposition service.

The more PARLOR MAID impressed the MSS, the more intelligence she might bring back to J.J., which in turn would increase his already lofty standing in the FBI. He might have allowed PARLOR MAID to take the documents "with a wink," one official speculated, allowing him to deny, truthfully, that he ever gave her any material from the files of the FBI.

There was no evidence produced by the FBI to indicate that Smith knew or suspected that PARLOR MAID was stealing the documents. But Wiser and his colleagues also recognized that they might never fully understand the dynamic of the complicated relationship between J.J. Smith and his prize asset.

A week after searching Leung's house, the FBI conducted the first of four interviews with Bill Cleveland. After retiring from the bureau in 1993, Cleveland had been hired by the Livermore lab as its chief of counterintelligence. Ironically, in light of his sexual relationship with PARLOR MAID, it was his job to protect the nuclear weapons laboratory from penetration by Chinese or other foreign espionage services. As such, he was in charge of the Security Awareness for Employees (SAFE) program at the lab, which encouraged employees to report suspected spies or anything "suspicious."

As part of the security awareness program, Cleveland briefed lab scientists on the importance of avoiding sexual entanglements that might prove embarrassing. He warned that foreign intelligence services could try to use the information to blackmail the scientists into revealing secrets.

At the first interview with Special Agent Duerst, Cleveland talked about how Leung had provided information to him, how he had met with her frequently in both San Francisco and Los Angeles, often with J.J. At this initial interview, however, he did not reveal his own affair with Leung.

Not until a second meeting with Duerst, on January 28, more than a month later, did Cleveland confess to his own long-term sexual relationship with PARLOR MAID. But he had difficulty recalling when it began. He thought it had started in 1991, but in the next interview, amended that to 1989. Finally on February 4, Cleveland was polygraphed and in the pre-interview he said the affair had begun in 1988, continued for five years until his retirement, and then was revived in 1997 and 1999.

Cleveland described how he had listened to the 1991 audiotape of the Luo and Mao conversation and recognized Leung's voice. He recounted his alarm at realizing that she was "passing information to the MSS without FBI authorization," as the affidavit of Special Agent Randall Thomas described it. How Smith, "visibly upset," had flown to San Francisco when he heard the news. And how J.J. later assured him that "the problem" had been resolved.

Bruce Carlson, after interviewing Leung for several days in December, concluded that her relationship with the MSS "cast doubt on all her previous reporting." The FBI had relied on her information "in the conduct of various foreign counterintelligence investigations. . . .

The FBI must now re-assess all of its actions and intelligence analyses based on her reporting."

The bureau, Carlson warned, would now have to figure out which counterintelligence cases had "been thwarted or compromised" by her passing information "to her PRC handlers, as well as by disinformation she may have provided her FBI handlers."

It was not a merry Christmas or a happy New Year for J.J. Smith, Katrina Leung, or William Cleveland. Wiser and his team had established the somber, unhappy truth. China's intelligence service, the MSS, had penetrated the Federal Bureau of Investigation.

There was no telling what would happen next. All the three could do was wait for the government's next move. It was a nerve-racking time, especially for J.J. and PARLOR MAID. It was only slightly less so for Cleveland, since there was no evidence that Leung had obtained documents or information from him. But his job at Livermore would be in jeopardy if his relationship with Leung became public.

It was better to try not to think about what the days or weeks ahead might bring, and J.J. dealt with the waiting by keeping busy. After he had retired, like many ex-FBI agents, he opened a private security firm out of his home in Westlake Village. His business card read "James J. Smith, Private Investigations and Security Consultant." On the reverse side, the same information appeared in Chinese.

Late in January 2003 J.J. and his old boss, Dot Kelly, who had also retired, were in separate cars conducting a surveillance in a northern Los Angeles suburb for a corporate client of the Emerald Group, a private security firm run by Tom Parker, an ex-FBI agent in Los Angeles. The streets in the area may have become a tad overcrowded, because at the time, and for several weeks, J.J. remained under surveillance by the FBI as he in turn conducted his own surveillance for Parker. It was a scene worthy of Mack Sennett, the celebrated silent film director who specialized in slapstick.

The comic relief would not last for long, however. Soon, Les Wiser, his work done, packed up the office in Santa Monica and prepared to head back East, after many months away from his family.

As daunting as the job had seemed in the beginning, he had done what he set out to do. The rest was up to the prosecutors.

## Chapter 15

# ROYAL TOURIST

IN JULY 1997 Robin Lee was annoyed when an outlet in the kitchen of her house in Manhattan Beach, California, suddenly stopped working. She unscrewed the faceplate to have a look; perhaps she could divine what was wrong and avoid the expense of an electrician.

She removed the plate and immediately saw something that struck her as extremely odd. There was an extra wire in the outlet, and it was unlike anything she had ever seen before.

Her husband, Peter Hoong-Yee Lee, a physicist and a graduate of the California Institute of Technology, had no difficulty recognizing the strange wire for what it was — a miniature bug, a microphone that had been disguised to pick up conversations in the room.

For Peter Lee, it was the first sign of danger, a harbinger of the major trouble that was soon to descend upon him. Until that moment, life had been good for the Lees. A respected scientist and expert on lasers who had worked at both the Los Alamos and Lawrence Livermore nuclear weapons labs, Peter Lee was then fifty-eight and employed at TRW, a Livermore contractor, in Redondo Beach, California.

A shy, introverted man who spoke and wrote Chinese fluently, Lee was born in Chongqing (then Chungking), in central China, in 1939, grew up in Taiwan, and immigrated to the United States.

Lee, a naturalized citizen, had briefly appeared on the FBI's radar screen in the early 1980s, while he worked at Livermore. On a trip to China, according to Paul Moore, the former FBI analyst, "at breakfast he tells a colleague that the strangest thing happened, somebody came to my hotel room and wanted to talk to me. The person he confided this to said, 'This is the kind of thing the security folks want to know about, be sure to put it in your trip report.' Lee didn't but the other guy did. The FBI came out to interview Lee. Bill Cleveland did the interview. Lee says, 'Oh yeah, I didn't put that into my report, I should have.' 'You kept a trip diary?' Lee says yes, but he can't find it, come back later. The FBI comes back and Lee says he doesn't want to get involved any further. So now Lee is on the FBI's records."

What Peter Lee did not know was that a decade later, in 1991, J.J. Smith had opened an FBI case on him after the bureau received information about Lee from an informant. The scientist was suspected of passing government secrets to China. The FBI gave the Peter Lee file the code name ROYAL TOURIST.

Chinese spy cases have tendrils that often seem to reach out and become entangled in other cases. The Peter Lee case was used as a pretext when the FBI ran a notably unsuccessful sting on Wen Ho Lee, with a bureau agent pretending to be a spy for the MSS. And the names of the agents who worked on the Peter Lee case were found in PAR-LOR MAID's bookcase in 2002, when the FBI was closing in on Katrina Leung and J.J. Smith.

At TRW, Lee worked on the Joint UK/US Radar Ocean Imaging Program, a $100 million effort by the United States in cooperation with Britain to use radars on satellites and aircraft to detect submarines moving underwater. The theory was that the remote sensing radars could detect submarine signatures by subtle changes on the surface of the ocean waves. The Pentagon program was based at the Livermore lab.

In February 1994 the FBI, with approval of the secret court established by the Foreign Intelligence Surveillance Act, began "technical surveillance" of Peter Lee, a euphemism for a wiretap. The bug in the kitchen was approved later, in August 1996.

In May of the following year, Lee and his wife visited China on a three-week trip that took them to Beijing, Shanghai, Guangzhou, and other cities. On his foreign travel form at TRW, Lee said he was going on a vacation and paying his own expenses. In fact, he had been invited to lecture by China's Institute of Applied Physics and Computational Mathematics in Beijing, which paid for his trip.

While in Beijing, Lee lectured on microwave scattering from ocean waves and talked about his work on the radar ocean-imaging project. He showed the scientists a photograph he had brought with him of the wake of a surface ship and drew a graph to illustrate his talk. In answer to a question, he said the technology could also be used to detect submarines moving below the surface.

Among the thirty scientists present were He Xiantu, Du Xiangwan, Chen Nengkuan, whom Lee had met on an earlier trip to China in 1985, and Yu Min, whom he had also met on the earlier trip and who was described by one Livermore official as the Edward Teller of the Chinese nuclear weapons program.

Apparently Lee realized he might get in trouble for his freewheeling lecture to the Chinese scientists, because before leaving the institute, he erased the graph and tore the photograph into small pieces. A few days later, he lectured to scientists in another city.

Back in California in late May, he filled out a questionnaire for TRW asserting that the Chinese had not asked "for technical information" or tried to persuade him to disclose classified data. However, he detected no sign of trouble — until Robin discovered the bug two months later.

J.J. Smith had assigned three agents to the ROYAL TOURIST investigation, Gilbert Cordova, Serena Alston, and Brad Gilbert. They were the same team that investigated Jeffrey Wang in the ETHEREAL THRONE case.

In late June, Cordova interviewed Lee, who insisted, as he had on his travel form for TRW, that he had paid his own expenses on what he described as a sightseeing and pleasure trip. He denied that he had engaged in any technical or scientific discussions with anyone in China.

By lying on both counts, Lee did not realize he was digging himself deeper into a hole.

Once Robin Lee had discovered the bug in the kitchen, the surveillance was obviously compromised. J.J. Smith and the other agents realized they had to move quickly. In August, the FBI interviewed Lee twice in a hotel room in Santa Barbara.

Lee was unaware that he had an audience. As Cordova and Alston questioned the scientist at Fess Parker's hotel, J.J. and his entire squad of about fifteen FBI agents from Los Angeles were crowded into the adjoining room, watching the proceedings on video.

Somewhat to the surprise of the FBI agents, Lee now admitted he had lied about the purpose of his trip and in denying that he had talked to the Chinese about technical matters. But he continued to insist he had paid for the trip himself. At the second of the interviews, on August 14, he was asked to provide receipts to verify his trip expenses.

Soon afterward, Lee sent an e-mail and fax to Guo Hong, a Chinese official, about an "extremely urgent matter." He asked Guo to send him receipts in English with his name and Robin's, showing that he had paid for the trip. The Chinese official obliged, and early in September, Lee submitted the phony receipts to the FBI.

A month later, Lee agreed to be interviewed again and to take a lie detector test. Told he had failed the polygraph, Lee then confessed on videotape that he had talked about classified information in China and lied on his post-travel questionnaire. He said he had revealed the information because China is "such a poor country" and one of the scientists had asked for his help. It was a classic example of *guanxi* and the "help China modernize" pitch that had worked in other cases.

But Peter Lee had an even bigger surprise in store for the FBI agents. Having decided to unburden himself, he began talking about the four-week trip that he had taken to China in January 1985.

At the time of the trip, Lee was working at Los Alamos. For eight years before that, however, he had been at the Livermore lab as a research physicist specializing in inertial confinement fusion, or ICF, the use of lasers to attempt to trigger what amounted to miniature, table-top thermonuclear explosions. In these experiments, powerful lasers are focused on a hohlraum, a small gold cylinder no bigger than a paper clip that holds a tiny capsule containing deuterium and tritium. The goal is to cause the fuel inside the capsule to ignite, creating for a fraction of a second a miniature star and producing new energy by fusion, the way the sun does. The process, if successful, could be used to produce nuclear energy to generate electricity, but it is also similar to what happens in a thermonuclear bomb.

The dance had begun on January 9, 1985, when Lee met with Chen Nengkuan of the China Academy of Engineering Physics, the agency that designed and developed the country's nuclear weapons. In Chen's hotel room in Beijing, Lee was asked questions by him that involved classified information. Chen told Lee he did not need to speak, he could just nod yes or no.

That would foil any eavesdroppers. But it would also allow Lee to claim that he never "talked" to Chen about any US secrets.

Chen, one of China's top scientists in its nuclear weapons program, had earned a PhD in physics at Yale in 1950. He drew for Lee a diagram of a hohlraum, and asked a series of questions about it. The business of just nodding yes or no was soon forgotten, and Lee answered questions about the dimensions of the cylinder and where the capsule was located inside it.

The next day, Lee was picked up at his hotel by Chen and driven to another hotel where a group of Chinese scientists was waiting in a small conference room. For two hours, Lee answered questions and drew several diagrams, including sketches of hohlraums. He also discussed problems the United States was having in its simulated nuclear weapons tests.

On the face of it, the government appeared to have an airtight case against Peter Lee. By his own admission, he had revealed classified information in 1985 on the laser program and in 1997 on the ocean-imaging project and its application to detecting submarines. He had lied about the purpose of his trip in 1997 and in denying he had discussed technical subjects in China. He then tried to deceive the FBI with phony travel vouchers to prove he had paid for the trip himself.

The case was assigned to Jonathan Shapiro, a young, gung-ho federal prosecutor in Los Angeles, a Harvard graduate with a law degree from the University of California at Berkeley and a Rhodes scholar. Shapiro, as he later testified to a Senate judiciary subcommittee chaired by Senator Arlen Specter, had "what I thought was a dead-bang case."

But Shapiro soon found himself at loggerheads with the Department of Justice in Washington. "It is no secret that in the Peter Lee prosecution," he testified, "I strongly advocated for the most aggressive approach in pursuing Mr. Lee on charges of espionage. It is also no secret that I had disagreements with my supervisors at the U.S. Attorney's Office and with the Department of Justice about how the case should be investigated and charged."

On hundreds of other cases that Shapiro had prosecuted, he did not need approval from Washington. But espionage was different. No spy case could move forward without a green light from the attorneys in the internal security section of the department.

And the lawyers in Washington quickly came to regard the ROYAL TOURIST case as a quagmire. The problem was that the information Lee had revealed in China on both occasions was classified at the time he had disclosed it, but later declassified and discussed publicly by US officials.

There is considerable misunderstanding about the classification system both in and outside the government. Documents are classified by executive order, not by law. Indeed, although the military classified documents starting in World War I, there was no civilian document-classification system until President Harry S. Truman issued the first presidential order on classification in 1951. Later chief executives have issued similar orders, providing that documents may be marked CONFIDENTIAL, SECRET, or TOP SECRET, depending on how much damage to national security their disclosure might cause.

But a whole superstructure of special intelligence classifications above TOP SECRET has sprung up, exotic code names like DINAR, UMBRA, or SPOKE, usually assigned to protect the methods used to gather intelligence, such as spy satellites or electronic intercepts.

An executive order, in short, is not a law. The classification system was not established by Congress. Created by the president, it applies only to employees of the federal government. Only Congress can pass laws. A president can instruct federal employees about how to mark a document TOP SECRET. But disclosing a classified document does not necessarily break any law.

The espionage statutes date back to 1917 and World War I, long before President Truman invented the classification system. With a narrow exception dealing with codes and communications intelligence, the statutes do not penalize disclosure of classified documents as such but of information "relating to the national defense." This is a crucial distinction, since many documents that should never have been classified in the first place are marked SECRET or TOP SECRET by overzealous bureaucrats. Sometimes officials wield the secrecy stamp on a document to feel important or because they know that otherwise their superiors may not even bother to read it.

To criminalize leaks of government information simply because the information is marked classified would be absurd: in 2008 the government classified 23,421,098 documents, a total that had more than doubled in six years. It is hardly likely that the government has that many real secrets to withhold from its citizens. Unnecessary classification is a fact of life in Washington. During World War II, the Army actually classified the bow and arrow as a "silent flashless weapon." One government agency classified the fact that water does not flow uphill. In the early years of the space program, the Pentagon classified the fact that it was sending monkeys into space, although a plaque on the cage of a macaque at the National Zoo announced to visitors that this particular monkey had been sent up two hundred thousand feet on an Air Force rocket.

When the government tries to invoke the espionage laws to prosecute someone, it must prove that a particular classified document fits the statutory definition of "relating to the national defense." It is not enough for prosecutors simply to show that a document is classified, since it may have been improperly classified. Otherwise, if publication or disclosure of classified information were illegal per se, the government would have total control over information and the First Amendment would become meaningless.

As a practical matter, however, prosecutors are usually reluctant to bring a case before a jury unless they can show that a defendant has revealed classified information. If the information is not classified, jurors might well wonder how the government can claim that the documents relate to the nation's defense and that their disclosure would harm national security.

And that was precisely the problem that the prosecutors faced in the ROYAL TOURIST case. A document that Lee had written in 1982, which he discussed in China in 1985, was classified. But scientists the world over were working on inertial confinement fusion, and by 1993 the ICF experiments that Lee spoke about had been declassified.

Moreover, by 1993 the Energy Department was encouraging other countries to simulate nuclear explosions in the laboratory — the ICF work that Lee was engaged in — in order to discourage other nations from conducting atmospheric nuclear tests. Michael Liebman, the Justice Department attorney responsible for the Lee case, worried that if Lee was prosecuted for his lectures in 1985, he could claim he was only trying to help persuade China not to conduct tests of nuclear weapons in the air.

The scientist's discussion about the ocean-imaging project and the use of radar to track ships and subs presented an even greater hurdle, in Liebman's view. But Lee had admitted telling the Chinese in 1997 that the radars could also be used to detect submarines. Liebman thought he could use that indiscretion to build an espionage case against Lee. Then Liebman was dismayed to discover a March 1995 article on the Livermore website, a date that was two years before Lee's trip to China.

Headlined "Radar Ocean Imaging," the article discussed Livermore's role in the joint US/UK program: "This project focuses on the detection by radars of surface manifestations of moving, submerged submarines." Oops.

It got worse. A few days later, Liebman found that in April 1994 Dr. Richard E. Twogood, who managed the ocean-imaging project at Livermore, boasted in an open session of the House Armed Services Committee that the program "has made important progress in the development of methods to detect submarine signatures with remote sensing radars" that could measure "surface effects produced by undersea disturbances."

When he testified before the Senate Subcommittee on Department of Justice Oversight in 2000, Twogood had difficulty deciding on the level of classification of the data about submarine tracking that Lee had disclosed in China. He had reviewed Lee's confession to the FBI. "When I saw the videotape and the audio tape, my immediate response was that it is at least confidential, and I thought it was likely . . . secret." Twogood said he told Bill Cleveland, then in charge of security at Livermore, that "it probably was secret." A document introduced at the hearing indicated that Twogood thought the information about detecting submarines was classified "Secret/Crimson Stage."

Shapiro was unhappy that Twogood was the only government witness provided to him who could testify that Lee had disclosed classified information. But Twogood waffled on the level of classification.

The prosecutor kept asking the Navy for someone who could clarify just how secret the submarine-tracking data was. Twogood, Shapiro told the judiciary panel, was "the best I could come up with." But, he added, "Nevertheless I had Twogood and I was going to use Twogood." The problem was that "Dr. Twogood's opinion evolved." As a witness, Shapiro fretted, Twogood was not too good. "Dr. Twogood, in my view, would have gone down in blue flames on cross-examination."

Shapiro also testified that he had wanted to arrest Lee when he confessed, but that the Justice Department vetoed him, saying it wanted more time to study the evidence. Shapiro said he wanted "to put the cuffs on him and let him taste incarceration. . . . My frustrations in this case began when I wasn't allowed to hook Mr. Lee up."

But the biggest blow to the prosecution came from an unexpected quarter — the United States Navy. John G. Schuster, head of the Navy's submarine security branch, wrote a memo evaluating the damage caused by Lee's disclosures to the Chinese. Although the memo purported to give "classification guidance," it was all over the lot. The memo said the radar techniques were unclassified unless applied to "submarine wake signatures," in which case they were SECRET. But it also said that, on the other hand, Lee's discussion was taken from a document marked CONFIDENTIAL. And since the subject had been discussed in unclassified briefings and publications, "it is difficult to make a case that significant damage has occurred."

Then came the kicker: "Further, bringing attention to our sensitivity concerning this subject in a public forum could cause more damage to national security than the original disclosure." For that reason, Schuster urged that Lee not be prosecuted for talking about radar to track subs. Or, as Schuster testified, he opposed "a prosecution that might risk exposure of other non-acoustic ASW [antisubmarine warfare] information."

If Shapiro thought that Twogood was a problem, the Schuster memorandum was an exponentially bigger obstacle. The Navy was saying, in effect, yes, ROYAL TOURIST disclosed SECRET information, but we don't want any court trial that advertises how to track subs.

In an interview, Shapiro confirmed that "the Navy's reluctance was a problem." It was, in fact, a huge obstacle, although only one among the many he faced.

The two principal espionage statutes are contained in Title 18 of the US Code. The penalties for each are very different.

Section 793, "Gathering, transmitting or losing defense information," is aimed at anyone who obtains defense information with the intent or reason to believe that it is to be used to injure the United States or help a foreign nation. It applies as well to anyone who has either lawful or unauthorized possession of such information and passes it to someone not entitled to receive it, or through "gross negligence" allows the data to be removed or lost. For violators, it provides fines or a ten-year prison sentence, or both.

Section 794, "Gathering or delivering defense information to aid foreign government," is much more draconian. It is aimed at anyone who, with intent or reason to believe that it is to be used to injure the United States or help a foreign nation, transmits to a foreign government information "relating to the national defense." Depending on the type of information passed, the penalty is either death or imprisonment up to and including life.

Shapiro believed he could convict Lee under 794. He reasoned that even though the secrets revealed in China by Lee were later declassified, he had broken the espionage law at the time he lectured to the Chinese scientists both in 1985 and 1997. But Shapiro's superiors at the Justice Department did not authorize him to move under that law. He was allowed only to threaten to use 794 for leverage in obtaining a plea bargain. If he failed to obtain a guilty plea, he was told he could come back to the department and the matter would be reconsidered.

On top of that, the FBI made it clear to the prosecutor that the bureau was more concerned with its counterintelligence mission than in convicting Peter Lee. Michael P. Dorris, a senior FBI official, said exactly that in a memo he wrote on November 25, 1997.

The memo emphasized that "the FBI is much more interested in the intel yet to be garnered than in punishing felons. Therefore, any plea agreement must contain language permitting a thorough consensual search and complete cooperation by RT [ROYAL TOURIST]. He must also agree to tell all. Maybe even submit to a polygraph, who knows. Anyway, I think you get the idea."

In his testimony to the judiciary subcommittee, Shapiro made no secret of his frustration in trying to move the case forward. Part of the problem, he said, was that "there were individuals who weren't interested in prosecuting Peter Lee so much as they were interested in garnering intel, getting intelligence. I'm a one-trick pony. I do one thing. I prosecute cases. They bring them to me. I prosecute them, I investigate them. I'm not an intelligence-gatherer."

Although in 1997 the ten-year statute of limitations on Section 793 had run out on his disclosures in 1985 Lee, perhaps to avoid a more drastic espionage charge, agreed to plead guilty to violating the lesser statute by having "willfully communicated" to China "information relating to the national defense" and having done so "with reason to believe that the information could be used to the advantage of the People's Republic of China." He also pleaded guilty to making a false statement on his travel form about his contacts with foreign officials during his 1997 trip. On the two charges combined, which the government recommended run concurrently, Lee faced ten years in prison and a fine of $250,000.

Lee thus was pleading guilty to revealing information in 1985 about his work with lasers on inertial confinement fusion. There was no mention in the plea bargain of the data he had revealed in 1997 about detecting submarines by radar. The Navy had prevailed; there would be no trial and courtroom discussion about tracking subs.

The Navy, however, wanted to have it both ways. Two years later, as the draft of the Cox Report on Chinese espionage was circulating behind the scenes to government agencies, senior Navy officials became alarmed at what they had wrought. The Cox draft, as well as the published version, said that the information Lee disclosed on detecting subs underwater could enable China's military "to threaten previously invulnerable U.S. nuclear submarines."

It seemed a reasonable conclusion; if radar could be used to peer beneath the ocean waves to find subs, they would no longer be invulnerable. From the Navy's viewpoint, however, it would not do at all if the public thought that nuclear-armed submarines, one leg of the triad of America's nuclear deterrent, were no longer safe.

Stephen W. Preston, the Navy's general counsel, wrote to Cox and Norm Dicks, the ranking Democrat on the committee, objecting to the language of the report. As Preston put it to the judiciary subcommittee, the Cox Report "had the potential of creating a widespread misperception that by virtue of Lee's disclosures the submarine force had been rendered vulnerable to adversaries."

As part of Lee's plea bargain, he had to agree to be debriefed by the FBI and answer all questions. In turn, the government said it would "recommend a short period of incarceration."

The deal was wrapped up by James D. Henderson, Lee's attorney, a former federal prosecutor in Los Angeles, and Shapiro. On the morning of March 26, 1998, Lee, Shapiro, and Henderson appeared before Judge Terry J. Hatter, in the federal district court in Los Angeles.

Henderson was at bat first. He did his best to try to persuade the judge not to send Lee to prison. "Not everybody needs to go to jail," he said. Lee, he argued, was "not the kind of person that belongs in a jail cell."

When Lee disclosed information in China, Henderson argued, he was in a teaching mode, just trying to aid other scientists and "was overcome by his desire to help them." It was just "a scientific thing." Lee's "ego got the best of him."

Shapiro wasn't buying it. "He lied," he said. "He compromised the security of projects he worked on. . . . Rather than serving the United States as he swore he would, he tried to help China." Shapiro said Lee had engaged in "a pattern of deception." In a dramatic flourish, the prosecutor displayed a hohlraum in court, linking it to "the design of nuclear weapons."

Finally it was Peter Lee's moment to speak. He admitted to an "egregious mistake" and added, "I got carried away with professional camaraderie. . . . I admit I violated a sacred oath not to discuss secrets. I am deeply sorry and regretful for my actions . . . and I would like to beg for leniency. Please, your honor, don't put me in jail."

Hatter was skeptical of Lee's explanation that he got "carried away" in speaking to the Chinese scientists. "Well, let me stop you for a moment," the judge said. "It isn't just an activity of thirteen years ago, but there is the other count, the false statement much more recently."

But Hatter, much to the open disappointment of Shapiro and the FBI agents in the courtroom, did not send Lee to prison. He sentenced Lee, instead, to one year in a halfway house, three thousand hours of community service, and a $20,000 fine. As a convicted felon, however, and without a security clearance, Lee's career as a scientist working for the nuclear weapons labs or defense contractors was effectively over.

Six months after Lee was sentenced, there was an odd postscript in the case. The Pentagon asked the Naval Criminal Investigative Service to conduct a "Project Slammer" interview with Lee. The little-known project, run by the government's intelligence agencies, conducts interviews of convicted spies to find out what makes them tick. The FBI, possibly not looking kindly on the Navy's interference in the Lee case, told NCIS to go away. There was no Project Slammer interview of Peter Lee.

Looking back on the case, James Henderson, Lee's attorney, said that his client was convicted for disclosing information that "should never have been classified." According to Henderson, "the director of one of the programs Lee worked on said to me the only reason it was classified was to get funding from Congress."

The defense attorney had his own view of ROYAL TOURIST. "He was no real spy," Henderson insisted, "just a guy who did something stupid because he wanted to be a big shot."

## Chapter 16

# RICHARD NIXON AND THE
# HONG KONG HOSTESS

I N 1967 DAN GROVE was the FBI's man in Hong Kong, a key
listening post for intelligence on China and Southeast Asia. Somewhat like Vienna after World War II, Hong Kong was a magnet for
spies and intrigue.

Grove, like all FBI agents stationed overseas, had the title of legal
attaché, or legat. He was later to play an important role in the TIGER
TRAP case when the student he recruited was entrusted with the letter
from Hanson Huang to Gwo-bao Min, the Livermore scientist.

In October 1967 Richard Nixon was in Hong Kong, a city he visited often as the senior partner in the New York law firm of Nixon,
Mudge, Rose, Guthrie, Alexander & Mitchell, where he worked during
the 1960s and plotted his way back to power. When Nixon traveled
abroad, as a former vice president he could, if he wished, receive political and military briefings at US embassies in the countries he visited.
He was briefed on China by officials at the US consulate when he traveled to Hong Kong in 1967.

As the FBI legat in the British colony, Grove sometimes worked
with Pericles "Perry" Spanos, the senior Treasury special agent in
Hong Kong. Spanos was primarily concerned with smuggling, coun-

terfeiting, and narcotics. One of the watering holes he kept a close eye on was the Den, the bar in the old Hilton hotel.

The US consulate in Hong Kong is on Garden Road. The Hilton, a landmark until it was demolished in 1995, was four blocks down the hill, below the consulate, at the corner of Queens Central Road. There were two bars in the Hilton: the Dragon Boat, shaped like a boat, was the regular bar; the Den, in the basement, was the cocktail lounge. Marianna Liu, a beautiful young Chinese woman, was the head hostess at the Den.

The Den was a place where patrons could enjoy a Filipino band, dancing, and drinks. "When the fleet was in," said one American diplomat, "US officers and aviators would book suites at the Hilton and there would be a lot of partying at the Dragon Bar and the Den."

Chinese intelligence did not overlook the fleet's fondness for the Hilton, according to Milton Bearden, who spent five years in Hong Kong during two tours for the CIA. "Hong Kong, the Hilton, the Dragon Bar, and the Den were hugely rich targets for the PRC. Intelligence was a cottage industry in Hong Kong. Everybody was involved. The Brits, the Americans, the Chinese, the fat cats. Everybody."

That included the FBI. "One day," Grove recalled, "Spanos comes across the hall to me about Liu. He says she's a source of mine on smuggling jewelry and different things out of China. He said there's all kinds of reports about her working for the other side. He said you got to look at this."

Nixon was in town, and Spanos told Grove that Liu had visited the former vice president in his suite at the Mandarin Hotel. "Spanos said she spent last night with Nixon. He said, 'I'm really concerned about this situation. Nixon spent the night with her at the Mandarin Hotel.' He said, 'He's shacking up with this girl and I know he got a security briefing.' That's what had Perry so distressed."

Grove resisted. "I said it's overseas, it's agency [CIA] jurisdiction. He said, 'Yeah, but Nixon is a US politician and just had a TOP SECRET briefing here.'" Grove finally agreed to accompany Spanos to the Den.

"I'll never forget," Grove said. "It was a very hot day — you could fry an egg on the sidewalk — we walked down to the Den." They were greeted by Marianna Liu. "She gives us a nice seat and Spanos says,

'I understand you spent the night with the big man last night.' She giggles. She laughed and giggled and said yes and pointed to the other girl and said she and the other hostess, Teresa, were with him and his friend. And the friend I found out was Bebe Rebozo."

Rebozo, a millionaire real estate developer who owned a bank on Key Biscayne, Florida, was Nixon's closest friend, his golfing, boating, and drinking partner, as well as his frequent travel companion. They both liked charcoal-broiled steaks and watching movies, which Rebozo would select.

Perry Spanos independently recalled the conversation about Nixon in the Den much as Grove had. "The main hostess was Marianna, a beautiful Chinese lady in her early thirties," Spanos said. "She was very coy, and said she and her friend Teresa met him, and she implied it was more than just a casual meeting. Teresa was nearby, Marianna pointed to her. She said, 'Myself and Teresa entertained Nixon.' I don't think Nixon was a ladies' man. So it surprised me."

Grove did not doubt that Liu and the other hostess had visited Nixon and Rebozo at the Mandarin. But he was skeptical of her giggling implication that they had spent the night. "Marianna Liu was Nixon's friend," Grove said. "I'm convinced she was working for the other side. I think she was also a communication channel, he was using her as a back channel to the Chinese. Before the opening to China. She swears they never even touched, and I believe her."

Nevertheless, Grove felt he had to tell FBI headquarters about his encounter with Liu at the Den. Before reporting the conversation to Washington, Grove decided it would be prudent to check with the British, on whose turf he was operating. He paid an official call on the Special Branch of the Royal Hong Kong Police.

"I went over to the Brits and asked if they had coverage of Liu, and they said she had been reported several times, always asking questions of Navy people down at the Den. When do you sail? and this kind of stuff. The Brits said it's been reported to us several times she was a possible CHIS [Chinese intelligence service] agent. We did not investigate because all her activities were directed at the US."

On October 12, Grove dutifully reported the British concerns about Liu and the conversation at the Den to FBI headquarters. He was well aware that the part about the hotel visit was the sort of salacious gossip that J. Edgar Hoover reportedly loved to collect to give him leverage over presidents and other public officials. Grove saw it another way. An old-fashioned FBI agent, reflexively loyal to the bureau, he argued that Hoover had a responsibility to inform high-level officials if the bureau learned of reports being spread about them.

Two years after Nixon resigned the presidency in 1974, his contacts with Liu in Hong Kong leaked out, but received little attention from the mainstream press. However, an FBI memo in July 1976 cited and restated Grove's 1967 report to headquarters. Referring to Liu, it said:

> Information concerning subject was originally brought to the attention of this Bureau by Legal Attache, Hong Kong, letter dated 10/12/67 wherein suspicions of possible Chicom intelligence involvement of subject were inferred but not substantiated by Special Branch, Hong Kong Police and a U.S. Customs representative in Hong Kong indicated he had heard from a former Customs representative in Hong Kong, that subject was a regular bedmate of Vice-President Nixon when he visited Hong Kong. The Customs representative indicated he had no firsthand knowledge, was furnishing the information in confidence and requested no further dissemination of the information. No active investigation of the subject was conducted by the FBI.

Grove's report, with its explosive line about Liu as "a regular bedmate of Vice-President Nixon," triggered an unexpected reaction from headquarters in 1967. "I got a screaming meemie cable from Bill Sullivan, saying, 'Mr. Nixon's private life is of no concern to this bureau.' Sullivan was hoping to get Hoover's job and he could see this ruining his chances." If Nixon became president, Grove reasoned, "Sullivan thought with this information Nixon would never get rid of Hoover."

Indeed, on December 16, 1968, a little more than a month after Nixon was elected president, he let it be known through his press secretary that he had asked Hoover to remain as FBI chief.

Hoover had guaranteed similar job security for himself during the Kennedy administration. Attorney General Robert Kennedy, the president's brother, intensely disliked the aging FBI director, and the Kennedys would have been pleased if Hoover had retired, which he had no intention of doing. On March 22, 1962, Hoover dropped by the White House for a private lunch with President Kennedy to inform him that the FBI knew of his sexual liaison with Judith Campbell (she later remarried and became Judith Campbell Exner), who was also bestowing her favors on Sam Giancana, a Mafia don. Giancana and Johnny Rosselli, another mobster, had been hired by the CIA to assassinate Fidel Castro and both later met untimely ends. Giancana was murdered in 1975 before he could testify to a Senate committee investigating the CIA's activities; a year later Rosselli's body was found stuffed into an oil drum floating in the ocean near Miami.

As documented by the Senate Select Committee on Intelligence, "the last telephone contact between the White House and the President's friend [Judith Campbell] occurred a few hours after the luncheon." Hoover remained director of the Federal Bureau of Investigation for a decade more, until he died in office on May 2, 1972, at the age of seventy-seven.

William C. Sullivan was an assistant director of the FBI, a Hoover sycophant who later broke with the FBI chief and became his bitter opponent. In his book, *The Bureau: My Thirty Years in Hoover's FBI*, Sullivan said that Nixon and Rebozo had taken two trips to Hong Kong "brightened for Nixon by his friendship with a Chinese girl named Marianna Liu." Sullivan described what he said happened when he gave Grove's letter to the FBI director:

" 'I'll handle this one,' Hoover said gleefully when I passed the letter on to him. He took the letter to the future president immediately. 'I know there's no truth to this,' he told Nixon. 'Someone must be misleading our legal attaché. I'll never speak of it to anyone,' Hoover concluded with great solemnity. It was one of his favorite speeches, one he gave often to politicians."

In an interview with Jack Nelson of the *Los Angeles Times* in 1973, Sullivan called Hoover "a master blackmailer." The minute Hoover would "get something on a senator he'd send one of the errand boys up and advise the senator that we're in the course of an investigation and we by chance happened to come up with this data on your daughter. But we wanted you to know this — we realize you'd want to know it. But don't have any concern, no one will ever learn about it. Well, Jesus, what does that tell the senator? From that time on the senator's right in his pocket."

In 2009 Marianna Liu was a peppy seventy-seven-year-old grandmother living modestly in Monterey Park, the heavily Chinese community east of downtown Los Angeles. In a lengthy interview with the author at her home, she confirmed that she and the other hostess had spent time with Nixon and Rebozo at the Mandarin Hotel, but disputed many of the stories that have swirled around her since her friendship with Nixon became known.

Thin, short, dark-haired, and brown-eyed, Liu said she exercised at the gym every day to stay trim. She spoke English in a rapid-fire, choppy style. "We were at Mandarin, yes," she said, "no love affair. We were friends."

"He was with Bebe Rebozo," she continued. "They were in the Den to have a drink. They said after work let's have a drink. I didn't want to go alone." So she asked her friend Teresa to come with her to Nixon's hotel.

"Around 9 P.M. after dinner we went to the Mandarin. We went there and just had a drink. Not very long, maybe an hour or less. Soft drink, I had, I don't drink." She did not recall what Nixon drank.

At the Mandarin, she said, Nixon introduced Bebe as his secretary. At some point in the hotel suite, Nixon "gave me a bottle of perfume." She added, "I did not spend the night with Nixon."

Although Liu insisted that she had only seen Nixon one evening, at the Den and then at the hotel, she apparently had a different recollection previously. According to a 1976 story in the *New York Times,* Liu said she had first met Nixon when he was vice president and she was working as a part-time tour guide for a travel agency. If so, this would date their first meeting to the 1950s, when Nixon was vice president.

The story reported that Liu said she had met Nixon several times thereafter, and that she thought they had seen each other on his trips to Hong Kong in 1964, 1965, and 1966. The story said Liu recounted that when she was hospitalized in April 1967, Nixon sent flowers to her room.

Although the visit to the Mandarin took place in October 1967, a photograph of Liu and Nixon smiling warmly at each other was taken at the Den in 1966, according to the files of the *Hong Kong Standard,* which published the photo. If the date is accurate, they had met at least in those two years.

Liu was asked in the interview with the author if she had ever provided information to China. "No, I would never do that," she replied. "I did not give information to PRC."

Told that the police in Hong Kong suspected she might have collected information for China, she laughed. "They say I'm a Red spy."

Her own background, Liu contended, did not support those suspicions. She was raised in Beijing, she said, and her father was a Nationalist general who had been killed by the Communists. She remembered that her father "limped one leg short from fighting the Japanese." According to Liu, in 1949, when Mao's forces prevailed, they told her father that if he surrendered and switched sides he could "stay a general. He refused. He ran away twice and third time they got him. He was shot somewhere in Shantung."

By 1951, Liu had moved to Hong Kong. After attending a Catholic school, she worked for a Swiss watch company, a travel agency, and an insurance company, then landed the job at the Hilton in 1963. She worked as a hostess at the Den for eight years.

According to the *Times* story, Liu said that Nixon had told her if she ever decided to emigrate to the United States and needed help, she could contact him. Liu did move to the United States and received permanent residence status on December 1, 1969, ten months after Nixon became president, but she told the newspaper that she had not asked Nixon for help. Her husband, Gorkey Faan, joined her a few years later.

Coincidence or not, Liu moved to Whittier, California, Nixon's hometown. She came to the United States as a domestic for Raymond F. Warren, an official of the Immigration and Naturalization Service in Los Angeles, who also lived in Whittier. Liu said she worked as a companion for Warren's wife, Helen, an invalid who was partially paralyzed.

Liu said in her interview with the author that she had contacted

Warren through a Chinese bartender she knew in Los Angeles who "was good friend of Ray Warren many years." She said she originally arrived in the United States on a visitor's visa, "and Warren got me papers to take care of his wife." She applied for naturalization in 1975 and became a citizen.

In the 1970s Liu and her husband bought a restaurant in Maywood, California, called Anderson's Cuisine, which served American food. They ran the place for three or four years.

But Liu's quiet life in Southern California took an unexpected and unhappy turn in 1976. The *National Enquirer* assigned a team of half a dozen reporters to dig into Liu's relationship with the by-then former president.

The supermarket tabloid trumpeted the first of two stories on August 10, with a sensational headline in large type: "Nixon Romanced Suspected Red Spy." Below the headline the paper ran the photo of Liu and Nixon and another banner: "Chinese Beauty: 'Yes, There Was Love.'"

The story, and a second article two weeks later, raised questions about how Liu's immigration to the United States had been handled, why she had been allowed into the country after the FBI reported suspicions that she was working for Chinese intelligence, and why she had been sponsored by an INS official from Whittier.

The tabloid quoted Liu as saying she and Nixon had gone dancing by moonlight on a yacht in Hong Kong harbor that was raided by police at 5 A.M. Liu and Nixon had been together "several times" at four different hotels in Hong Kong, the story claimed. It quoted Liu as saying, "Yes, there was love. . . . It could easily have developed into a very strong love affair, but I wouldn't let it. He had an important career and a wife and family to think of, and I cared too much for him to let him spoil that. . . . We had many opportunities to make love — we were alone in his hotel room at least six or seven times — but I wouldn't let it happen." The story also claimed that Liu had visited Nixon twice in the White House in 1970.

In her interview with the author, Liu denied many of the assertions in the tabloid's account. There was, she said, no dancing on a yacht in the harbor, by moonlight or otherwise, and no police raid. "Never happened," she said. She denied she had been at four hotels with Nixon. "No, only the Mandarin," on the one occasion she talked about.

And the "Yes, there was love" quote? "No, they made it all up. Don't believe a word of the *Enquirer*."

Liu also insisted she had never visited Nixon at the White House, never saw him after she came to the United States, and did not travel to Washington for his inauguration, as one FBI report suggested.

By 1976, Dan Grove was in the FBI's office in Berkeley. The *National Enquirer* had contacted him when it was researching its stories on Liu, and in July, the month before the stories were published, Grove sent two airtels alerting FBI headquarters to the tabloid's investigation and detailing his conversations with one of its reporters.

Grove's alerts, sent from the San Francisco field office, triggered an internal memo at FBI headquarters, which said that although the Liu file had not been forwarded to Attorney General Edward H. Levi, he was aware of its contents. The FBI memo, the same one with the reference to Liu as "a regular bedmate" of Nixon, also said there would be no counterintelligence investigation of her. As for any allegations about Liu's immigration, the memo continued, that was a problem for INS or the State Department, not the FBI.

And that was probably the last official record of the saga of the Hong Kong hostess and the thirty-seventh president of the United States. Only Marianna Liu knows the truth about their relationship.

But perhaps it was more than a drink one night at the Mandarin. "When he died," she said, "I went to the cemetery a couple of times, to show some people, some friends. He is buried in Yorba Linda and that's where I went to cemetery."

Her most recent visit to Nixon's burial place, on the grounds of the Nixon Library, took place in 2007. "Two years ago I took some friends to see Mr. Nixon's grave," she said. "Ladies from San Francisco. They wanted to see his grave."

She paused for a moment. Then she added softly: "They did not know I knew him."

# Chapter 17

# ANUBIS

**I**N EGYPTIAN MYTHOLOGY, he is the familiar jackal-headed god who was believed to protect the dead. His likeness guarded the tomb of King Tutankhamen for twenty-two centuries.

Perhaps the code name ANUBIS was chosen by the FBI with a touch of whimsy, because he was an RIP, although in bureau language that did not mean "rest in peace." It meant "recruitment in place."

His true name was Wen Ning. He was born in Shanghai in 1949. At Qing Hua University in Beijing he earned a bachelor's degree in thermal engineering in 1976. He did two more years at a university in Shanghai, and married his high school sweetheart, Lin Hailin.

Because he finished at the top of his class, in 1980 Wen was allowed to come to the United States for graduate studies. During the next four years, he earned a master's degree and a PhD in engineering from the University of California at Berkeley. After leaving Berkeley, Wen and his wife returned to China for a few years and he entered the diplomatic service. In 1986, with his command of English and his graduate degrees, he was posted to the Chinese consulate in San Francisco. His wife also worked there, as a receptionist. Two years later, when China opened its consulate on Shatto Place in Los Angeles, Wen was transferred there as the science and technology attaché. But the family was forbidden to bring their only child, Sharon, with them to the United States.

In 1989, a year after the consulate opened, Wen apparently became disillusioned after the Chinese leadership brutally suppressed the protests in Tiananmen Square, killing hundreds of students and workers. He told an American friend that he was disappointed in the Chinese government's actions.

The friend introduced Wen to Steve Johnson, an FBI agent in Los Angeles who normally worked criminal cases. Johnson persuaded Wen to remain as a diplomat in the consulate, providing information to the FBI. The intelligence he passed to the bureau through Johnson went to J.J. Smith, who became the acting supervisor of the China counterintelligence squad in April 1990.

In convincing ANUBIS to continue at his post, Johnson was able to play a powerful card. He offered to help Wen's daughter get a US visa. The FBI then arranged for Sharon to come to Washington, DC, to live with her uncle there. In return, Wen agreed to meet clandestinely with Johnson on a regular basis until his tour ended.

A recruitment who stays on the job, becoming an agent in place, is the ultimate prize, the crown jewel of any counterintelligence operation. At great personal risk, a recruitment in place is in a position to provide continuous and up-to-date information. By contrast, a defector, while usually welcome, is of less value. Once debriefed of the information he or she knows, and with no further access to secrets, a defector has diminished worth.

By all accounts, the information that Wen passed to the FBI was valuable. Among other things, by virtue of his position, he had access to the code room. How much he obtained of the traffic between Shatto Place and Beijing is unknown. Code rooms are typically secured. The consulate had a husband-and-wife communications team, and the male, so that he could keep a close eye on the code room, was never allowed to leave the building.

But nothing in the counterintelligence world is uncomplicated.

ANUBIS became aware that Katrina Leung had a relationship with the FBI, which she certainly made no effort to conceal and in fact advertised. And ANUBIS did not trust PARLOR MAID.

Leung, in turn, knew and socialized with a number of officials at the Los Angeles consulate — she had, after all, helped to select the site for the building. She knew Wen Ning.

In investigating the PARLOR MAID case in 2002 and 2003, Les Wiser and his team in Santa Monica had to consider whether Leung had learned that ANUBIS was an FBI source inside the consulate.

J.J. Smith may not have directly told PARLOR MAID about ANUBIS, but he worked closely with Leung, treating her almost as a member of his squad. From the informed, detailed questions he asked her, it must have been obvious to Leung that the FBI had a source inside the consulate.

Wiser and his team concluded that Leung would have figured out the identity of ANUBIS. That, in turn, led to the next question: if she did become aware that Wen was feeding intelligence to the FBI, did she tell the Chinese? Leung did not reveal everything she learned to Beijing. But the investigators could not determine whether PARLOR MAID, if she knew about ANUBIS, shared that information with the MSS. Like so much in the wilderness of mirrors that is counterintelligence, there was no unequivocal answer.

A lot of the intelligence that ANUBIS provided, however, was in the form of documents that he smuggled out of the consulate. Despite the later concerns over PARLOR MAID's role, the FBI did not conclude that any of the documents were fake, or that Wen was under MSS control and deliberately handing the bureau misinformation. He was considered an important source.

ANUBIS was very busy. In 1991, unknown to the FBI, and while still a consulate official, he began shipping computer chips to China that had potential military use. He did so without obtaining the necessary export licenses. Whether he was moonlighting to make money on the side or acted at the direction of the Chinese government was not clear.

It had begun when a Chinese official asked Wen to help "a friend" in China. Wen was then contacted by Qu Jian Guo, who worked for an electronics company in Beijing. Wen, while continuing to work in the consulate and simultaneously serving as a secret FBI informant, sent thirteen shipments to Qu at his company, Beijing Rich Linscience Electronics.

By early 1992, however, ANUBIS had decided to call it quits as a recruitment in place for the FBI. "His tour was coming to an end, close to over," one bureau insider said. "They had a rule you had to rotate home before you could come back to the US. It was after Tiananmen, a lot of people were afraid to go home. He thought he might never get out again."

In March, Wen decided to defect. The FBI got him out and J.J. stashed him for a time in a safe house in the Valley. The Chinese may or may not have known that Wen had been spying for the FBI, although they certainly must have suspected as much when he walked out. But they realized he was gone for good.

Wen did not burn his bridges completely, however. Before leaving, he wrote a five-page letter to consulate officials. In it, he said that although he was resigning he still hoped he could "make actual contributions to my motherland." He had been offered high-tech jobs at a good salary and that way could "take advantage of the American funds" to continue to help China.

In his letter, Wen admitted that he was worried that if he went back to China, "I might not be able to obtain an approval" to return to the United States and work abroad. "I decided to act before seeking approval," Wen said. He left three addresses of relatives, two in the States and one in Canada, where he could be contacted. "We will not be hermits 'hiding in the woods,'" he wrote.

What to do with ANUBIS? The FBI wanted to help Wen and his wife and daughter to start a new life in the United States, and it wanted to keep tabs on him as well. The bureau helped him obtain a job in Manitowoc, Wisconsin, a small city far away from Los Angeles on Lake Michigan, north of Milwaukee. The couple moved there and settled into a modest condominium on the city's south side. And they were reunited with their daughter.

Wen also continued to report to the FBI as a bureau asset. Special Agent Melvin Fuqua, from the FBI's Milwaukee division, was assigned as ANUBIS's new handler. Fuqua had worked counterintelligence most of his career, in Boston and Kansas before Milwaukee. Over the next decade, he met with or spoke to Wen on the telephone perhaps one hundred times. Early on, the families socialized together, enjoying dinner around Christmas at a Chinese restaurant in Milwaukee.

In 1992 Wen established Wen Enterprises, an export company that he and his wife operated out of their home. From Manitowoc, Wen began shipping computer chips to Qu and Wang Ruo Ling, Qu's wife, who also worked for the Beijing electronics company. Under federal law and Commerce Department regulations, some dual-use products, which have both military and civilian applications, are restricted and cannot be exported without a license. In addition, exporters must file a declaration if the item is valued over $2,500. Wen and his wife used various subterfuges to get around these requirements and ship chips without export licenses.

For example, many of the computer chips they sent to China were valued at more than $10,000, or in one case more than $20,000, but they would typically falsify invoices and list the value at $2,457 or another amount just under $2,500. To pay for the shipments, money was wired to Wen Enterprises by a construction company in Beijing or a mysterious "Ms. Tsui Kan" in Hong Kong.

Wen, meanwhile, went to work in 1993 for the Manitowoc Company, one of the nation's largest manufacturers of cranes and ice machines. In 2000 the company sent Wen back to China as president and general manager of its refrigeration company in Hangzhou, in the Yangtze River delta south of Shanghai. The job required him to spend ten months out of the year in China.

It was an unexpected bonanza for the FBI, which now found itself with a long-term asset inside China who could travel freely back and forth between the mainland and the United States.

For Agent Fuqua, ANUBIS now became much more interesting. Wen was reporting to him on contacts in China and on his dealings with officials of the Chinese government. Wen became a naturalized American citizen in 2000 and his wife became a citizen the following year. In Wisconsin, they listed their names in American style, surnames last, as Ning Wen and Hailin Lin.

From Hangzhou, Wen kept a close eye on his export business, telephoning his wife frequently. Wen Enterprises may have been a mom-and-pop shop, but it was very lucrative. In just one two-year period between 2002 and 2004, almost $2 million was wired to Wen Enterprises from China. With a 20 percent markup on the computer chips, Wen's firm was earning about $10,000 a month, in addition to his salary from the Manitowoc Company.

Wen and his wife prospered. In 2002 they bought a $400,000 home on a leafy cul-de-sac in the upscale Lakeshore neighborhood on the north side of town.

The only downside of his job was all the months he had to spend in Hangzhou. Three times a year he was able to visit his wife in Manitowoc for a few weeks and once a year she joined him in China. The job was demanding; Wen was working fourteen hours a day and in charge of more than a hundred employees.

But Wen was looking forward to the 2008 Beijing Olympics. "There are about three hundred big hotels in the city, but that will double," he told an interviewer for the local paper in Manitowoc. "They will need ice machines. There will be big growth for our products."

As matters turned out, ANUBIS never made it to the Beijing Olympics. Wen Enterprises first showed up on the Commerce Department's radar screen in 2001 when a US company that had sold an electronic part to Wen tipped off the Office of Export Enforcement that the component had been shipped to China and ended up in the "54th Research Institute," which, according to the US Defense Intelligence Agency (DIA), specializes in telephone exchange systems for China's public security forces, satellite communications equipment, and communications jamming equipment.

Because the Commerce Department has designated shipments to the 54th Research Institute as posing an "unacceptable risk in the development of missiles," exports to the institute are subject to greater restrictions than components sent to other end users.

The Commerce Department sleuths did not get very far with their investigation of Wen Enterprises, however, until 2003, when an agent gained access to a database that showed about fifty shipments of integrated circuit chips to Qu's Beijing firm.

In March 2004 the Department of Commerce called in the FBI, the

US Attorney's Office in Milwaukee, and Homeland Security. The FBI obtained a FISA authorization and began tapping Wen's home telephone and his faxes and e-mails. The bureau recorded thirty-seven hours of conversations between Wen and his wife. Without Wen's knowledge, he was removed from the bureau's informant rolls.

That same month, Agent Fuqua, Wen's FBI handler, learned that his prize asset was being investigated. In all the years they had met, Wen somehow never thought to mention that he and his wife were running an illicit export business. Fuqua got the news in a phone call from an immigration agent. "I was shocked and just about fell out of my chair," Fuqua later claimed. "I had no idea that was going on."

In April an FBI counterintelligence agent began searching Wen's trash. The search turned up a note from Qu to Hailin Lin telling her to ship items in two different packages, using two shippers, and to report false values.

On the wiretaps, the FBI heard a woman who was one of Qu's associates in Beijing warn Wen's wife about one shipment of an expensive part. "Risk. The risk is big," the woman said. Lin agreed, replying, "Risk, yeah."

Hailin Lin complained in one phone conversation that Qu was slow to wire money from China to pay for the goods he had ordered. On May 28, Wen and his wife had a long conversation about a faster way to get the money. If Qu would share his Visa card number with her, Wen said, "You can use it to get cash from an ATM machine."

"This is a better way," Wen assured his wife. "You get money from the bank, the bank won't know. You get money directly from ATM. It's better."

Hailin Lin was dubious, since she knew that ATMs only disbursed "a couple of hundred dollars" at a time. Wen did not deny it would be inconvenient. "Yeah . . . you have to make several trips to get more money."

In another conversation on July 15, Qu and Hailin Lin discussed falsifying shipping documents. Qu reminded her that as long as the value "doesn't exceed $2,500" there would be no problem. Hailin Lin replied, "Yeah, I have to make up the figure every time."

On August 17, the wiretap picked up the most interesting conversation, between Wen and his wife. Hailin referred to tensions between China and Taiwan, saying that both sides were busy with "military maneuvers."

Wen replied, "China now is desperately purchasing weapons, developing weapons." He then asked, "How is Qu Jian Guo's business? Well, if the war breaks out, his business will be booming."

From overhearing conversations on Wen's telephone, the FBI learned that Qu and his wife, Wang Ruo Ling, planned to take a trip to four US cities and then visit Wen and his wife in Manitowoc in September. Hailin Lin had made the plane and hotel reservations.

But on September 30, when the couple from Beijing, both Chinese nationals, got off a Greyhound bus in Milwaukee, the FBI arrested them. Other agents arrested Wen and his wife at their home in Manitowoc. The government simultaneously seized their home and almost $1 million in assets in five different bank accounts.

A criminal complaint charged the four with using their businesses "to illegally transfer sensitive, national-security controlled items to the People's Republic of China . . . without obtaining required export licenses." The products, the complaint said, "can be used in a wide variety of military radar and communication applications."

The Manitowoc Company lost no time in washing its hands of its star executive in China. "The charges against the Wens are unrelated to the Manitowoc Company or Mr. Wen's responsibilities as general manager of Manitowoc Hangzhou," Maurice Jones, the senior vice president of the parent firm, announced.

A month later, a federal grand jury handed down an eight-count indictment charging the four with conspiracy to violate the export laws and money laundering. Wen was later charged with making false statements as well.

In May 2005 Qu and his wife pleaded guilty to reduced charges, avoiding potentially long prison terms. Qu pleaded to a single count of conspiring to export restricted electronics without a license. He was sentenced to forty-six months in prison and fined $2,000. Wang, who admitted to a single count of undervaluing a shipment, was sentenced to six months, which she had already served, and a $1,500 fine.

Wen's wife, Lin Hailin, pleaded guilty to conspiracy and money laundering and was sentenced to three and a half years in prison and fined $50,000. Wen alone decided to stand trial.

The case took an intriguing twist in July when Wen claimed diplomatic immunity because he had been an official in the Chinese consulate in Los Angeles from 1987 to March 1992, part of the time covered by the conspiracy charges. His attorney filed a motion to dismiss the case on those grounds.

Once the diplomatic immunity gambit was raised, the case became entangled with the State Department. Wen's lawyers got a court order blocking the department from talking to the US Attorney's Office in Milwaukee. When Erica O'Neil, the assistant prosecutor handling the case, tried to find out whether Wen could validly claim diplomatic immunity, the State Department informed the Justice Department that it could not make a decision in the matter without discussing the case with the prosecutors — something it was prohibited from doing by the court order.

The prosecutors solved the problem with a simple stratagem — they obtained a superseding indictment that moved the export violations and other charges to Wen's actions after March 16, 1992, the date he left the consulate. That disposed of any diplomatic immunity issue.

Wen's decision to stand trial was a gamble he lost. The government's evidence was strong. During the trial, FBI agent Ryan Chun read parts of the transcripts of eight telephone calls intercepted by the FISA wiretaps. The prosecution presented extensive documentary evidence of the various dodges Wen and his wife had used to circumvent the law and export regulations. In September, Wen was convicted of violating export controls, money laundering, and making false statements.

On January 18, 2006, Wen stood before Judge William Griesbach in federal court in Green Bay for sentencing. He faced up to twenty-five years in prison. Griesbach was sympathetic, up to a point. He called Wen a "diligent, hardworking person," which he said made the sentencing "difficult."

But the judge rejected Hailin Lin's testimony at the hearing that she often did not tell her husband about the day-to-day operations of Wen Enterprises because he was "very busy" making ice machines in Hangzhou. "I do not find it credible," Griesbach said, "that he didn't know the violations going on."

He then sentenced Wen to five years in prison and fined him $50,000. ANUBIS was sent to the minimum-security federal prison camp in Duluth, Minnesota. His lawyers appealed. Chicago attorney James Geis argued Wen's case before the Seventh Circuit Court of Appeals.

When the Foreign Intelligence Surveillance Act was passed in 1978, the special FISA court it established was authorized to approve wiretaps if the government can show probable cause that the target is a foreign power, or an agent of a foreign power, and that "the purpose" is to obtain foreign intelligence. After 9/11, the Patriot Act amended that language to allow surveillance if "the significant purpose" was obtaining foreign intelligence.

Geis argued that under the broader language the government used FISA to conduct a criminal investigation of Wen. The district court, in refusing to throw out the wiretaps, Geis maintained, had disregarded the requirements of the Fourth Amendment.

In December 2006 the Chicago appeals court ruled against Wen, a decision that expanded the government's power to use wiretaps aimed at foreign targets in criminal cases unrelated to espionage. Less than a year later, however, in September 2007, a federal judge in Oregon struck down the expanded provisions of the Patriot Act that Geis had contested.

In the world of spies, nothing is entirely predictable. But in the annals of Chinese counterintelligence cases inside the FBI, the saga of ANUBIS is surely one of the strangest. Not every crime is prosecuted or presented to a grand jury. Prosecutors have discretion and great leeway with respect to whom they choose to go after. Wen Ning had been a secret FBI asset for fifteen years, yet that did not prevent the Justice Department from prosecuting him after another arm of the government, the Commerce Department, uncovered his sins. His five-year prison term was not likely to encourage others to risk their lives to become sources for the FBI.

But ANUBIS for more than a dozen years had been illegally sending computer circuits to China that could be used in missiles and other weapons systems. And that, in the words of Erica O'Neil, the assistant prosecutor, "will not be tolerated."

One FBI agent remarked, sorrowfully, "We brought him out, got him a job in Wisconsin, and he went sideways up there."

A few months before Wen was arrested, the local newspaper did a friendly feature story on him, as a Manitowoc resident whose unusual job took him to China most of the year. He did not then know that the full weight of the United States government was about to come crashing down on him. But in retrospect, the comment he made as he sat in the living room of his house was prescient.

"Of course, I am Chinese by birth," he said, "but I am not a Chinese citizen any more. I'm afraid sometimes China doesn't recognize me as Chinese and America doesn't recognize me as an American. Just who am I?"

# Chapter 18

# ENDGAME

THEY KNEW IT would come, and on April 9, 2003, it did. PAR-
LOR MAID and J.J. Smith were arrested at their homes by the FBI,
taken downtown, and in handcuffs appeared separately in federal
court. Both were charged under the espionage statutes.

Gail Smith had to cancel her trip to attend a reunion of the Daffodil
Queens in Washington State. She had planned to go with her ninety-
three-year-old mother. Her spunky mother insisted on going alone,
and did.

US magistrate Victor B. Kenton ordered Katrina Leung held without bail after Rebecca Lonergan, an assistant US attorney, contended
she was "a serious flight risk." PARLOR MAID sat in the courtroom
with her head in her hands. She was charged with unauthorized copying of national defense information with intent to injure the United
States or benefit a foreign nation.

J.J. Smith was charged with "gross negligence in handling documents related to the national defense." Magistrate Stephen Hillman set
bail at $250,000 and ordered J.J. to surrender his passport. He was re-
leased that night after pledging his home as bail.

For the first time since the start of his investigation, Les Wiser surfaced publicly. "This is a sad day for the FBI," he told reporters. "Mr. Smith was once a special agent sworn to uphold the rule of law and the high ethical standards of the FBI." According to the charges, Wiser added, "he betrayed the trust we all placed in him."

In Washington, Robert Mueller, the FBI director, agreed. The charges that J.J. Smith "caused the loss of classified information, as well as his personal indiscretions with Ms. Leung, are very serious," he said.

The lawyers for Leung and J.J., as might be expected, had a rather different view. PARLOR MAID had hired Janet Levine, a smart, tough Los Angeles criminal defense lawyer, and her courtly older partner, John D. Vandevelde, to represent her. Levine knew her way around the criminal courts — she had defended drug dealers and other clients accused of fraud, money laundering, and racketeering.

"Katrina Leung is a loyal American citizen," the two defense lawyers said in a statement. "For over twenty years she has worked at the direction and behest of the Federal Bureau of Investigation. She repeatedly endangered herself in order to make significant contributions to the security and well-being of the United States and her fellow citizens." When "the full story" became known, they predicted, she would be cleared and "her heroic contributions to this country will be revealed." Understandably, they made no mention of her heroic contributions to the MSS or the $100,000 she received from the Chinese government.

J.J. Smith's attorney, Brian Sun, who later successfully represented Wen Ho Lee in his lawsuit against the government, called his client a "loyal, patriotic, and dedicated former agent." He did not mention J.J.'s long-term affair with PARLOR MAID, but the FBI affidavits detailing their relationship and describing the bureau documents found in her home were released to the press.

The government took no action against Bill Cleveland, but the day after the arrests, Cleveland resigned from his job as chief of counterintelligence at the Lawrence Livermore lab and his office was sealed. While Cleveland "has not been charged with any wrongdoing, due to the seriousness of the situation, a thorough review of his work is now under way," Susan Houghton, the lab's spokesperson, announced.

It was a close call for Cleveland. While he had not initially volunteered his affair with PARLOR MAID, he later admitted it. He had worked in tandem with Leung, but the FBI had no evidence that she had obtained documents from him, although he had told her about his trip to China, which she then revealed to Mao Guohua, her MSS handler. "He was guilty of poor judgment," one FBI agent said, "but not a crime."

In J.J.'s quiet Westlake Village neighborhood, residents could not believe that he had been arrested. The Smiths were regarded as solid members of the community, fixtures at the annual barbecue block party.

A month later, on May 7, J.J. was indicted on charges of "gross negligence" for allowing classified documents to end up in Leung's hands. Two counts of the indictment specifically cited the documents revealing a classified location used in the ROYAL TOURIST investigation — the Peter Lee case — and the June 12, 1997, electronic communication from the FBI legat in Hong Kong, classified SECRET and found in Leung's second-floor bookcase.

The indictment also accused J.J. of defrauding the FBI and United States of his honest services by having "an improper sexual relationship with Katrina Leung" and failing to report to the FBI her "unauthorized contacts with the PRC" and her admission "that she had secretly passed information to the PRC without authorization." In addition, the indictment charged J.J. with four counts of wire fraud for transmitting his periodic evaluation reports on PARLOR MAID assuring headquarters she was a "reliable" asset. J.J. was not accused of knowing that Leung was taking the documents from his briefcase or that she was passing information to China. The six-count indictment carried a possible maximum penalty of forty years in prison, although federal sentencing guidelines made a much shorter sentence likely.

The next day it was PARLOR MAID's turn. A federal grand jury handed down a five-count indictment, accusing her of illegally copying classified defense documents with "intent and reason to believe" that the data would be used "to the injury of the United States" and to the advantage of a foreign power. As in the case of Smith, one of the documents cited revealed the classified location used in the ROYAL TOURIST investigation, and another was the 1997 report from the Hong Kong legat.

Three more counts charged that Leung had "willfully retained" three documents — the transcripts and summaries of her conversations with Mao, the ROYAL TOURIST document, and the 1997 report from Hong Kong. If convicted, she faced a possible maximum sentence of fifty years in prison, but more likely ten to fourteen years.

Although both Smith and his lover were charged under the laws that as a group are commonly called the "espionage statutes," neither was indicted under the more severe provisions that can carry penalties of life imprisonment, or in some circumstances, death.

Debra W. Yang, the US attorney in Los Angeles, soon assigned the prosecution of Leung to Michael W. Emmick, a twenty-year veteran of that office who had handled several major fraud and public corruption cases. The lead prosecutor in the case against J.J. Smith was Rebecca Lonergan, who had been an assistant US attorney in Los Angeles for a decade and had worked on a number of national security cases. John B. Owens, an assistant US attorney in the fraud and public corruption section, worked with her.

On the morning of June 19 PARLOR MAID, who had been in jail since her arrest, appeared in federal court in downtown Los Angeles for a bail hearing before Judge Florence-Marie Cooper. By the time the press and public were admitted, Katrina Leung was already seated on the right side of the courtroom at the defense table next to her attorneys, Levine and Vandevelde. Leung wore an oversize green shapeless jacket. She looked small, not much over five feet, a tiny woman with jet-black hair pulled back in a tight bun, a thin, chiseled face, with high cheekbones and a firm chin. She wore a little lipstick and a hint of rouge. She followed the proceedings attentively with absolutely no expression until the very end of the hearing.

The government's team marched in looking grim, crewcut men in suits, and Diana Pauli, a tall, blond assistant US attorney. The platoon of prosecutors was led by Emmick. From the FBI there was Les Wiser and Peter Duerst.

Judge Cooper, a white-haired, sixty-two-year-old Canadian-born jurist, had been nominated to the bench four years before by Bill Clinton. She announced she had "reached a tentative decision to grant release with a $2 million bond." That sounded like good news for Leung.

But wait—Cooper said new information had given her "some doubt," chiefly two letters Leung wrote to Chinese leaders in 1998. They showed her close relationship with the top officials, which the court found "particularly troubling." In one of the letters, Leung said she wanted to make a major real estate investment in Shenzhen, a booming industrial area just north of Hong Kong, and asked that the local government be instructed to grant her the right to buy the land. She wrote that "my Hong Kong Fulichang International Company in Hong Kong has raised $500 million Hong Kong dollars from U.K. and U.S. banks (if necessary it can be increased to 1 billion)."

The second letter about the same land deal expressed her appreciation for "the tremendous support you have given me over the years." Each time, she said, "you have come forward to resolve the problems on my behalf."

Judge Cooper clearly enjoyed the sort of suspense that television programs often employ in courtroom dramas. The outcome is not revealed to the audience until the end.

Levine took the podium and claimed that the letters that worried the judge were all part of Leung's work for the FBI. Leung's husband had been "not subtly threatened" with tax prosecution. With some passion, Levine argued that Leung was a political hot potato; there was no way China would want her.

Emmick, in turn, rose to argue that bail of $2 million was not enough. The Leungs had sold their San Marino residence for $1.8 million. They owned several apartment buildings, he said; they were trying to sell three that would raise more cash and make it easier for her to disappear.

Even if Leung were required to wear a tracking device, she might give the feds the slip, the prosecutors argued. A tall, gangling government technician explained to the court that the Global Positioning System is not foolproof; GPS can tell within thirty feet where people are. But in downtown Los Angeles, the system is blocked. You can go into this building, cut the bracelet off, go out a different exit, and the person is gone.

Judge Cooper then summarized the situation. Leung and J.J. Smith "had a sexual relationship"; the defendant, although not charged with espionage, faced up to fourteen years in prison, by the government's estimate. Leung "could reasonably conclude" she might be convicted. The government, Cooper noted, found that the Leungs had sixteen foreign bank accounts, she had made false statements, took fifteen trips not authorized by the FBI, and got $100,000 from the PRC. She and her husband were targets in a pending tax case.

All of this sounded like Cooper would not let PARLOR MAID out of jail, after all. But, on the other hand, Cooper said, there were elements to support granting bail: Leung had cooperated with the government and made no attempt to flee when she could have.

Cooper then announced her decision. The court concludes that it is likely the defendant will make appearances, she said. She set bail at $2 million and required Leung to wear an electronic bracelet with GPS capability and remain confined to her residence, except for trips to her attorney's office, the court, or the secure facility in the courthouse where she could read government documents to help prepare her defense. She could not go to seaports, airports, or bus terminals. She also had to surrender her passport.

Leung had no reaction to the judge's ruling, which meant her three-month stay in jail was about to end. But as soon as the hearing was over, she stood up and hugged both of her lawyers. For the first time, she was smiling.

Months of legal maneuvering between the government and the lawyers for Leung and J.J. followed. PARLOR MAID made bail, and the Leungs moved into one of the apartments they owned.

Although Leung was out of jail, a few weeks later, Cooper signed an order imposing further restrictions on her. She was not to go within one mile of the Chinese consulate or come closer than one hundred yards to any consular car. And she was not to "knowingly have any contact" with anyone from the PRC.

Even before PARLOR MAID was released on bail, her lawyers made it clear that their strategy would be to try to force the government to reveal secrets. Classified information would be "central to defending our client in this case," they warned. Levine and Vandevelde asked the government for access to Leung's "briefings to the FBI over the past 20 years."

"We expect the government will have to make hard decisions about whether to publicly disclose 20 years worth of spying secrets in order to pursue an ill-advised prosecution of a loyal American," the attorneys said. It was a classic graymail tactic. Typically, in national security and espionage cases, defense counsel try to box the government in by threatening to reveal its secrets.

Under the Classified Information Procedures Act (CIPA), a judge may examine in camera documents sought by the defense if prosecutors claim the material contains government secrets. The law was designed to prevent disclosure of classified information in espionage cases. But the court may rule the documents are relevant to the defense and must be released. Faced with that choice, in a number of cases, the government has dropped charges or scaled them back substantially rather than risk exposing intelligence or other classified data to win a conviction. And the law is often used by defense attorneys as leverage to reach a plea bargain.

Unlike Leung, J.J. Smith had not spent any time behind bars. His attorneys were busy trying to keep it that way. J.J. had been working Chinese counterintelligence cases for two decades. He knew everything there was to know about the FBI's China program. And he had two very smart lawyers. If the case against him went to trial, the government was well aware that its secrets might be aired in court.

The government did not want that to happen. The prosecution worked out a plea deal with J.J.'s attorneys that meant there would be no trial for the former counterspy. There was always a chance, however, that a judge would sentence him to prison.

On May 12, 2004, J.J. pleaded guilty to only one felony count, lying to the FBI about his sexual affair with Katrina Leung. The charge of "gross negligence" was dropped. He would have to "cooperate fully" with the FBI and answer all questions in debriefings. As part of the plea deal, J.J. would have to testify in court against his longtime lover if she stood trial.

But the Smith plea bargain contained within it the seeds of disaster for the prosecution of PARLOR MAID. Lurking on page 7 of the 16-page plea agreement was a single paragraph that, as it turned out, was a land mine. The key sentence requiring the defendant to "withdraw from any joint defense agreement (written or oral) relating to this case, including any such agreement with Katrina Leung, counsel for Katrina Leung, or the employees of counsel for Katrina Leung, and to have no further sharing of information relating to this case with Leung, counsel for Leung, or the employees of counsel for Leung."

Leung's lawyers had been handed an unexpected gift — by the prosecutors. The "no further sharing" language could be read as meaning that Leung's attorneys could not interview J.J., a potential witness against her. The Sixth Amendment of the Constitution provides clearly that accused persons have the right "to be confronted with the witnesses" against them and to compel witnesses to testify for the defense. Levine and Vandevelde saw their opening and pounced. In November, they filed a motion to dismiss the case on grounds of "prosecutorial misconduct" because of the "no further sharing" prohibition.

The government scrambled for a way to respond. Emmick, the Leung lead prosecutor, fired off e-mails to the Justice Department and the other prosecutors to try to find out who had inserted the disastrous language in the J.J. Smith plea and why.

A government brief attempting to explain the history of the controversial paragraph said that the "no sharing" language had been suggested by Lonergan, but written by John Owens, her associate on the case. According to Lonergan, "Owens did the first draft of the plea agreement and then we worked together on the entire plea agreement."

The two prosecutors told Emmick that the language was intended only to require Smith to withdraw from any joint defense agreement with Leung's attorneys. Lawyers for defendants in separate cases sometimes enter into such cooperative arrangements, which are usually secret, to help each other.

"That clause was never intended to stop the defense from interviewing J.J. or using him as a witness for Leung," Lonergan said. "Of course not. That's Law School 101." The intent, she said, was to prevent the lawyers for two defendants from sharing classified information through a joint defense agreement. All of this was happening behind the scenes. Then, in January 2005, in a stunning surprise move, Judge Cooper threw out all charges against Katrina Leung, saying that the government had engaged in "willful and deliberate misconduct" by inserting the "no further sharing" language in J.J.'s plea bargain. Access to a prosecution witness is a basic constitutional right, Cooper noted, which had been denied to the defendant.

The government, the judge said, had repeatedly insisted that it never intended to bar Smith from talking to Leung's attorneys, it was just that the language was "inartfully drawn." Cooper wasn't buying it. There was nothing ambiguous about the clause, she ruled: "Smith is being told not to talk to Leung or her attorneys."

The prosecutors, she added, had "misrepresented" the purpose of the clause. In language seldom heard in a federal court, Cooper made no attempt to conceal her anger. "In this case, the government decided to make sure that Leung and her lawyers would not have access to Smith. When confronted with what they had done, they engaged in a pattern of stone-walling entirely unbecoming to a prosecuting agency."

The target of her wrath was the mild-mannered Michael Emmick. Three months later, however, Judge Cooper backpedaled, conceding that Emmick had been improperly singled out since he had not drafted the plea bargain. But she rejected the government's motions to reconsider the dismissal of the case.

It was a bizarre and unexpected development. Why had the federal prosecutors bungled so badly? Surely they knew that the Sixth Amendment of the Constitution gives defendants the right to confront the witnesses against them. Was it a deliberate attempt to torpedo the case against Leung, to avoid the revelation of intelligence secrets in court — and salacious details of a spy and sex scandal?

It made a plausible theory for the conspiratorially minded, but more likely it was the result of bad grammar and an incredible bureaucratic snafu. Emmick, who was dismayed to see the most sensational case of penetration of the FBI by Chinese intelligence go out the window, offered his own explanation of why the "no sharing" language was included in the plea.

"The goal of the clause was to prevent Smith's lawyers from helping Leung's lawyers with their defense motions. Unfortunately the clause was written in a way that was grammatically awkward and ambiguous." The "no sharing" language, Emmick added, "could be interpreted to mean Smith *himself* could not be interviewed by Leung's lawyers.

And that was not the intent and would be an obvious violation of both the Constitution and legal ethics rules."

Be that as it may, the case against PARLOR MAID had been tossed out of court, a black eye for the government in a case that had been widely publicized when J.J. Smith and Leung were arrested and charged.

Whenever there is a foul-up inside the government, the first reaction of the bureaucrats is to point fingers at one another. True to form, the government, in its response to the dismissal of the case, was quick to say that officials in the counterespionage section of the Justice Department had no role in drafting the Smith plea, it was all done by the prosecutors in Los Angeles. However, it stretches credulity to think that Justice Department officials in Washington did not closely monitor and approve the plea bargain.

One question remained, almost overlooked in the court battle over the odd language in J.J. Smith's plea. Katrina Leung, by her own admission to the FBI, had been passing information to the MSS and working for Chinese intelligence for years. China had paid her $100,000. She was supposed to be spying for the FBI, which paid her $1,718,889 in expenses and other money over nineteen years. In her house she had classified FBI documents that she claimed she had pilfered from her lover. Given that set of facts, why had she not been charged under the more serious espionage statute?

Contrary to public perception, there is no crime of "espionage" in US law. The word appears nowhere in the US Code statutes (only in the heading of Chapter 37, Title 18). Although half a dozen laws are usually referred to as the "espionage statutes," only Section 794, aimed at anyone who transmits information to "any foreign government," carries the more draconian penalties. That is the section that prosecutors mean when they talk about "espionage."

Within the Justice Department, there had been a division of opinion on whether to throw the book at Leung or charge the case more cautiously. Bruce C. Swartz, a senior department official, was said to have pushed for charging Leung with espionage. Officials in the department's counterespionage section, John Dion, the chief and a veteran of many spy cases, Ron Roos, and Robert E. Wallace Jr., were involved in the discussions, as was the US Attorney's Office in Los Angeles. In the end it was decided to indict PARLOR MAID for the lesser charge of taking and retaining classified defense information.

None of the Justice Department officials involved in the sensitive decision would comment. Emmick would only say that there were discussions between Los Angeles and Washington "about whether more serious espionage charges were supported by the evidence or were advisable as a matter of strategy." It was decided "not to charge espionage or to otherwise broaden the charges."

Lonergan, too, would not discuss the decisions made by the Justice Department and the prosecutors. But she indicated that ultimately, the decision was made in Washington. "When a case has high-level attention, it follows that high-level people will be involved in the decision making," she said. "I would not say that case was under our [the prosecutors'] control.

"In any espionage case you want to charge as narrowly as you can," Lonergan continued. "Otherwise you have a huge graymail problem. You open the door to secrets being disclosed.

"Trying to prosecute national security cases is like walking a tightrope. The more serious the charge the government brings, the greater the risk that sensitive secrets will be disclosed. We've got all this evidence, but can we use it? As a prosecutor, you're twisted into a pretzel trying to prove some of these cases. Many of the most serious cases never get charged."

Lonergan, who became a law professor at the University of California after leaving the US Attorney's Office, added, "The more sensitive the information that somebody took, the more likely it is that the intelligence agencies will not want it to be disclosed during a criminal trial." What the public sees "is usually the tip of the iceberg. You're not going to charge your most serious stuff because you do not want to risk exposing the most serious stuff."

Emmick agreed that graymail was a huge problem in the Leung case. "The problem is always to make the charge narrow enough to avoid graymail and broad enough to reflect the seriousness of the conduct." The decision was made "to charge the case narrowly so all we needed to do was to establish she had possession of these documents, they were classified documents, she knew they were classified. This would be a narrow, scalpel-like way to charge the case.

"We would reduce the likelihood that classified information would be discovered. We wanted to reduce the risk of being graymailed. There were discussions within the office and within DOJ as to whether to charge more broadly, charges that actually involved espionage, or conspiracy that might involve the Chinese government as well.

"She went to China on a number of occasions and had discussions with representatives of their intelligence service. Information was apparently passed. But the more the charges focused on the passing of information, the more classified information would be involved, and the more vulnerable the case would be to being graymailed."

When government secrets are disclosed in court, Emmick said, it created an additional problem. "You have to declassify documents in order to bring them into a trial, and when you declassify, you lose jury appeal." A jury would think, "If it's no longer secret, then what does it matter? How could it be so important?"

There was another, and at least equally compelling, reason that the government did not charge Leung with spying, despite her admissions to the FBI. The prosecutors certainly described her as a Chinese spy. In one court document, the government termed her "an agent for the PRC" and said that while still an FBI asset "she began to work for the Ministry of State Security ('MSS'), which is the PRC's spy service." And according to the FBI affidavits, she confessed to stealing documents from J.J. Smith's briefcase and "admitted that she provided intelligence she gained in this manner to the MSS." But the affidavits conspicuously omit a description of any specific document she may have provided to China. The clear implication is that PARLOR MAID was careful not to admit passing any specific document to the MSS — otherwise the FBI affidavits would presumably have included that key information. "The fact that there was no specific document admitted by her was a factor," Emmick confirmed.

On July 18, 2005, J.J. Smith stood before Judge Cooper for sentencing. "I have nobody to blame but myself for my being here today," he told her. "I stand before you ashamed and humiliated."

Lonergan argued for a brief prison term, asserting that Smith had endangered national security by his affair with PARLOR MAID. The government, she said, "will be scrambling for years to come to determine what damage was done here."

The judge decided on no jail time for J.J. Smith. She sentenced him to three months of house arrest, three years probation, and fined him $10,000. Under his plea bargain he could have been sent to prison for six months. With tears in his eyes, he turned to his wife and son, who were sitting in the courtroom, and apologized to them.

The prosecutors, meanwhile, were not ready to give up their pursuit of Leung. After Judge Cooper dismissed the indictment against PARLOR MAID, the government appealed the case to the Ninth Circuit. At the same time, the FBI continued to dig into the Leungs' finances. A likely tax charge was still hanging over the couple.

In the original complaint filed to arrest Leung, the government outlined three tax cases against her. It charged that she had failed to pay taxes on at least $435,000 of the more than $500,000 she had received from the FBI for her services as an asset. In addition, the complaint charged that she had paid no taxes on $1.2 million that Nortel had paid to her through Merry Glory, Ltd., a Hong Kong company she controlled. Leung had entered into an agreement to represent the giant Canadian telecom in a joint venture to sell Nortel's digital switching systems in China.

Finally, the government contended that Leung had engaged in a tax scheme to take annual deductions on mortgage interest of about $40,000 on her home by making monthly payments to an account in the name of Right Fortune, Ltd., in the Hang Seng Bank in Hong Kong. Although Right Fortune supposedly held the mortgage on the Leungs' luxurious home in San Marino, the company was actually controlled by Katrina Leung. Each month Leung duly sent a check for $6,000 to the Hong Kong account. As the FBI put it, Leung "was making the mortgage payments to herself and then deducting the interest portion of those payments."

With the three tax cases looming, and the possibility that the appeals court would reinstate the case that Judge Cooper had thrown out, Leung and her lawyers decided it was time to strike a deal. If the government brought the tax charges it would mean perhaps years of expensive litigation for Leung and her husband.

In December, before the appeals court could rule, Leung agreed to a deal. She pleaded guilty to lying about her love affair with J.J.—she had, at first, said he was nothing more than "a good family friend" and that theirs was a "business relationship," and she had denied traveling overseas with him although they had gone to Hong Kong and London together.

In addition, she pleaded guilty to failing to report $35,000 in income from the FBI on her 2000 tax return. She also agreed that in the seven-year period after 1995 she had not reported $207,000 in payments from the FBI. She had to consent to nine debriefing sessions and to take a polygraph if required. In return, the government agreed not to pursue criminal tax charges against Kam Leung and to settle the back taxes owed by the couple.

On December 16, PARLOR MAID stood before Judge Cooper for the last time. She was sentenced to three years probation, two hundred hours of community service, and fined $10,000. Essentially, both Smith and Leung had walked. And the government was spared an embarrassing courtroom spectacle.

Small wonder that Katrina Leung announced to the judge, "I love America."

But J.J., although he had avoided prison, had lost his reputation. The star of the Los Angeles counterintelligence squad had been arrested by his fellow FBI agents and hauled before a federal judge in handcuffs. The personal toll it took on him was revealed in an e-mail he sent to friends when he agreed to plead guilty.

Although his lawyers said he would probably get a minimal sentence or probation, J.J. was worried. "With my luck the judge's husband just ran off with his thirty year old secretary and I'll get five years breaking rocks—in stripes."

With his wife and son watching, he wrote, he had to tell the court, "'I entered into an unauthorized intimate relationship with Katrina and then lied about it to my employer.' Argh!"

Although he could "start working on my tattered relationship with Gail, Kelly, family . . . I am near broke, my relationships are shattered

. . . and will perhaps have to testify against someone I believed in for eighteen years and she will go away for a long time."

His wife stayed with him, despite everything. Gail Smith believed strongly in family. Their son, Kelly, worked as a bartender, graduated from law school, and, ironically, became a prosecutor.

Bill Cleveland and his wife separated. Having lost his six-figure job at the Livermore lab, he turned to teaching criminal justice.

As for Leung's husband, he still loved his wife. Kam Leung appeared to be faithful and true to Katrina, despite her extramarital adventures. "I am a very ordinary human being tossed into this extraordinary situation," he said. "She is my charge, a brilliant person, vulnerable and insecure. It is my job to see it through and protect her."

Was his, then, an open marriage? "No, not an open marriage, I am Chinese by culture. This is the greatest love story. It is my mission, my role. As though I were put in the cosmos to take care of her."

Katrina Leung, the object of all this adoration, kept a very low profile, shunning the public eye in which she had once reveled. She had pleaded guilty to two felonies. She no longer enjoyed her prestige and status as a prominent leader of the Chinese American community in Los Angeles.

Les Wiser, after twenty-three years in the FBI, retired in 2007 from his last post as special agent in charge in Newark, New Jersey. He was hardly pleased that the cases he had built so carefully against J.J. Smith and Katrina Leung ended as they did. But Wiser was an FBI agent; he was not in charge of the prosecution. He could take comfort from the fact that he had done his difficult job, and done it well.

The sheriff had caught the bad guys.

# Chapter 19

# EAGLE CLAW

**T**HE PARLOR MAID CASE was dramatic enough, combining as it did sex, spies, secret reports to the White House, and millions of dollars, but it was not the first time that China had penetrated an American intelligence agency.

Three decades before Katrina Leung passed FBI secrets to the MSS, Chinese intelligence had recruited a long-term spy inside the CIA. His name was Larry Wu-Tai Chin, and his pursuit and eventual detection and capture was given the code name EAGLE CLAW.

Tall and so skinny that his classmates at Yenching University, where he studied English, called him Grasshopper, Chin lived a double life in more ways than one. To his colleagues at the CIA's Foreign Broadcast Information Service, the bespectacled Chin appeared quiet and color-less. But he was not only a Chinese spy — over the years Beijing paid him about a million dollars — he had multiple girlfriends, a penchant for sex toys, gambled tens of thousands of dollars in Las Vegas, and stored gold bullion in a bank account in Hong Kong.

It is not often that the key to unlocking an espionage mystery is lit-erally a key, but it was in the case of Larry Chin. The FBI learned that an American spying for China, his identity not yet certain, had stayed in room 533 of the Qianmen Hotel in Beijing. By 1983, a year after the EAGLE CLAW case file was opened, Chin was under suspicion. In May of that year, as Chin was leaving from Washington for Hong Kong, the FBI searched his luggage at Dulles International Airport and found a key to room 533. It was a major break in the case.

Chin, who was born in Beijing in 1922, began working for the United States in 1944, during World War II, when he was hired as a translator for an Army liaison office in Fuzhou, China. It was then, he later admitted, that he was recruited by Chinese intelligence. After the war, in 1948, he became an interpreter at the US consulate in Shanghai. A year later, he was transferred to Hong Kong, and then to Korea in 1951, where he interviewed Chinese war prisoners.

In Korea, he carefully noted the names of those who cooperated with the United States and of others who were willing to return to China as American agents, and he passed that information to the Chinese, for which he was paid $2,000. The FBI believed that his betrayal of the POWs may have cost many lives when they were repatriated.

In 1952 Chin joined the Foreign Broadcast Information Service in Okinawa. Now China had a mole inside the CIA itself. FBIS monitors broadcasts and publications throughout the world, but Chin's access was not limited to such open sources. In time, he routinely received CIA reports, including those from covert agents. He made frequent trips to Hong Kong, where he met with his Chinese handler, Ou Qiming. Then in 1961, Chin was transferred by FBIS to Santa Rosa, California. Over the next decade he made half a dozen more trips to Hong Kong, where he met and was paid by Ou for his services.

In 1965 Chin became an American citizen, which meant that he could receive a security clearance after a background check. He passed a polygraph—so much for the accuracy of the lie detector tests by which the CIA sets great store—and was given his clearance. Chin later said he might not have passed if the questions had been asked in Chinese, but they were not.

With his TOP SECRET security clearance, Chin now routinely received classified CIA documents, which he regularly gave to the Chinese. In 1970 he transferred to the CIA's FBIS office in Rosslyn, Virginia, not far from the agency's Langley headquarters.

Chin owned thirty-one properties in the Washington area, and two condominiums in Las Vegas. To coworkers and friends, he explained his wealth by saying that he played blackjack and was an expert card counter, allowing him to beat the odds in the casinos. Since he was a high roller, he boasted, the casinos paid for his airfare to Las Vegas and his hotel stays.

Chin was handled by officers of the Ministry of Public Security, China's principal intelligence agency until the MSS was created in 1983. His method of stealing documents was simple; he squirreled them in his clothing or briefcase and walked out of the building. At FBIS, there were only occasional spot checks of briefcases.

Chin then photographed the classified documents and passed the films to Chinese agents in a series of meetings in a Toronto shopping mall. He also met Chinese intelligence officers in Hong Kong, Macao, and Beijing.

He kept meticulous diaries of his travels and his meetings with his handlers. One entry noted the dishes he ate when he dined in Beijing with three senior intelligence officers. The meal included "Bears' feet" and "muttonpot."

Among the most important documents that Chin fed to the Chinese were classified memos on President Nixon's secret preparations in 1971 for the historic opening to China. Nixon announced on television in July that he would go to Beijing in an effort to normalize diplomatic relations between the two countries. He traveled to China in February 1972. Chin was suspected of having passed to Chinese intelligence the secret Presidential Review Memorandum outlining Nixon's plans and objectives for the China trip.

In July 1981, after almost thirty years as a Chinese mole inside the CIA, Chin retired at age fifty-nine. To show its appreciation — Chin was regarded as the CIA's best translator — the agency's deputy director, Bobby Inman, personally presented the Career Intelligence Medal to Chin at a retirement ceremony attended by his coworkers. A week later, Chin flew to Hong Kong, met with a Chinese intelligence contact, and was paid $40,000.

Chin could look back on his espionage career with satisfaction. He was wealthy, his services greatly appreciated by China's intelligence service, which treated him royally, he had many playmates, and best of all, his spying over three decades had not been detected.

That, however, was about to change. Inside the Ministry of Public Security, a senior official was becoming nervous about his future. His name was Yu Zhensan, and he was no ordinary intelligence officer. His background was unusual.

Yu's father had reportedly once been married to Jiang Qing, an actress who used the stage name Lan Ping (Blue Apple) and was involved at one point with Kang Sheng, the legendary head of China's intelligence services. She joined the Communist revolution and met Mao Zedong, whom she married. Jiang was one of the central instigators of the Cultural Revolution, and after Mao's death in 1976, she was placed on trial as one of the infamous Gang of Four, blamed for the chaos and thousands of deaths during the period. She was convicted, her death sentence commuted to life, and she committed suicide in 1991 while receiving medical treatment outside the prison.

Before Jiang married Mao, Yu's father had been at odds with her, and until her downfall, she was a dangerous enemy. Yu Zhensan himself had become increasingly resentful of the Chinese Communist Party and its leadership. He contacted the CIA and warned the agency that Beijing had a spy inside American intelligence. He was taking a huge risk, but viewed the information as his ticket out of China.

The CIA did not tell the FBI right away; it held on to the disturbing news for two or three months while it investigated, then concluded that the penetration could not be inside the CIA and was probably in the military.

In September 1982 the CIA notified the FBI that there might be a Chinese spy inside a US intelligence agency. The notice landed on the desk of I. C. Smith, the Louisiana native and FBI veteran who was in Shenyang with Bill Cleveland when they encountered Gwo-bao Min, the TIGER TRAP suspect.

Smith gave Yu Zhensan the code name PLANESMAN. He assigned Special Agent Tom Carson, who was known as a tenacious investigator, to try to ferret out the mole inside US intelligence.

An Alabama native, Carson had joined the FBI in 1970, working foreign counterintelligence cases for most of his twenty-eight years in the bureau. Carson started on the daunting assignment, but it was slow going and the initial information from the CIA lacked details.

But then the CIA came up with a clue. PLANESMAN, Yu Zhensan, said that the mole had flown to Beijing on a Pan Am flight that left New York on February 6, 1982, and returned to the United States on February 27.

Carson began checking flight manifests but was frustrated to find that there was no Pan Am flight on February 6. It looked like a dead end. But Carson, true to his reputation, kept digging. He finally discovered that there had been a flight by China Airlines scheduled to leave for Beijing on February 5. But a snowstorm had enveloped JFK airport, and the flight was delayed for hours. It did not actually leave until February 6.

There was no way to check the names of the passengers on the China Airlines flight; the company did not provide its manifests to US authorities. Carson did not give up. There was a Pan Am return flight to New York on February 27, and checking the list of passengers, Carson found only four US citizens. One was a male with a Chinese name, who lived in Alexandria, Virginia. The passenger was Larry Wu-Tai Chin.

The FBI asked the CIA if Chin worked for the agency. The CIA, after checking its rolls, said, He's not ours. Well, was he ever? the FBI asked. The CIA checked again and was dismayed to find the answer. Chin had worked for the agency for three decades, but had retired a year earlier.

Now EAGLE CLAW had a suspect. But having a name was far from what was needed to build an espionage case. Chin was placed under FBI surveillance, and his telephone tapped after a FISA warrant was issued. Bruce Carlson, the FBI China specialist, was assigned to the Chin investigation. Carlson spoke Mandarin so fluently that he was often mistaken on the telephone for a native Chinese.

From the wiretaps, the FBI learned that Chin was planning a trip to Hong Kong in the spring of 1983. "We got a FISA warrant to search his luggage at Dulles," Carson said. But there was a problem; it would take about forty minutes to retrieve and discreetly examine Chin's luggage. There wouldn't be time enough to do all that before the plane took off.

"We delayed the flight at Dulles enough to take the luggage from the time he put it through the chute and search it, unpack it, and put everything back the way it was, without him knowing." The airport authorities cooperated and the passengers were given some bogus but plausible reason for the delay.

Carson had hoped to find classified documents in Chin's luggage but there were none. "We found the hotel key and took a picture of it. I didn't know what it was or realize it was important. It turned out to be the smoking gun."

"Back to the office, I asked Bruce, 'What are the Chinese words on the key?' He said it was the name of the hotel, the Hotel Qianmen. And there was a room number on the key, 533.

"It rang a bell, and I went back and looked through our files and that's where he had stayed on his first trip to China, one year after he had retired." PLANESMAN, the CIA's source inside the Chinese intelligence service, had provided that detail. Finding the key corroborated Yu Zhensan's information and, beyond that, it buttressed and tended to validate the other information he had provided. It also indicated that Chin was planning to travel on from Hong Kong to Beijing.

Why Chin was returning his room key was unclear. "In this country we don't care much about hotel keys," Carson said, "but maybe he thought he should return it."

A few months later, Chin flew to Hong Kong to meet with Ou Qiming, his handler. Chin suggested to Ou that the Chinese might want to try to recruit Victoria Liu Morton, a woman he had known at the CIA. She had once mentioned to him that she had a brother on the mainland; perhaps, Chin suggested, that could be used as leverage against her. Ou decided one mole was enough and he rejected the idea. Morton was not approached or recruited by the Chinese.

At the same meeting, Chin mentioned his marital problems to Ou. If the Chinese would give him $150,000, he said, he could pay off his wife and get a divorce. Ou declined.

Yu, meanwhile, had more tidbits for the CIA. He said that the mole had an emergency contact in New York, a Chinese sleeper agent named Father Mark Cheung, a Roman Catholic priest at the Church of the Transfiguration on Mott Street, in the heart of New York's Chinatown. Cheung had arrived in 1972, invited by the church as assistant pastor. He must have impressed the diocese because later Cheung was promoted to parish administrator, the first Chinese priest to hold that position.

The FBI investigated, trying to figure out whether Cheung was an actual priest, or simply posing as one. "Mark Cheung was a real priest," Carson said. "The Chinese intelligence service sent him to a seminary. He was co-opted by them before he became a priest. He was a mole in the church." He was also, as far as is known, the first Chinese "illegal" who was also a Catholic priest.*

Cheung had moved to Hong Kong, and two FBI agents, Pat Dooley and Larry Goff, interviewed him there. But Cheung was not helpful. "Then he skedaddled," Carson said. He left Hong Kong and disappeared into the mainland. The FBI learned that Cheung, although a priest, was married, with a wife in China. When he visited her, he switched his clerical garb to civilian clothes.

The FBI could not determine whether or how Cheung was supposed to help Chin flee the United States if his spying was discovered or he sensed he was under suspicion. "We never figured out what his role would be," Carson said.

In 1984 another FBI agent, Ken Schiffer, took over as supervisor of the Chin case. PLANESMAN, Schiffer said, "was a headquarters desk officer with supervisory responsibility." But he was not the handler of China's mole inside the CIA — that was Ou Qiming — and as in all intelligence agencies, Chin's name would have been closely held inside the Chinese spy agency.

But Yu took risks. "He went into his colleague's files," Schiffer said. "He rifled his colleague's desk and got all the information about [Chin's] travels, hotels, people he met but not the name of the source." That was finally learned when Carson checked the manifest of the Pan Am return flight.

---

* In intelligence parlance, an "illegal" is a spy operating without benefit of diplomatic cover. If caught, an illegal can be prosecuted, imprisoned, or even executed; by contrast, a diplomat can only be declared persona non grata and expelled by the host country.

Although Chin had retired from the CIA, he continued to work as a translator on a government contract. But he realized his value to the Chinese had diminished once he left the CIA. So he falsely told Beijing that he had obtained a job with the National Security Agency. Since he had never worked for the NSA, he bought a copy of *The Puzzle Palace,* a groundbreaking book by James Bamford about the code-breaking agency. He translated parts of the book into Chinese, and passed them along to his handlers.

All was not well in the Chin household, however, thanks to Chin's extramarital wanderings. He was charged with assault in 1983, for allegedly fondling a teenage girl in the laundry room of his apartment in Alexandria, Virginia. The charge was eventually dropped.

Chin was married in 1949 and divorced after ten years; he and his first wife, Doris, had three children. In Okinawa, he met his second wife, Cathy. Their relationship was stormy. She was aware of his affairs and disturbed over his unexplained trips.

After catching him in their apartment in bed with a mistress, she called a friend, desperately asking what she should do. The FBI wiretap recorded the friend's suggestion that Mrs. Chin throw a pot of cold water on the couple; that would definitely cool their ardor. The friend remained on the line while Chin's wife carried out her advice.

A moment later the wiretap picked up Cathy screaming, "He's killing me! He's killing me!" Soaked and naked, Chin was furiously beating his wife with the pot.

Chin often engaged in telephone sex with a "niece" in New York, who would sometimes travel to Washington, DC, and spend the afternoon with him in a motel. Once, talking on the tapped phone to a girlfriend, Chin told her to be sure to bring the "machine." The FBI agents were excited — was a confederate, perhaps another spy, about to deliver a code machine? This could be a big break in the case.

But in later conversations, Chin and the girlfriend talked in titillating detail about how they would use the "machine," and it became clear it was not a spying device, but a sex toy, a battery-operated vibrator.

As the FBI continued to watch Chin and gather evidence of his espionage, there was no longer any doubt that he was the mole who had burrowed into the CIA. But there was a problem. There was no way the bureau could move until Yu Zhensan was safely exfiltrated from China. Neither the CIA nor the FBI was about to blow a source who would, if uncovered, surely be executed or sent to prison for life.

When Yu had first approached the CIA, according to Schiffer, "the agency was cautious it might be a setup." Intelligence agencies often send "dangles" offering information, sometimes true, sometimes not, to rival spy agencies. The goal is to infiltrate or confuse the opposition.

"But when PLANESMAN provided details on a Chinese American who was a US government employee, that convinced the agency," Schiffer recalled. "He was still in place when we identified Chin. We sat on the case — we could not move on Chin for about a year until PLANESMAN got out. They [the CIA] arranged for him to travel south from Beijing through China, maybe to Hong Kong."

Although it has never previously been disclosed, another Chinese defector came out soon after Yu Zhensan. He was a coworker of PLANESMAN, but neither knew about the other. The second defector brought with him a list of the names of Chinese intelligence agents in the United States. The FBI tracked all the names down. Some were kept under surveillance and others quietly deported.

As the cases described in this book make clear, espionage is a very difficult crime to prove, unless a spy is caught in the act, or confesses, because counterintelligence agents seldom have direct proof that a suspect passed documents to a foreign power. For all the evidence that the bureau had compiled on Chin, without a confession it would be difficult to convict him. With PLANESMAN safely in the United States, the way was clear for the FBI to confront Chin. Everything would depend on how well and carefully that was done.

Ken Schiffer decided that the approach to Chin would be made by agents Rudy Guerin, Terry Roth, and Mark Johnson. Guerin was a veteran counterintelligence agent at the FBI's Washington field office and later head of the China section at headquarters. Roth was his regular partner, and Johnson had worked closely with Carson on the investigation.

Late in the afternoon of November 22, 1985, the trio knocked on the door of Chin's condominium in Alexandria. They identified themselves as FBI agents. They said they were investigating a leak of classi-fied information to China's intelligence service and hoped Chin might be able to assist them. Chin invited them in and the four men sat down around Chin's dining room table.

Guerin lost little time in coming to the point. He told Chin that the FBI suspected *he* was the spy.

Chin denied it, and claimed to have had no contact with Chinese intelligence. Then he was told that the FBI knew of his flight to China on February 6, 1982, and his return flight on February 27. While you were there, the agents said, you were the guest of honor at a banquet and received an award.

Now Chin knew he was in trouble. He was shown a picture of Li Wenchong, the senior Chinese intelligence official who had given him the award. He was told the FBI also knew of his meetings with a Chi-nese contact in Toronto.

And then he was shown a photo of the key to room 533 of the Qian-men Hotel. We know you were checked into that room in June 1983, the agents informed him.

As the agents had hoped, Chin was rattled by the picture of the hotel key. "He realized somebody on the inside had betrayed him," Ken Schiffer said. The hotel key was just one of the specific facts that we had, but it was a very powerful one. Because it indicated to Chin that someone had inside access to his case in [Chinese intelligence] headquarters."

Mark Johnson ratcheted up the pressure. In September, he said, Chin met in Hong Kong with Ou Qiming, his handler. He had talked to Ou about whether the Chinese might want to try to recruit Victo-ria Liu Morton, the CIA employee who had a brother in China. And, Johnson added, he had requested $150,000 to get a divorce.

That did it. "You have details that only Ou knew," Chin said. He asked where the agents had gotten that information, then answered his own question. Ou Qiming must have defected, Chin said.

"He thought Ou Qiming had defected and was the one who had dimed him out," Schiffer said, referring to the pre–cell phone days when it cost a dime to use a pay phone. "Rudy and Terry allowed him to think that." But it was Yu Zhensan, not Ou, who had defected.

Chin stalled, asking the agents to come back the next day. They refused, and Chin, convinced that his handler had betrayed him, began talking. He talked, and talked, and talked.

Schiffer and Tom Carson were standing by. They received a phone call from Guerin. Chin had confessed. After getting the green light from the Justice Department, the two agents arrived at the apartment. Carson saw his quarry for the first time. He arrested and handcuffed Chin. The agents drove him to the Arlington County jail.

The trial of Larry Wu-Tai Chin on seventeen counts of spying and conspiracy opened three months later in federal district court in Alexandria. Chin took the stand during the four-day trial, and claimed he had spied to improve relations between the United States and China. His defense attorney, Jake Stein, believed Chin's explanation of his supposed motive offered the best, albeit slim, hope of swaying the jury.

When Chin saw a classified message from President Nixon about his plan for the opening to China, he said he believed "if this information is brought to the attention of the Chinese leadership . . . it might break the ice. I wanted Chou En-lai to see it." The prosecutors, however, said Chin's motive was money, and pointed out that he had been well paid.

Perhaps the most interesting revelation during the trial was the testimony by Special Agent Mark Johnson that Chin had no contact with Ou Qiming from 1967 to 1976 because Ou was in prison. The chaos of the Cultural Revolution had ensnared even Chin's handler.

Joseph J. Aronica, the assistant US attorney prosecuting Chin, asked him if he was "stealing documents from the CIA and giving them to the Chinese?"

"Right," Chin answered.

"You knew the documents you gave . . . would go to the highest levels of the Chinese government?"

"Yes."

"Your intent was to help the People's Republic of China?"

"Yes and . . . the U.S., too."

Chin's admissions did not leave much for the jury to deliberate. They took just three hours to find him guilty on all seventeen counts. His wife, Cathy, sitting in the gallery, broke into sobs. Chin was escorted back to jail, facing two life terms in prison. Sentencing was set for March 17.

Why had he done it? Although he claimed he wanted to bring about a rapprochement between Washington and Beijing, the FBI agents who worked on the case thought that, even aside from the money, Chin, who toiled in obscurity in a CIA backwater, hungered for recognition, a sense of importance that he got from his Chinese intelligence admirers.

Two weeks after he was convicted, on the morning of February 21, Chin ate breakfast at 6:30 A.M. A little over two hours later, a guard found Chin in his cell. He had tied a plastic trash bag over his head with a shoelace. Efforts to revive him were unsuccessful.

He had left a note for Cathy.

"This morning I had a dream of a celestial world which makes me comfortable mentally and physically. . . . When I thought of the fact that I don't need to do anything after waking up and can . . . keep on sleeping, it's extremely comfortable.

"So, Little Fish, don't worry about me. . . . Isn't it a happy thing in the life. . . . Except that I can't stay with you, I already have everything."

It was over. The spy inside the CIA had been caught after three decades, and sentenced himself. At FBI headquarters, the EAGLE CLAW case file was closed.

# Chapter 20

# RED FLOWER

O N OCTOBER 19, 2005, Tai Wang Mak, chief engineer in Los Angeles for the Chinese-language television channel that broadcasts by satellite to the United States, placed a telephone call to a contact in Zhongshan, China.

"I work for Red Flower of North America," he said. Since Mak worked for the Phoenix North America Chinese Channel, not for a florist, it sounded like a line from a spy movie. To the FBI, however, the phrase was not scripted in Hollywood but an apparent code name for a family of spies headed by Chi Mak, Tai's brother. The group had been under intense FBI surveillance for more than a year.

The phone call to Zhongshan, a bustling city in southern China across the Pearl River from Hong Kong, was answered by Pu Pei-Liang, a researcher at Zhongshan University who the FBI believe was actually an intelligence officer for the People's Liberation Army — and Chi Mak's longtime handler.

According to FBI documents, Chi Mak, who worked for Power Paragon, a major defense contractor in Anaheim, had been secretly passing sensitive Navy data on US weapons systems to China for more than twenty years.

Nine days after the "Red Flower" phone call, FBI agents pulled Tai Mak and his wife, Fuk Li, from a security line at Los Angeles International Airport as they waited to board a midnight flight to Hong Kong. Both were arrested. At the same moment, other FBI agents swooped down on Chi Mak's home in Downey, a Los Angeles suburb, and arrested him and his wife, Rebecca Chiu.

Chi Mak, then sixty-six, was born in Guangzhou, educated in Shanghai, naturalized as a US citizen in 1985, and since 1996 held a SECRET security clearance at Power Paragon. He was the lead project engineer on research for the Quiet Electric Drive, or QED, a propulsion system designed to allow the Navy's submarines to run silent, and to make surface ships quieter and harder to detect as well.

In an affidavit filed for the arrest warrant of the Maks, FBI special agent James E. Gaylord described the QED as "an extremely sensitive project," with the technology banned from export to denied countries, including China. The QED was also labeled NOFORN, meaning "not for release to foreign nationals," so that the data was restricted and could not be divulged to other countries or foreigners.

The FBI charged that Chi took data about the QED and other Navy projects to his home, copied the information onto three CDs with his wife's help, and passed them to his brother, Tai, who encrypted the CDs. Tai was planning to deliver them to Pu Pei-Liang in Guangzhou, his ultimate destination, had he been permitted to board the flight from LAX.

Chi Mak's home had been wiretapped for months through a FISA warrant, and a video camera had been secretly installed over his dining room table. Gaylord's affidavit said that on October 23, 2005, five days before Tai Mak was to fly to Hong Kong with the CDs, Rebecca reminded her husband that the items Chi was asking his brother to take "are certainly against the law."

Months earlier, the FBI had recovered two lists from the trash at Chi Mak's house. The documents, in Chinese, which had been torn into small pieces, were reassembled and translated by the bureau. The FBI concluded that these were "tasking lists" from Chinese military intelligence, documents or information his handlers wanted him to collect. In secret searches of Chi Mak's home, the FBI found documents about several of the weapons systems on the lists.

One list of the items sought included a space-based missile-intercept system, submarine torpedoes, and aircraft carrier electronic systems. The second document asked for "ship submarine propulsion technology . . . early warning technologies, command and control systems technology, defense against nuclear attack technology . . . shipboard internal and external communication systems, establishment of high frequency, self-linking, satellite communications . . . submarine HF transient launch technology," and information about the DD(X), the Navy's next-generation high-tech destroyer.

According to court documents, after Chi Mak was arrested he admitted passing to China data on electric converters and a circuit breaker for submarines, an electromagnetic aircraft launch system (EMALS), to launch aircraft from carriers using magnets instead of steam, and data about the Aegis combat system, the Navy's most advanced command-and-control system, which uses computers and the powerful AN/SPY-1 radar to guide missiles to their targets.

A month after the arrests, Chi Mak, his wife, and his brother were indicted by a federal grand jury in Los Angeles for acting as unregistered "agents of a foreign government, namely the People's Republic of China." They were not, however, charged under the espionage laws.

The prosecutors had run into a problem. Although much of the information the Maks were said to have transmitted to China was sensitive, and some marked NOFORN, none of it was classified, weakening the prosecution's case. Chi Mak had been careful not to filch any documents stamped SECRET or otherwise classified.

The government was not about to back off for that reason, however. In June 2006, Tai Mak's wife, Fuk Li, and their son, Billy Mak, twenty-six, were indicted on charges of lying to the government and acting as unregistered agents of China. In October, a superseding indictment was handed down, naming all five family members and adding charges of conspiracy to export defense information to China, and making false statements to federal investigators.

The trial of Chi Mak began in March 2007. The prosecution unveiled surprise testimony that tied Chi Mak to Dongfan "Greg" Chung, another Chinese American defense worker who was later prosecuted and convicted for illegally passing sensitive information to China.

FBI agent Gaylord testified that in the FBI's search of Chi Mak's home, a letter was found written by Gu Weihao, an official of China's Ministry of Aviation, to Chung, an engineer who worked at the Boeing plant in Huntington Beach on the space shuttle.

Gu, who was a relative of Chi Mak's wife, Rebecca, had introduced Chung to Chi Mak. In the 1987 letter, Gu wrote that China was planning to build commercial aircraft and a space shuttle. "I hope these products will be flying sky high soon. There are some difficult technical issues that need your assistance."

The letter indicated that Mak had been instructed to deliver it by hand to Chung. "You can discuss the time and route of your trip to China with Mr. Mak in person. . . . You may use 'traveling to Hong Kong' or 'visiting relatives in China' as reasons for traveling abroad."

Then came language that directly implicated Chi Mak. "Normally, if you have any information, you can also pass it on to me through Mr. Mak. This channel is much safer than the others. . . . I hope that you will . . . provide advanced technologies and information."

Chi Mak took the stand and denied that he had passed information to China. The encrypted disks, he claimed, were meant for two "friends." Pu Pei-Liang, to whom Tai Mak placed the "Red Flower" phone call, and who was supposed to meet him at the airport in Guangzhou and receive the disks, was simply another friend who was taking care of Tai Mak's sick mother-in-law. How encrypted information about a system to make submarines run silently would have proved beneficial for her health was not made clear.

After the six-week trial in Santa Ana, the jury on May 10, 2007, found Chi Mak guilty of conspiracy to violate the export control laws, acting as an unregistered agent of China, and lying to the FBI.

With Chi Mak convicted, the rest of the family pleaded guilty in rapid succession. In March 2008 Chi Mak was sentenced to twenty-four years in federal prison. His wife, Rebecca, pleaded guilty to acting as an agent of China, received a sentence of three years, and was to be deported afterward. Tai Mak was sentenced to ten years. His wife, Fuk

Li, received three years probation, and their son, Billy Mak, was sentenced to time already served. All three were also to be deported after serving their sentences.

Having discovered the link to Boeing and the space shuttle in the search of Chi Mak's residence, the FBI opened an investigation of Dongfan Chung. A native of China, Chung came to the United States in 1962 and was a naturalized US citizen who had worked in the aerospace industry in Southern California for thirty years with a SECRET security clearance. Before Boeing, he had been employed by Rockwell International.

Chung was a volunteer spy. Around 1979 he sent a letter to Professor Chen Lung Ku at China's Harbin Institute of Technology. "I don't know what I can do for the country," he wrote. "Having been a Chinese compatriot for over thirty years and being proud of the achievements by the people's efforts for the motherland, I am regretful for not contributing anything. . . . I would like to make an effort to contribute to the Four Modernizations of China" — a reference to Deng Xiaoping's 1978 plan to spur economic development in agriculture, industry, technology, and defense.

Chen wrote back in September 1979. "We are all moved by your patriotism. . . . Your spirit is an encouragement and driving force to us. We'd like to join our hands together with the overseas compatriots in the endeavor for the construction of our great socialist motherland."

Chung lost no time in sending materials to China, among them twenty-four manuals from Rockwell on the B-1 bomber. In turn, the Chinese sent him elaborate tasking lists, with detailed questions. Example: "How many types of loaded flights are used for the fatigue test of small fighter planes? When performing loading test, are the sequences of the loading random or are they derived manually?"

Among other topics, the Chinese asked for "aircraft design manuals, fatigue design manuals . . . space shuttle design manuals . . . the space shuttle's airtight cabin, the space shuttle's heat resistant tile design, lifespan . . . analysis of U.S. fighter planes and airborne equipment; and S-N curves for fighter plane cabin plexiglass and cabin canopies."

In 1985 Chung was invited to lecture in China, on a trip paid for by the Chinese. Among the topics he said he would discuss was "Space

Shuttle Heat Resistant Tiles, Brief Introduction and Stress Analysis." He also planned to lecture on "Fatigue Life" and "F-15 Jet Fighters."

"It's a great honor and I am excited to be able to make some contributions to the four modernizations of the motherland," Chung wrote. He looked forward to a trip "of several weeks to take a good look at the motherland with my own eyes."

Two years later, Gu Weihao, the aviation ministry official, appears to have become Chung's chief contact. "It is your honor and China's fortune that you are able to realize your wish of dedicating [yourself] to the service of your country," Gu wrote.

The Chinese official asked that Chung "collect information on airplane design for the trunkline and the development of the space shuttle." Once in Guangzhou, he would be able to meet with Gu and Gu's colleagues in a "small setting, which is very safe."

Perhaps as a cover story for his trip, Gu suggested, Chung's wife, an artist, could be invited to visit an art institute in China. Chung could then accompany his wife as his reason to visit the PRC. In 2001 Chung again traveled to China to lecture on the space shuttle, and he made two more trips there in 2002 and 2003.

When FBI agents interviewed Chung in 2006 and searched his home in Orange, California, they were astonished to find three hundred thousand pages of Boeing documents squirreled away in his residence, containing information about the space shuttle, the Delta IV rocket, used to boost unmanned vehicles into space, the F-15 fighter jet, the B-52 bomber, and the Chinook helicopter. Some of the documents were in a crawlspace underneath the house.

On February 11, 2008, Chung was arrested after being indicted on charges of economic espionage, acting as a foreign agent of China, and making false statements to the FBI. After a ten-day bench trial without a jury in July 2009, Chung, then seventy-three, was found guilty by US District Court judge Cormac J. Carney. In a scathing opinion, Judge Carney declared: "Mr. Chung has been an agent of the People's Republic of China ('PRC') for over thirty years. Under the direction and control of the PRC, Mr. Chung misappropriated sensitive aerospace and military information belonging to his employer, the Boeing Company, to assist the PRC in developing its own programs."

The judge minced no words. "As federal agents sifted through the hundreds of thousands of pages of documents in Mr. Chung's home, the story of Mr. Chung's secret life became clear. He was a spy for the PRC."

China's Foreign Ministry released a short statement. "The allegation that a so-called Chinese person stole trade secrets in the United States and gave them to China is purely a fabrication."

Chung was the first person to be convicted in a trial under the Economic Espionage Act of 1996. In February 2010 he was sentenced to fifteen years and eight months in prison. Judge Carney said he imposed the long sentence because he wanted to send a signal to China to "stop sending your spies here."

Chinese spy cases have often proved to be linked or overlapping in some fashion. Chi Mak and Dongfan Chung were closely connected. On the same day that Chung was arrested in California, at the other end of the country, in Alexandria, Virginia, the government charged three people under the espionage laws with spying for China in what the press reported was "an unrelated case."

But it was not unrelated. For, as it turned out, Lin Hong, a Chinese intelligence official based in Guangzhou and Hong Kong, was the puppet master pulling the strings in the cases on both coasts and a fourth that was revealed a year later, in May 2009.

The three people arrested in February 2008 were Gregg W. Bergersen, a Defense Department employee, Tai Shen Kuo, forty-eight, a New Orleans businessman acting as a spy for China, and Yu Xin Kang, his young Chinese girlfriend who worked for Kuo's furniture company and served as a cutout between Kuo and his handler in China, Lin Hong.

Bergersen, a Navy veteran with a TOP SECRET clearance who liked to gamble in Las Vegas, worked in Arlington, Virginia, for the Defense Security Cooperation Agency, the Pentagon unit that manages the vast program of US arms sales to foreign countries. He began his military career in naval intelligence, and served on a CIA committee (COMEX) that monitored technology transfer to the Soviets and eastern Europe. For that work, he received a Meritorious Unit Citation from then CIA director Robert Gates.

With a family to support, Bergersen, fifty-one, longed after he retired to move into the world of "beltway bandits," the military and intelligence companies and consultants that surround Washington and
thrive on government contracts.

It seemed as though his prayers were answered when he met the
free-spending Tai Shen Kuo, who cultivated Defense Department officials and claimed he was developing a consulting company to obtain
defense contracts. He told Bergersen, "When my company get to the
point . . . where I can pay you three, four-hundred thousand a year,
you come out" and retire. He also held out the prospect that Bergersen
might become part owner of the company.

Born in Taiwan, Kuo, short and charismatic, came to the United
States in 1972 to attend college in Louisiana on a tennis scholarship.
He became a naturalized US citizen eight years later and held both
American and Taiwanese passports. Kuo went into business import-
ing Chinese furniture. He lived in New Orleans but traveled regularly
to China and had an office in Beijing. His wife, Jane, was the daughter
of a high-ranking Kuomintang general, Hsueh Yueh, who fought the
Japanese during World War II and fled to Taiwan after the Communists took over the mainland in 1949.

After the FBI arrested Kuo, he sought out Plato Cacheris, a prominent criminal attorney in Washington, renowned for representing defendants in espionage cases, among them Aldrich Ames and Robert
Hanssen. According to Cacheris's younger partner, John Hundley, Kuo
was first approached by Chinese intelligence in the 1990s.

"He was trying to sell cotton and other products to China and
working with an associate on the West Coast," Hundley recounted.
"They made several exploratory trips to China to promote their business, and his associate introduced him to Lin Hong as someone Kuo
needed to know to do business in China. Lin was described to him as
an executive with the Guangzhou Friendship Association, a government organization that helped North American businessmen conduct
business in China. It didn't take him long to realize that Lin was in the
Chinese government." In fact, Lin Hong was an intelligence officer of
the People's Liberation Army.

In the 1990s Kuo had embarked on a new business venture to develop a defense communication system between the United States and Taiwan. Lin Hong pressed him for information about the work, holding out the prospect of a "big project" in China if he delivered what Lin wanted. Over the next several years, Kuo passed defense information to Lin.

And it was in the early 1990s that Kuo developed another reason to travel to Beijing. He met Yu Xin Kang, a slim nineteen-year-old Chinese girl, and their relationship blossomed into an affair. Kuo supported Kang, using her as a go-between with Lin Hong. She met with Lin in Beijing and passed messages between the Chinese spymaster and Kuo, who used her apartment in Beijing for meetings with Lin.

Yu Xin Kang moved to New Orleans in 2007 to work as a secretary for Kuo. In the United States, Kang, now thirty-two, answered to the name Katie and obtained a green card as a legal permanent resident alien. With money from Lin Hong, Kuo continued to support her.

The spy business was proving more lucrative than Kuo's other uncertain enterprises. According to court documents, Lin Hong paid Kuo $50,000, and Kuo in turn entertained Bergersen in the casinos and expensive shows of Las Vegas, and paid him small amounts of cash. Bergersen, in turn, provided Kuo with Pentagon documents and information, some classified. Kuo told Bergersen that the data he provided was going to Taiwan. Bergersen did not know that Kuo passed the information to Beijing.

In April 2007, on a trip to Las Vegas, Kuo handed Bergersen $3,000 in cash to play poker, and Bergersen exchanged the money for casino chips. The next day, Kuo reported to Lin Hong that Bergersen had agreed to provide the Pentagon's projected five-year arms sales to Taiwan. In a phone call to Bergersen in July, Kuo reminded Bergersen it was the Defense Department's document he wanted: "I want your . . . paper. I don't want CIA, I got CIA's paper."

Kuo flew to Washington in July, and the FBI managed to plant both audio and video surveillance in the car he rented. As they drove to Dulles International Airport later that day, Kuo put a thick stack of bills into Bergersen's shirt pocket. Bergersen brought along the Taiwan arms sales projection and had cut the "SECRET" markings off the document. He told Kuo he was reluctant to let him have it, "because it's all classified," but Kuo could "take all the notes you want."

If anyone found out, Bergersen warned, "Fuck, I'd go to jail, I don't wanna go to jail."

"I'd probably go to jail, too," Kuo replied, chuckling.

Back in Louisiana the next day, Kuo e-mailed his Chinese handler, Lin Hong, that he was not able to keep a copy of the Taiwan arms sales projection—it was "very, very sensitive"—but he was allowed to take notes about it. He said that Bergersen had also let him look at the plans to improve Taiwan's command-and-control and intelligence capabilities.

Five days later, Kuo flew to Beijing, where he was met at the airport by Yu Xin Kang. Kuo personally delivered to Lin Hong the handwritten notes he had taken from the documents that Bergersen had let him see.

In August, there was a domestic scene right out of *Fawlty Towers*. In a telephone conversation with Kuo, Bergersen lamented that when he returned from a trip, his wife went through his wallet and found an unexpected amount of money. Not wanting to explain its source, he told her that he won it gambling. In that case, his wife said, she was entitled to half the money—and she took it as her share. Kuo offered to make up the difference, but Bergersen declined, saying he could not put it in the bank anyway, because, "I don't want any record."

In March 2008, a month after he was arrested, Bergersen pleaded guilty under the espionage statutes to a single count of conspiracy to disclose national defense information. He was sentenced to just short of five years in federal prison.

Tai Shen Kuo pleaded guilty to conspiracy to deliver national defense secrets to China. He was sentenced to almost sixteen years, later reduced to five for cooperating with prosecutors, and fined $40,000.

Yu Xin Kang received a much lighter sentence of eighteen months in prison for aiding and abetting an unregistered agent of the Chinese government. Prosecutors recognized that she had been used and controlled for years by Kuo, her lover and sole financial support.

Lin Hong was safely out of reach, in China. But an FBI affidavit in the Bergersen/Kuo case made clear that the spymaster also ran the Chi Mak operation on the West Coast. Rebecca Chiu had admitted that Lin Hong and others had provided them with the tasking lists of information Chi Mak was to gather. Lin Hong's name and phone numbers appeared in two of Chi Mak's address books and also on a document in Mandarin Chinese seized from Kuo.

Lin Hong's web of spies on both coasts included a second Pentagon official, James W. Fondren Jr., whom he gave the code name Fang. On the day that Kuo and Bergersen were arrested, Kuo was staying at Fondren's home in Annandale, Virginia. Like Bergersen, Fondren was one of several current and former government employees and contractors cultivated by Tai Shen Kuo.

A lieutenant colonel in the Air Force, Fondren retired in 1996 and two years later set up a consulting business from his home. But his only client was Tai Shen Kuo. With a search warrant issued when Kuo was arrested, the FBI took Fondren's computer and discovered it contained many "opinion papers" containing classified information that he had written and e-mailed to Kuo for payment.

In March 1999 Fondren and Kuo had traveled together to China. Kuo introduced him to Lin Hong, whom he described as a "political researcher" and consultant to the Chinese government.

After the trip, Fondren began exchanging e-mails directly with Lin Hong, who responded cryptically in April: "Everything OK with you? The weather outside is not so kindly, please take care while working."

In May, Fondren assured Lin Hong that he was trying his best to obtain a Theater Missile Defense report before it was released. That same month Kuo gave him a check for $1,150. Fondren would have had to be exceptionally dim not to realize that his new friend Lin Hong was acting for, or an official of, the Chinese government. In fact, Fondren boasted to a friend that "the PRC government . . . has already adopted some of my suggestions."

Then in 2001, Kuo and Lin got good news. Fondren was hired by the Pentagon as deputy director of the Washington liaison office of the US Pacific Command (PACOM), the unified armed forces command for the Asia-Pacific region. Now Fondren held a TOP SECRET and Sensitive Compartmented Information (SCI) clearance.

With Fondren on the inside, Lin Hong suggested that Kuo mislead him into thinking the information he was providing was going to the Taiwan military. Fondren kept batting out the classified "opinion papers" for Kuo, who said he would now have to pay him in cash.

In late October 2006, Kuo telephoned Fondren asking for a copy of a Pentagon antiterrorism publication. Although marked "For Official Use Only," Fondren agreed to get it. A week later, Lin Hong e-mailed Kuo asking where the publication was. The next day, the FBI intercepted a package sent by Fondren to Kuo with the document.

Then in February 2007, Lin complained to Kuo by telephone that his superior was not pleased with two of the papers Fondren had written and believed they did not reflect what Fang knew. In the future, Lin said, Fang should simply send the documents and not write papers, which took too much time.

That same month, Kuo asked Fondren to snag an advance copy of the Defense Department's annual report on the Chinese military. Early in March, Kuo called Fondren at home and asked if he had obtained the draft. Fondren replied, "I can't talk about uh — that stuff over the phone." So Kuo flew to Washington, stayed at Fondren's home, and Fondren gave him the report, saying: "Let people find out I did that, it will cost me my job."

In August, the FBI conducted a pretext interview of Fondren, saying they were talking to government employees familiar with Asia. Fondren told them he knew and had worked with Kuo, but he smelled a rat. He sent an e-mail to Kuo reporting that the agents "wrote down only that information and didn't take notes when I talked about Vietnam and other Southeast Asia countries."

Despite the suspicious FBI visit, Fondren continued to send classified data to Kuo. Then on May 13, 2009, the prosecutors acted. Fondren was charged with conspiring to disclose classified defense information to an agent of China. He surrendered to federal authorities and was released with electronic monitoring.

Fondren's trial in federal district court in Alexandria opened in

September 2009. The chief witness against him, appearing in a green prison jumpsuit, was Tai Shen Kuo. At the end of the five-day trial, the jury, on September 25, convicted Fondren on one count of unlawfully communicating classified data to an agent of a foreign government and two counts of making false statements to the FBI. In January 2010 Fondren was sentenced to three years in federal prison.

By the fall of 2009 Red Flower, Fang, and the other players in the bicoastal spy drama were history. Chi Mak and four other members of his family, as well as Dongfan Chung, Tai Shen Kuo, Gregg Bergersen, Katie Kang, and James Fondren — ten people in all — had been caught and convicted. Lin Hong's spy network had been broken.

# Chapter 21

# THE CYBERSPIES

I N T H E  T W E N T Y - F I R S T  C E N T U R Y, spies have finally achieved what practitioners of their ancient craft could only dream of in the past: thanks to the Internet, they have become truly invisible.

From the Pentagon to the State Department, from the Sandia nuclear weapons laboratory to the Department of Homeland Security, intruders have managed to hack into US government computers with increasing frequency. Many of the attacks appear to have originated in China.

In 2009 a group of Canadian researchers at the University of Toronto called "Chinese cyber-espionage" a "major global concern." Their report strongly implied that the Chinese government, not just individual hackers, was behind widespread computer attacks aimed at the United States and 102 other countries.

The Chinese hackers, the researchers said, broke into computers in the United States, Taiwan, India, and other nations, directing them to download a Trojan horse — a destructive program masquerading as useful software — called Ghost Rat. As in typical hacker assaults, the program then allowed the attacker to gain real-time control over the computers, turning them into zombies or proxies, unknown to their owners.

Once the computers were controlled, the intruders could search and download files, and even covertly operate "microphones and web cameras," the Canadian report noted. According to Nart Villeneuve, one of the authors of the report, that Orwellian capacity means that if a computer has a webcam, it can peer into a bedroom or office and allow the attacker secretly to watch what is happening, with sound. If a computer only has a microphone, that can be activated to eavesdrop on the room where the PC is located.

Beginning in 2003, a series of attacks on the Pentagon and other government agencies from websites in China was given the code name TITAN RAIN by US investigators. The government classified the attacks and has said very little about them. The veil was partially lifted on TITAN RAIN, however, by an extraordinary episode at the Sandia National Laboratories site in Albuquerque, New Mexico.

In 2004 Shawn Carpenter, a thirty-six-year-old computer security analyst at the nuclear weapons lab, studied a series of break-ins at Sandia and tracked them to servers that appeared to be located in Guandong Province in southern China. On his own time he continued to trace back the technologically sophisticated, rapid intrusions to their source, sharing his information first with Army counterintelligence and later the FBI.

Instead of appreciating what Carpenter had done to protect the lab, Sandia yanked his Q clearance and fired him for going outside established channels. Carpenter sued, and in 2007 won a whopping $4.7 million jury award in a New Mexico court. The jury found that his firing by Sandia was "malicious, willful, reckless, wanton, fraudulent or in bad faith."

The attacks on the Defense Department and other government computers are ongoing. Air Force general Kevin P. Chilton, head of the US Strategic Command, said in 2008 that defense networks were taking a million suspicious "hits" a day. Without pinpointing China, he said he believed the break-ins could be attributed to "espionage work."

It is not only defense-related targets that are vulnerable to computer attacks. The *Wall Street Journal* reported in 2009 that cyberspies from China, Russia, and elsewhere had penetrated the power grid in the United States, and inserted malware, or malicious software, programs that could be used to disrupt the system. It quoted unnamed officials as saying that water, sewage, and other infrastructure systems were also at risk.

Later that year, former CIA director James Woolsey drew a stark portrait of what could happen. "Taking down the grid for months comes as close to a nuclear attack with many weapons on the United States as anything could. You'd have mass starvation and death from thirst and all the rest."

A year earlier, Tom Donahue, the CIA's chief cybersecurity official, told a meeting in New Orleans of security officials from utility and energy companies that hackers had in fact breached the computers of power companies in another country and caused a power outage in several cities, a report later questioned.

In 2008 the Tennessee Valley Authority, which provides power to nine million people in seven southern states, was criticized by the Government Accountability Office for lax security. The chairman of the House panel on cybersecurity said that the TVA, the nation's largest generator of electric power, "risks a disruption of its operations as the result of a cyber incident."

And the nation's electrical grid is vulnerable. Researchers at DOE's Idaho National Laboratory demonstrated in 2007, in an experiment called the Aurora Generator Test, that a cyberattack could in fact knock out a power system. In a startling video released by the Department of Homeland Security, a power turbine like many in use across the United States was forced to overheat and shut down after receiving computer commands in a simulated hacker attack. In the video, the huge turbine shakes and shudders and belches black-and-white smoke as pieces fly off.

President Obama confirmed in 2009 that "cyber intruders have probed our electrical grid" and "in other countries cyber attacks have plunged entire cities into darkness." Although he did not elaborate, CBS News reported that an attack in Brazil in 2005 affected three cities and another in 2007 in that country caused blackouts affecting more than three million people, but the CBS report was disputed by Brazilian officials, who blamed the blackouts on sooty insulators.

China has vehemently denied responsibility for any computer attacks directed against the United States or other countries. In answer to reports that Beijing had broken into the Pentagon's computers, for example, Jiang Yu, the spokesman for the Chinese Foreign Ministry, declared: "The Chinese government has always opposed any Internet-wrecking crime, including hacking, and cracked down on it according to the law."

The denials are frequent but not entirely persuasive. The Chinese government tries to tightly control all aspects of the Internet in that country, sharply restricting the web content that its citizens may view. In recent years, Internet activists outside China have provided software that has enabled a relatively small percentage of Chinese computer users to circumvent the government's firewall. Even so, it is not credible that large numbers of private Chinese hackers, supposedly acting on their own, could engage in repeated attacks on US defense and intelligence agencies — unless the government of China either organized, directed, or encouraged those intrusions, or at the very least condoned them.

In a book published more than a decade ago, two Chinese Internet specialists acknowledged that "using hackers to obtain military information from computer networks is a very effective method." A more recent book published in China in 2003, *Deciphering Information Security,* discusses a university specializing in computer security, a sort of "Hacker U," with courses on "Computer Virus Program Design and Application," and "A Study of Hacker Attack Methods."

Efforts to prove that the Chinese government might be behind the TITAN RAIN–type attacks on the United States run up against what computer security experts call the problem of "attribution." Because it is relatively easy for hackers to disguise their country of origin and precise location, today's cyberspies can hide behind a virtual cloak, and their dagger is electronic. A hacker in eastern Europe can make it appear that his e-mail has been sent via a server in Shanghai.

For that reason, when Google early in 2010 revealed attacks on its e-mail service and on thirty-four American companies, many of them engaged in defense work, it did not pinpoint the precise source but made clear that it believed the intrusions had originated in China. Later, some investigators thought the attacks could be traced to two schools in China, one with close ties to the military.

FBI director Robert Mueller described the problem in a speech in San Francisco in 2009. "At the start of a cyber investigation, we do not know whether we are dealing with a spy, a company insider, or an organized criminal group," he said. "Something that looks like an ordinary phishing scam may be an attempt by a terrorist group to raise funding for an operation."

The government has tried to thwart assaults on critical defense networks. NASA, the target of cyber intrusions at both the Kennedy Space Center in Florida and the Johnson Space Center in Houston, initiated a program code-named AVOCADO to block suspected Chinese computer attacks. The Department of Homeland Security's EINSTEIN program has provided government agencies with sensors designed to detect computer intrusions.

In 2002 the US Naval War College was the site of a war game called Digital Pearl Harbor. Mock attacks by computer security experts simulated attacks by other countries on vital US infrastructure. The exercise found that the Internet and digital financial networks were the most vulnerable. Other experts have warned that telecommunications networks and the air traffic control system could be disrupted by cyberattacks.

Like the United States, China has devised plans to disrupt the digital networks of an adversary in a war. According to the 2009 report by the University of Toronto researchers, "China is actively developing an operational capacity in cyberspace, correctly identifying it as the domain in which it can achieve strategic parity, if not superiority over the military establishments of the United States and its allies."

The role of the People's Liberation Army was also highlighted in the Defense Department's 2008 annual report to Congress on Chinese military power: "The PLA has established information warfare units to develop viruses to attack enemy computer systems and networks." The report added that the PLA sees computer network operations "as critical to achieving 'electromagnetic dominance' early in a conflict."

Although the evidence is murky, Chinese hackers may have targeted that country's critics in the United States. Two Republican members of Congress claimed in 2008 that the computers in their offices on Capitol Hill had been penetrated by hackers they believed were in China. The two representatives, Chris Smith, of New Jersey, and Frank Wolf, of Virginia, both conservatives, were longtime vocal critics of China's human rights record.

And in an Atlanta suburb in 2006, Peter Yuan Li, a computer technology specialist, naturalized American citizen, and critic of the Chinese government, was robbed, beaten, tied up, and blindfolded by three or four armed Asian men who invaded his home and took two laptop computers, leaving behind other valuable items. He required fifteen stitches to treat a facial injury suffered in the attack.

Li was a locally prominent follower of Falun Gong, a spiritual movement that China has outlawed as an "evil cult." The FBI and Fulton County detectives investigated the robbery and attack on Li, but there were no arrests. Li, for one, had no doubt about why he was targeted. He blamed China for the break-in, which he claimed was designed to silence him. He expressed surprise "that in the US they could do such things."

In 1987 Li came to the United States for graduate studies at Princeton, where he received a PhD in electrical engineering. For several years he has worked with other activists to combat Internet censorship in China. "Initially we provided e-mails to China, we had twenty million e-mail addresses and sent articles to them," he said. "Around 2004 proxy servers didn't work anymore, they were easily blocked, and we had to go to more sophisticated methods."

Along with his group, Li then began supplying Internet users in China with software that allowed them to navigate around the government's firewall. There were various ways to get the software into China. "They block e-mails, but we can still send some, either through e-mail or Skype." Inside China, he said, the software is passed along by word of mouth or on the Internet. When a computer user in China clicks on a link provided in an e-mail, the user can download software that connects to a computer overseas, which then reroutes the traffic to the restricted Chinese website.

In Li's view, cyberattacks on the Pentagon and other US agencies are originating in China. "The Chinese government regards hackers as heroes," he said. "The government does not crack down on the hackers. The way for students to show genius is to do hacking. I believe they [the Chinese government] are organizing these attacks."

Most concerns over cyberspying aimed at US defense and intelligence networks have been focused on software, the use of programs that can disable or steal data from the target computers. But computer security experts today are increasingly worried about the compromise of hardware — computer chips that control missiles, aircraft, and radars.

One reason is that only about 2 percent of the integrated circuits purchased every year by the military are manufactured in the United States. And even most American chip makers have moved offshore, where labor is cheaper. A computer chip made with a hidden, malicious flaw could sabotage a weapons system. And the compromised hardware is almost impossible to detect.

A chip might even be embedded with a "kill switch," allowing the weapon to be disabled by remote control. When the Israeli air force attacked a suspected nuclear reactor site in Syria in 2007, observers wondered why the Syrian air defenses did not respond. Later, there were unconfirmed reports that a kill switch, provided by the United States to Israeli intelligence, had been used to disarm the Syrian radars.

The United States has been slow to discern the threat to national security of cyberspies and hackers. President Obama, recognizing the problem, declared in May 2009, "We're not as prepared as we should be as a government or as a country." He spoke ruefully of how, during his presidential campaign a year earlier, "hackers gained access to emails and a range of campaign files, from policy position papers to travel plans."

He talked about "spyware and malware and spoofing and phishing and botnets." And, he warned, "In today's world, acts of terror could come not only from a few extremists in suicide vests but from a few key strokes on the computer — a weapon of mass disruption."

Obama announced that he would appoint a White House cybersecurity coordinator to work with federal, state, and local government agencies and the private sector to defend against cyberattacks on the nation's infrastructure. The following month, the Defense Department ordered the creation of the nation's first military cyber command. The appointment of Lieutenant General Keith B. Alexander, who was also director of the National Security Agency, to head the new command stirred controversy. A powerful argument can be made that the NSA, already snooping on e-mails and phone calls under a secret program instituted by President George W. Bush and later approved by Congress, should not exercise control over computer security.

At the same time, the creation of a White House "cyber czar" and a military cyber command were long overdue, given the continuing computer attacks against the United States. And there was plausible evidence that many of the intrusions originated in China.

In examining cyber espionage, the detailed 2009 report by the University of Toronto researchers, while appropriately cautious in not blaming every hacker attack on the Chinese government, noted that the cyber assaults on 103 countries were targeted against diplomats, military personnel, the staff of prime ministers, and journalists.

"The most logical explanation, and certainly the one in which the circumstantial evidence tilts strongest, would be that this set of high profile targets has been exploited by the Chinese state for military and strategic intelligence purposes. . . . Many of the . . . high-value targets that we identified are clearly linked to Chinese foreign and defence policy.

"Like radar sweeping around the southern border of China, there is an arc of infected nodes from India, Bhutan, Bangladesh and Vietnam, through Laos, Brunei, Philippines, Hong Kong, and Taiwan."

There was one other key piece of intelligence uncovered by the academic researchers. The attackers' Internet Protocol (IP) addresses, the identifying numbers assigned to all computers and servers, "trace back in at least several instances to Hainan Island."

There is a reason the finding was especially significant in the continuing effort to pinpoint the source of the cyberspies. The location is a tourist attraction, but it is also something more. Hainan Island, in the South China Sea, is the site of China's Lingshui signals intelligence facility and the Third Technical Department of the People's Liberation Army.

Perhaps the strongest evidence linking China to cyberspying against the US was provided by WikiLeaks, which began making public 250,000 confidential American diplomatic cables in late November 2010. Among them was a cable to Washington from the US embassy in Beijing, dated in January of that year, reporting that a Chinese contact said that hacker attacks against Google were directed by the Politburo, the highest level of China's government.

The cable stated: "A well-placed contact claims that the Chinese government coordinated the recent intrusions of Google systems. According to our contact, the closely held operations were directed at the Politburo Standing Committee level."

The trove of cables, made public by Julian Assange, the founder of WikiLeaks, described a global, coordinated campaign of computer attacks run by Chinese government officials, and Internet hackers recruited by China's government. The documents described previously secret intrusions of American government agencies, attacks code-named BYZANTINE CANDOR and BYZANTINE HADES by US investigators.

One 2008 State Department cable quoted an analysis of Chinese cyberattacks by Germany's security service, which surmised "the intention of PRC actors is espionage, and the primary attack vector used in their malicious activity is socially engineered e-mail messages containing malware attachments and/or embedded links to hostile websites." The cable added that the emails "were spoofed to appear targeted specifically to the recipients' interests, duties, or current events."

The WikiLeaks cables provided further confirmation of what had long been suspected: that China, despite its loud denials, was actively engaged in cyberspying against the United States and other targets around the world.

# Chapter 22

# AN AFTERWORD

IN JANUARY 2010 Google made a surprise announcement that reverberated across Washington, Beijing, and other world capitals. The technology giant threatened to pull out of China because of attacks on its computer systems and thirty-four American companies, mostly in Silicon Valley. The cyberattacks were traced to half a dozen servers in Taiwan, but Google strongly suspected that the assaults, aimed partly at Gmail accounts of Chinese human rights activists, had originated in China.

The attacks aimed at the US companies in California, including Northrop Grumman and Dow Chemical, appeared designed to scoop up information about weapons systems, and perhaps their vital "source codes," or computer programming instructions. Google turned to the National Security Agency, the nation's eavesdropping and code-breaking arm, for help in investigating the attacks.

Google also made clear that it would no longer cooperate with Chinese Internet censorship. Soon afterward, the company closed its search engine service in China, google.cn, and automatically routed users to its uncensored website in Hong Kong, google.com.hk, although Google said it was "well aware" that China could block access there as well at any time.*

The United States treaded lightly at first in response to the initial Google announcement. The White House was silent. A week went by before Secretary of State Hillary Clinton made a speech calling for global "Internet freedom" and asking the Chinese authorities to "conduct a thorough investigation of the cyber intrusions." China responded angrily, saying that Clinton's "groundless accusations" were "harmful to US-China relations."

Aside from the difficulty of proving that the Chinese government, rather than individual hackers, was behind the spying, there were geopolitical and financial reasons for the muted response by Washington. In 2010 China held more than a trillion dollars of US debt. If the United States were a house, China would hold the mortgage. The Google episode, more than anything else, captured the ambiguous and mutually dependent nature of the relationship between the United States and China in the twenty-first century.

Politics aside, in the espionage war, as this history has demonstrated, China has often, although certainly not always, been successful. Indeed, China may be America's single most effective and dangerous adversary. It managed over the years to penetrate both the CIA and the FBI. It acquired highly classified and guarded nuclear weapons secrets. The FBI's counterintelligence agents have also won significant battles, detecting several of China's spies, including a number who have been arrested and successfully prosecuted. Yet the record of China's achievements is formidable.

What is strikingly different about many of the Chinese spy cases is how they overlap and interlock, a tangled web of espionage with tendrils spreading in different directions. The threads of the Chi Mak, Dongfan Chung, Tai Shen Kuo, Gregg Bergersen, and James Fondren

---

* Six months later, in July 2010, the crisis eased with a compromise: China renewed Google's license and allowed it to operate some services on its google.cn website. Chinese Internet users would no longer automatically be routed to the uncensored Hong Kong website, but could click on a link that would take them there.

cases, for example, were all held by a single spymaster in China, Lin Hong.

There is a controversial subtext to Chinese spying in the United States. Asian Americans have good reason, historically, to be skeptical of the US government. For sixty years, beginning in 1882 and lasting into World War II, Chinese were barred from immigrating to the United States by the Chinese Exclusion Act. In 1917 Congress created an Asiatic Barred Zone, prohibiting immigration from much of East Asia and the Pacific Islands; the law was not abolished until 1952. Thousands of Japanese Americans were shunted off to internment camps in the paranoia after Pearl Harbor, a blot on Franklin D. Roosevelt's otherwise admirable record as a peacetime and wartime leader. Xenophobia, particularly with respect to those who look different, is embedded in US history.

When the FBI investigates or arrests a Chinese national or an American of Chinese background, it inevitably opens itself up to charges of racism. When Katrina Leung was arrested, even though she was exposed as someone working for the MSS, using a Chinese code name and reporting to a handler in Beijing, some prominent Chinese Americans in Los Angeles leaped to her defense and implied that she was being singled out because of her ethnicity and gender.

In the backlash after the government's unconscionable treatment of Wen Ho Lee, who was no hero, many Chinese Americans and others concluded that the government and the FBI were in the business of targeting ethnic Chinese as spies.

The fact that Lee's background was ethnic Chinese may well have influenced the Department of Energy to single him out, although the evidence on that point remains ambiguous and may never be fully resolved. Yet, as already noted, there were good reasons, unrelated to Lee's ethnicity, that he became a suspect. He had worked on the W-88 nuclear warhead in the most secret division at Los Alamos, the vault where nuclear bombs are designed. So had others. But Wen Ho Lee stood out as the subject of two previous FBI investigations, for telephoning the TIGER TRAP spy suspect and lying about it, and for failing to report that he had been questioned about key US nuclear secrets when China's top bomb designer visited him privately in a hotel room in Beijing.

The record of Chinese espionage against defense and intelligence agencies in the United States demonstrates that it is China, rather than the FBI, that targets ethnic Chinese. In any number of cases, the MSS and the intelligence arm of the People's Liberation Army have sought, sometimes successfully, to recruit Chinese Americans, by appealing to their roots and family ties to the "motherland." Of course, that reality should not obscure the fact that the vast majority of Chinese Americans are loyal to the United States.

As noted, inside the FBI, the agency with the greatest responsibility for uncovering China's spies in America, counterintelligence is not regarded as the most fruitful career path. Pursuing terrorists or white-collar criminals is a better track toward promotion. And for decades, even within the counterintelligence division, the Chinese target was an orphan. Moscow's spies, not Beijing's, were perceived as the main enemy.

Only a minuscule number of FBI agents specialized in Chinese cases. If the bureau lacked an understanding of China, that was not true of the small group of China hands. Some became so fascinated by their subject that they stayed in the Chinese counterintelligence program, knowing that as a result they would never make it to the level of a special agent in charge of a field office or a desirable headquarters post.

Bill Cleveland, until his career was derailed by his singular lack of judgment in the PARLOR MAID debacle, was known inside the FBI as a serious student of China, who over the years became immersed in its language, culture, and history. J.J. Smith, who unwisely bet his counterintelligence career on a source with whom he became emotionally entangled, and who ultimately betrayed him, was also well versed in the byways of Chinese culture and society. Perhaps for both men, China, as much as Katrina Leung, became a kind of fatal attraction.

As an institution, the FBI was overly dependent on its informants. In the PARLOR MAID case, the FBI's prime source on China, whose reports went all the way to the White House, was secretly working for the MSS.

In the ETHEREAL THRONE case, Jeffrey Wang, an innocent man, lost his job and was subject to a lengthy FBI investigation when he was falsely accused as a Chinese spy by a longtime bureau informant who had a personal, family grudge against him. And Denise Woo, the Asian American FBI agent who became convinced of Wang's innocence and rightly tried to help him clear his name, was fired and prosecuted for her efforts.

In the wake of these twin disasters, the FBI ordered an overdue review of the bureau's use of informants. Changes were made, among them a rule that the files of bureau assets be reviewed every sixty to ninety days. An informant review panel was established by the attorney general. None of which was any help to Jeff Wang or Denise Woo.

Rudy Guerin, a former veteran FBI counterintelligence street agent, talked about the risks of running informants too long. "After PARLOR MAID, one of the procedures we put in place, you should not run a source for more than a couple of years."

Asked about the informant who fabricated the story about Jeff Wang, Guerin replied: "This source had been run for a long period of time. Agents bond with their sources if they run them for a long time, as happened with PARLOR MAID. Agents tend to take things their sources tell them and write it up and say it's gold. Maybe you have to use bad guys in drug cases, but when working espionage and someone sets up a US citizen, you can't do that."

No recent president, Bill Clinton, George W. Bush, or Barack Obama, has wanted to make a high-decibel issue of Chinese espionage. With the United States struggling in 2010 to recover from the worst economic crisis since the Great Depression, Washington could hardly afford to alienate its banker. Indeed, a year earlier, Chinese premier Wen Jiabao lectured the United States about its economic policies. "We have lent a huge amount of money to the U.S. Of course we are concerned about the safety of our assets. To be honest, I am definitely a little worried."

Aside from the US-China economic embrace, the Obama administration was seeking Beijing's help in curbing North Korea's nuclear weapons and preventing Iran from building a bomb. Short of a revelation that China has planted a mole in the White House, or wired

Bo, the Obama family dog, Washington is not likely to fuss too loudly about Chinese spies.

How damaging to national security is Chinese espionage?

When the question was put to FBI director Robert S. Mueller III at a 2007 hearing of the House Judiciary Committee, he replied: "I can probably say more in a classified setting. I can say that it is a substantial concern. China is stealing our secrets in an effort to leap ahead in terms of its military technology, but also the economic capability of China. It is a substantial threat."

In an earlier report to Congress, the FBI said, "Penetrating the US intelligence community is a key objective of the Chinese." Ironically, at the time of that warning, the MSS had already done exactly that through PARLOR MAID.

Aside from classic espionage, China has benefited from the widespread export of military equipment in violation of US laws. The instances are far too numerous to catalog. In the three years from 2006 to 2009, there were literally dozens of prosecutions for illegal shipments to China of defense equipment, including integrated circuits, thermal imaging cameras, night-vision goggles, restricted computer software, smart-bomb components, and parts for radar and missile systems.

Infiltrating the CIA and the FBI, and stealing the secret measurements of the W-88 nuclear warhead and the design details of the neutron bomb are flagrant examples of China's espionage successes.

"If we're talking about violations of U.S. law, the Chinese are surpassing the Russians," according to Harry J. Godfrey III, the former head of Chinese counterintelligence at FBI headquarters. "We know they are running operations here. We have seen cases where they have encouraged people to apply to the CIA, the FBI, Naval Investigative Service and other defense agencies."

Porter J. Goss, former chairman of the House Intelligence Committee and later director of the CIA, said of Chinese espionage against the United States, "It's pervasive, ubiquitous, constant."

Joel Brenner, the former counterintelligence chief for the director of national intelligence, has a gift for talking in sound bites. Referring to the tasking list that the Chinese gave to Chi Mak, Brenner said: "You can get to know the dragon by its claw, and the list was a clear picture of the dragon's claw."

Harold Agnew, a physicist who worked on the Manhattan Project, flew over Hiroshima on August 6, 1945, in an observation plane behind the *Enola Gay,* and watched the uranium bomb devastate that Japanese city. As head of the weapons division at Los Alamos, and later director of the laboratory, he designed most of the nation's nuclear arsenal. In the 1980s he was the first American scientist allowed to visit Lop Nor, China's secret nuclear test site.

"They had everything," he told an oral history project in 2005. "They're in our knickers and there's maybe one under the couch."

The "dragon's claw" and Harold Agnew's colorful metaphors are eye-catching hyperbole, but they also contain a good deal of truth. Without exaggerating the danger of Chinese espionage, or magnifying the threat, it is a fact that China's spying on America is ongoing, current, and shows no sign of diminishing. The conflict is no less real for being mostly unseen.

Two decades ago, a revealing handbook for spies was published in China by two veteran intelligence researchers, Huo Zhongwen and Wang Zongxiao. The book, *Sources and Techniques of Obtaining National Defense Science and Technology Intelligence,* tells how to gather secret information in the United States. Most intelligence can be collected from open sources, the authors explained, although about 20 percent must be obtained by "special means," including "electronic eavesdropping, and the activities of special agents (purchasing or stealing)." But, by mining "the vast amount of public materials and accumulating information a drop at a time, often it is possible basically to reveal the outlines of some secret intelligence."

They noted that some years ago, the Department of Energy had mistakenly declassified almost twenty thousand documents, including "at least eight highly secret items regarding thermonuclear weapons." They admitted, however, that gathering defense and technology information can be difficult because of security classifications.

Difficult, but not impossible, they wrote. The authors of the espionage guide reminded their readers of a common Chinese saying: "There are no walls which completely block the wind."

# AUTHOR'S NOTE

When, years ago with Thomas B. Ross, I coauthored *The U-2 Affair*, the story of the CIA spy plane shot down over the Soviet Union, I did not realize at the time that I was embarking on a career of writing books about espionage and intelligence.

For most of the intervening years, I studied and reported on the Cold War battle between the CIA and the FBI and the Soviet, now Russian, intelligence services. I wrote of moles and men, of Edward Lee Howard, Aldrich Ames, and Robert Hanssen. To follow the trail of those stories, I traveled to Moscow four times and to many other locales.

Only in the past decade did I come to the growing realization that there was another narrative waiting to be written, the largely unexplored story of China's espionage against the United States. With the encouragement and support of Sterling Lord, my longtime literary agent, I expanded my initial research on the PARLOR MAID case into a broader examination of Chinese espionage spanning the last several decades, up to and including the present.

Like all or most countries, including the United States, China steals secrets. The Chinese have had some notable successes, and some failures as well. The risks posed by their activities in the United States, and the damage done to national security, should not be exaggerated, or ignored.

To write this book, I conducted almost five hundred interviews, with more than 150 people. Given the sensitive nature of counterintelligence, and the ingrained reluctance of CI officers and agents to talk about their work, some declined to speak with me. Many others agreed to be interviewed only on condition that they not be identified. I have respected their wishes.

For their generous assistance on this book I wish to thank Plato Cacheris, and also John F. Hundley, of Trout Cacheris, Lily Lee Chen, Stacy Cohen, John D. Cline, Christopher Cox, James A. Geis, Marc S. Harris, James D. Henderson, Mark C. Holscher, Henry V. Huang, Marianna Liu, Angela Machala, Jonathan E. Medalia, Robert S. Norris, Mary Palevsky, Philip D. Polsky, David Ryan, Federico C. Sayre, Jonathan Shapiro, Perry J. Spanos, Jerry Stockton, Brian A. Sun, Nart Villeneuve, Michael Woo, and Peter Woo.

Katrina Leung declined to be interviewed, but her husband, Kam Leung, spoke to me openly and at length over a period of two days in 2003, and the biographical details about his wife that he provided, as well as his account of their life together and their trips to China, were invaluable and much appreciated.

My especial thanks go to Michael P. Kortan, the FBI's assistant director for public affairs, who did his best to pry loose an occasional morsel from the bureau's famously reticent counterintelligence division. I also appreciate the assistance I received from his predecessor, John J. Miller, and from Bill Carter and Susan T. McKee of the Public Affairs Office. In Los Angeles, Laura Eimiller of the FBI's Public Affairs Office was always helpful.

A number of former FBI agents and bureau officials were willing to share their insights and experience, including Robert M. "Bear" Bryant, Bruce Carlson, Tom Carson, Edward J. Curran, Stephen W. Dillard, Neil J. Gallagher, Harry J. Godfrey, Dan Grove, Rudy Guerin, John L. Hoos, Sheila Horan, Jack Keller, Jay Koerner, John F. Lewis Jr., T. Van Magers, John J. O'Flaherty, Phillip A. Parker, Kenneth J. Schiffer, I. C. Smith, Raymond H. Wickman, and Leslie G. Wiser Jr.

I am greatly indebted as well to the many other former FBI counter-intelligence agents who preferred not to be quoted or have any material attributed to them. This book would have been incomplete without their generous time and assistance. I thank them all; they know who they are.

Among the former CIA officials and officers interviewed were Porter J. Goss, who served as Director of Central Intelligence in 2004–5, Milton A. Bearden, Jennifer Millerwise Dyck, Colin R. Thompson, and Robert S. Vrooman.

At the Department of Justice, I appreciate the help I received from Dean Boyd, the public affairs officer for national security, and in Los Angeles, from Thom Mrozek, the media spokesperson for the US Attorney's Office. Michael W. Emmick, the former assistant US attorney in Los Angeles who was the lead prosecutor of Katrina Leung, was especially patient with my questions, as was Rebecca Lonergan, the former assistant US attorney in that office and the lead prosecutor of J.J. Smith. I also appreciate the assistance I received from Erica O'Neil, an assistant U.S. attorney in Milwaukee.

From the Department of Energy, I benefited from conversations a decade ago with then-secretary Bill Richardson, Lawrence H. Sanchez, director of the Office of Intelligence, and Notra Trulock, the acting deputy director of that office. I also thank Stephen Wampler, of the Public Affairs Office at the Lawrence Livermore National Laboratory.

In threading my way through the intricacies of the science and control of nuclear weapons, I am indebted to Thomas B. Cochran, of the Natural Resources Defense Council, Richard L. Garwin, George A. "Jay" Keyworth, the former White House science adviser, and Daryl G. Kimball, executive director of the Arms Control Association.

Several friends and members of the news media were helpful, including Pete Williams of NBC, Matthew Barakat of the Associated Press, and Greg Krikorian, formerly of the *Los Angeles Times*.

Chen-yieh Catherine Yu, assistant professor of Chinese at Georgetown University, graciously answered several questions about Chinese language and usage. Jeffrey T. Richelson of the National Security Archive was more than generous with his help and guidance. My thanks as well go to Ian M. Cunningham, who provided me with skillful research assistance at several points along the way. Alexandra and Elizabeth Evans cheerfully kept my newspaper files current.

I especially want to thank Bruce Nichols, senior vice president and publisher of Houghton Mifflin Harcourt, whose steadfast support and enthusiasm for this project made it possible, and is deeply appreciated by me. The manuscript also benefited greatly from the skillful editing of Martin Beiser. Others at the publishing house deserve my thanks as well, including assistant editor Christina Morgan, production editor Rebecca Springer, Laura Brady, who presided over the photo section, and Melissa Dobson, the dedicated copyeditor.

And finally, I am enormously grateful to my wife, Joan, who over these many long months heard more about Chinese spies than she may have wanted to know but who was always patient and supportive. Her love and understanding deserve the most thanks of all.

— DAVID WISE
Washington, DC
October 1, 2010

# NOTES

Unless otherwise noted, the interviews cited were conducted by the author. The Intelligence Resource Program of the Federation of American Scientists (http://www.fas.org/irp) archives a variety of resources relating to intelligence matters. Links to documents available at the FAS website have been included in notes where possible.

*Key to abbreviations for documents cited in* PARLOR MAID *case:*

RT: Affidavit of FBI special agent Randall Thomas for complaint and arrest warrant of Katrina Leung, April 8, 2003.

RT2: Affidavit of FBI special agent Randall Thomas for search warrant of Leungs' bookstore and home, December 20, 2002.

OIG DOJ: Office of Inspector General, Department of Justice, Unclassified Executive Summary, "A Review of the FBI's Handling and Oversight of FBI Asset Katrina Leung."

## PRELUDE

page

1 *VIP audience of one thousand at the Biltmore Hotel in Los Angeles:* Matt Krasnowski, "Ambivalence, Excitement, Anger to Greet Chinese President Jiang in Los Angeles," Copley News Service, October 31, 1997; K. Connie Kang and David Rosenzweig,

"Plain-Faced L.A. Consulate Is No Ordinary Installation," *Los Angeles Times*, November 2, 1997, p. A14.

*"One silver moon over the window sill"*: the description of President Jiang Zemin's vocalizing is from Kam Leung interview, June 26, 2003.

2  *"You won't believe who I just ran into. . . . It was Gwo-bao Min"*: I. C. Smith interviews, May 1, 2003, July 1, 2003, and July 7, 2010. See also I. C. Smith, *Inside: A Top G-Man Exposes Spies, Lies, and Bureaucratic Bungling in the FBI* (Nashville, TN: Nelson Current, 2004), p. 121. In his book, Smith refers to Min as "Mr. Lee," and writes that the FBI would not allow him to use "Mr. Lee's" true name or the code name of the investigation.

3  *"the same guy kept showing up"*: Smith interview, May 1, 2003.

4  *"Neither one of us believed in coincidences"*: Ibid.

## 1. "A THOUSAND GRAINS OF SAND"

7  *The secret headquarters of the Ministry of State Security:* Discussion of the history and organization of the MSS draws upon the Intelligence Resource Program of the Federation of American Scientists, http://www.fas.org/irp; multiple interviews with former US counterintelligence agents; Jeffrey T. Richelson, *Foreign Intelligence Organizations* (Cambridge, MA: Ballinger Publishing Co., 1988), chap. 9; Patrick E. Tyler, "Cloak and Dragon; There Is No Chinese James Bond. So Far," *New York Times*, March 23, 1997, sec. 4, p. 1; Lo Ping, "Secrets About CPC Spies — Tens of Thousands of Them Scattered Over 170-Odd Cities Worldwide," *Cheng Ming* (Hong Kong), January 1, 1997, pp. 6–9 (US Foreign Broadcast Information Service [FBIS] Daily Reports, CHI-97-016, January 1, 1997); Tan Po, "Spy Headquarters Behind the Shrubs — Supplement to 'Secrets About CPC Spies,'" *Cheng Ming*, March 1, 1997, pp. 34–37 (FBIS Daily Reports, CHI-97-047, March 1, 1997).

*Chien Men, which means "front door"*: Chien Men is also the name of Beijing's main gate, the scene of heavy fighting by US Marines in August 1900 during the Boxer Rebellion.

8  *Geng Huichang, fifty-six . . . moved up to become MSS chief:* Jim Yardley, "China Replaces Key Ministers," *New York Times*, August 31, 2007; see also Xinhua News Agency, August 31, 2007, cited in "Who's Who in China's Leadership," China Internet Information Center, http://www.china.org.cn/english/MATERIAL/222718 .htm.

9  *Zou spoke of the "tens of thousands of nameless heroes . . ."*: Ping, "Secrets About CPC Spies."

*Sun Tzu . . . is credited with writing the classic treatise Ping-fa, or The Art of War:* The discussion of Sun Tzu's five kinds of intelligence agents is adapted from Allen Dulles, *The Craft of Intelligence* (New York: Harper & Row, 1963), p. 13.

10  *"Know the enemy and know yourself . . ."*: There are various versions of this quotation attributed to Sun Tzu. One rendering often quoted and paraphrased appears in *Sun*

*Tzu on the Art of War,* translated from the Chinese with an introduction and critical notes by Lionel Giles (London: Luzac & Co., 1910), chap. 3, par. 18: "If you know the enemy and know yourself, you need not fear the result of a hundred battles."

*Kang Sheng was the sinister and powerful spymaster:* David Wise and Thomas B. Ross, *The Espionage Establishment* (New York: Random House, 1967), pp. 176–79; Roger Faligot and Remi Kauffer, *The Chinese Secret Service* (New York: William Morrow & Co., Inc., 1987), pp. 10–14ff.

*"a thousand grains of sand":* Paul Moore interview, July 2, 2003.

11  *a modern complex in Yasenevo:* The description of the KGB's foreign intelligence headquarters off the Moscow ring road is based on personal observation. The author was the first Western writer allowed to visit the complex. See David Wise, "Closing Down the K.G.B.," *New York Times Magazine,* November 24, 1991, pp. 30–32, 68.

12  *"China has a different approach to intelligence":* Moore interview, August 19, 2008. Moore's quotes in this chapter on Chinese intelligence methods and how they differ from Russian tradecraft are from this interview and the July 2003 interview cited earlier.

13  *"You may be talking about a different kind of espionage":* John F. Lewis Jr. interview, July 26, 1999.

*"discreetly dipping their ties":* Terrorism and Intelligence Operations: Hearing Before the Joint Economic Committee, *Congress of the United States,* 105th Cong. (May 20, 1998), statement by Nicholas Eftimiades, http://www.fas.org/irp/congress/1998_hr/eftimiad.htm.

14  *the most bizarre example . . . is the case of Bernard Boursicot:* Richard Bernstein, "France Jails 2 in Odd Case of Espionage," *New York Times,* May 11, 1986, p. 7; "France Pardons Chinese Spy Who Pretended to Be Woman," *New York Times,* April 10, 1987; Richelson, *Foreign Intelligence Organizations,* pp. 300–1. *M. Butterfly,* the Broadway play based on the Boursicot story, is discussed in Jeremy Gerard, "David Hwang: Riding on the Hyphen," *New York Times Magazine,* March 13, 1998.

16  *[Footnote] "After he showed me the code keys":* Boris Solomatin interview, Moscow, September 24, 1991.

*American technology companies "are purchased outright by Chinese state-run firms":* Terrorism and Intelligence Operations: Hearing, Eftimiades statement.

17  *More than 127,000 students:* Institute of International Education, data for 2009–2010, http://www.iie.org.

*"over 25,000 Chinese visit the United States each year as members of official delegations":* Interagency OPSEC Support Staff, *Intelligence Threat Handbook,* June 2004, http://www.fas.org/irp/threat/handbook/index.html.

*[Footnote] the Census Bureau survey:* US Census Bureau, S0201, Selected Population Profile in the United States, Population Group: Chinese Alone Data Set: 2009 American Community Survey 1-Year Estimates. Released September 28, 2010. Data for 2009.

*"all individuals of Chinese ancestry as 'overseas Chinese'"*: In "Report to Congress on Chinese Espionage Activities against the United States," December 12, 1999, http://www.fas.org/irp/threat/fis/prc_1999.html.

18 *"They are no more likely to commit espionage than any other American"*: Bruce Carlson interview, February 5, 2009.

## 2. PARLOR MAID

20 *"they knew we were coming before we even left"*: I. C. Smith interviews, May 1, 2003, and August 26, 2008.

*code name Luo, and . . . Mao*: The intercepted conversations between Leung and her Chinese spy handler are described in RT. During interviews with the FBI, "LEUNG stated . . . that 'Mao' was her MSS handler, and 'Luo' was her MSS alias." RT, p. 11. A brief excerpt of one recorded conversation appears in Bill Gertz, *Enemies: How America's Foes Steal Our Vital Secrets — and How We Let It Happen* (New York: Crown Forum, 2006), pp. 22–23.

21 *He had become Katrina Leung's lover three years earlier*: The FBI conducted four interviews with William Cleveland. During the second interview he "admitted that he had a long-term sexual relationship with LEUNG." In the fourth interview he said it had begun in 1988. The FBI documents do not name Cleveland but clearly describe the subject as the former special supervisory agent in charge of the Chinese counterintelligence squad in San Francisco. RT, pp. 18–19.

*Almost from the start, J.J. had begun a sexual relationship of his own with Ms. Leung*: The relationship began in August 1983, a year after J.J. first interviewed her. OIG DOJ, p. 6.

24 *"I made the recommendation we move forward with the case"*: Paul Moore interview, August 19, 2008.

26 *the FBI's technicians had succeeded in bugging the consulate's copying machines*: Interviews with former FBI agents. According to the *Newsweek* article, the $3,000 check from the Chinese consulate was paid to the Hollywood Metropolitan Hotel, owned by Ted Sioeng.

*"if we close it down, does she stop going to China?"*: Moore interview, August 19, 2008.

27 *She also agreed from then on to provide everything she knew about FBI operations to the MSS*: RT2, pp. 20–22. Exactly when the MSS recruited Leung is unclear. A 2003 government "Memorandum of Points and Authorities" states that "in 1990 . . . she began work for the Ministry of State Security ('MSS'), which is the PRC's spy service" (Memorandum, pp. 7–8). Similarly, a Justice Department review says that "according to Smith's contemporary notes, he confronted Leung about her alias and . . . Leung responded that the PRC had discovered her relationship with the FBI in 1990 and had coerced her into cooperating with them" (OIG DOJ, p. 10). Since Leung, in the confrontation in her kitchen, claimed she had begun cooperating with the MSS in 1986 or 1987, it is uncertain why Smith's "contemporary notes"

would have fixed the date as 1990. However, Leung knew from the confrontation with Smith that her conversation with Mao had been intercepted in 1990. Since that date appeared to be the FBI's first irrefutable, documented evidence that she had been working for China, she or Smith would have had no incentive to disclose that she had cooperated with the MSS prior to that time, if she had done so.

28  *J.J. . . . made her apologize to Cleveland in a San Francisco hotel room:* RT2, p. 21.

## 3. THE RECRUITMENT

29  *It was there that Katrina Leung was born:* Biographical details of Katrina Leung's early life, immigration to the United States, and marriage are from Kam Leung interviews, June 25, 2003, and June 26, 2003.
   *"Katrina sleepwalks":* Kam Leung quotes in this chapter are from the interviews cited above.

30  *Kam Leung was born in Hong Kong in 1951:* Details of Kam Leung's background are from Kam Leung interviews cited above.

32  *the FBI began a full field investigation of Katrina:* The two FBI investigations of Katrina Leung prior to her recruitment by the FBI are described in OIG DOJ, pp. 3–4.

## 4. DOUBLE GAME

35  *"But J.J. was a rare duck, he went into FCI":* John L. Hoos interview, June 10, 2003.
   *By August 1983 they had hopped into bed:* OIG DOJ, p. 6.
   *in June 1983 convicted of espionage in a Beijing court:* Richard Bernstein, "China Said to Jail Ex-U.S. Attorney," *New York Times*, January 20, 1984; Michael Weisskopf, "Peking Imprisons Harvard-Educated Hong Kong Lawyer as Spy," *Washington Post*, February 1, 1984, p. A27.

36  *J.J.'s first major assignment for Katrina:* I. C. Smith interview, August 26, 2008.
   *"I said, 'Dammit, J.J., where's the fucking beef?'":* Ibid.

37  *"she knocked on the door of the MSS":* Kam Leung interview, June 25, 2003. This is the source of all quotes from Kam Leung in this chapter.

38  *contributing $10,000 to Los Angeles mayor Richard J. Riordan and $4,200 to Bill Simon Jr.:* Margaret Talev, "Spy Case Arrest Shocks GOP Friends," *Sacramento Bee*, April 11, 2003, p. A3.
   *the Leungs contributed some $27,000 to the Republican Party during the 1990s:* Dan Eggen and R. Jeffrey Smith, "Lieberman Seeks Donations Probe," *Washington Post*, April 27, 2003, p. A12.

39  *"She was the one who put the trip together":* Peter Woo interview, June 18, 2003.
   *"When you need to get something done with China":* K. Connie Kang and David Rosenzweig, "Plain-Faced L.A. Consulate Is No Ordinary Installation," *Los Angeles Times*, November 2, 1997, p. A14. The quote is attributed in the story to an unidentified "high-ranking Los Angeles city official."
   *more than half, $951,000, was paid to her after the FBI learned in 1991 that she had*

*passed unauthorized information to Mao Guohua:* RT, p. 26; United States v. James J. Smith, United States District Court for the Central District of California, original indictment, May 7, 2003, p. 15.

*Nortel, a major Canadian telecom company . . . paid her $1.2 million:* RT, pp. 21–22. *the Chinese government also paid her $100,000:* RT2, p. 22.

40 *J.J. would leave his briefcase open:* RT, pp. 14–15. The description of how Leung removed and copied documents from Smith's briefcase was provided by her in a series of videotaped interviews with the FBI in December 2002, and summarized in the FBI affidavits filed with the court.

## 5. DESTROY AFTER READING

43 *"He was the best I ever knew":* Kenneth J. Schiffer, quoted in Ian Hoffman, "Colleagues Taken Aback at FBI Agent's Indiscretion," *San Mateo County Times,* April 13, 2003.

*"he was holier than thou, you couldn't swear around him":* Interview with former FBI special agent, October 2008.

*With a reported bankroll of $250,000:* The account of the TIGER TRAP case, and the tasks the FBI believed had been given to Chien Ning, is based on multiple interviews with former US counterintelligence agents.

*It clearly had the backing of the Chinese government at the highest level:* The description of *Science and Technology Review* is from Anthony Polsky, "China Science Journal Starts — Has Blessings of Chinese, US Governments," *Washington Post,* May 29, 1980, p. D3; "Science and Technology Review Put On Sale in China," Xinhua General News Service, January 28, 1980; and "New Science and Technology Journal," BBC Summary of World Broadcasts, February 9, 1980.

44 *With his Q clearance, he also had access to the design of every US nuclear missile:* Interviews with former FBI special agents; Select Committee on US National Security and Military/Commercial Concerns with the People's Republic of China, H.R. 105-851 (Cox Report) (1999), p. 87, which states that "the suspect" worked at Lawrence Livermore National Laboratory "and had access to classified information including designs for a number of US thermonuclear weapons"; Dan Stober, "How FBI Wiretap Launched Spy Case China Probe: Wen Ho Lee Phoned Nuclear Espionage Suspect, Now Identified," *San Jose Mercury News,* April 13, 2000, which names Gwo-bao Min as "the FBI's prime suspect in the alleged loss of neutron bomb secrets"; and Dan Stober and Ian Hoffman, *A Convenient Spy: Wen Ho Lee and the Politics of Nuclear Espionage* (New York: Simon & Schuster, 2001), chap. 5. The author telephoned Gwo-bao Min at his home in California on September 14, 2008, and asked to interview him for this book. He interrupted, said, "I'm not interested," and hung up. Two further attempts to contact Min, by a telephone message that day and by letter the next day, were unsuccessful.

45 *His work brought official recognition:* The role of Jerry Chih-li Chen, the TV-repair-

shop owner in Oakland, was described in Dan Grove interviews, November 25, 2008, December 20, 2008, and April 7, 2009, and by other FBI sources.

46  *Chien introduced him to Hanson Huang:* Chien Ning interview, March 26, 2009.
    *He was given several questions to take back to the States with him:* Interviews with former FBI special agents.
    *"there was reason to suspect me of that . . . but that's not true:* Chien interview, March 26, 2009. Other Chien quotes in chapter, as well as biographical details on Chien, are from this interview.
    *"I don't remember this person":* Doroteo Ng interview, April 16, 2009.

47  *Huang flew to San Francisco and met twice with the Livermore engineer:* Hanson Huang's role in the TIGER TRAP case is chronicled from multiple interviews with former FBI counterintelligence specialists. The author located Hanson Huang in Hong Kong, and exchanged e-mails with him on December 26, 2008. In his reply Huang wrote, "If you need any corroboration or confirmation on my part, please do not hesitate to contact me." But when the author responded the same day with specific questions about his relationship with Katrina Leung and Gwo-bao Min and asked to interview him, he did not reply.

48  *"He was always somebody with a cause":* Henry V. Huang interview, November 18, 2008.

49  *"This letter should be destroyed after reading":* Interviews with former FBI special agents, 2008 and 2009.

## 6. "HOLY SHIT, MR. GROVE!"

50  *the All-China Games in Beijing:* Also known as the National Games, the sports event was inaugurated in 1959 and held at four-year intervals thereafter. The games, a sort of mini Olympics, were designed to demonstrate the prowess of Chinese athletes to invited guests and dignitaries from other countries.

51  *"They're going to be after you":* Dan Grove interview, October 28, 2008.
    *"Holy shit, Mr. Grove! You'll never guess what I have":* Ibid.

52  *The measurement technique was based on "Teller light":* See W. E. Ogle, *An Account of the Return to Nuclear Weapons Testing by the United States after the Test Moratorium 1958–1961* (Las Vegas, NV: Department of Energy Nuclear Testing Archive, 1985), pp. 59, 60, 62; Samuel Glasstone and Philip J. Dolan, *The Effects of Nuclear Weapons,* 3rd ed. (Washington, DC: US Department of Defense and Energy Research and Development Administration, 1977), pp. 73, 75–76, 343–45.

53  *"If the FBI found the wrong things in his baggage he would be arrested":* Paul Moore interview, August 19, 2008.

54  *A highly dedicated FBI agent reconstructed the cards:* Ibid.

56  *"I wish to congratulate you":* Interview with former counterintelligence agent, October 2008.

57  *seventy-six spies had been prosecuted, and all but one convicted:* George Lardner Jr., "Spy Nemesis Crosses Last Bridge," *Washington Post,* July 31, 1997, p. A13.

58 *Robert McFarlane, who held that post under President Ronald Reagan:* McFarlane pleaded guilty to withholding information from Congress about the Iran-Contra affair, and was later pardoned by President George H. W. Bush.

59 *"Put it in a ball and throw it on the floor and it will go off":* George Keyworth interview, November 10, 2009.

*"he was made aware of certain gaps in US intelligence":* Kenneth J. Schiffer interview, May 26, 2009.

*"how it was possible to circumvent their question":* Keyworth interview, November 10, 2009. Nineteen years after his 1980 trip to China, a congressional committee investigating the transfer of nuclear weapons technology to China (the Cox Committee), without naming Keyworth, excoriated him for "the inadvertent, bordering on negligent, disclosure of classified technical information" to the Chinese. Select Committee on U.S. National Security and Military/Commercial Concerns with the People's Republic of China, H.R. 105-851 (Cox Report) (1999), p. 91. Keyworth told the author, however, that the Cox Committee "never interviewed me." See also James Risen, "In China, Physicist Learns, He Tripped Between Useful Exchange and Security Breach," *New York Times,* August 1, 1999, p. 10. The story quotes Keyworth as saying that the simple physics analogy he provided the Chinese was "absolutely unclassified."

60 *He offered to find out who had "squealed" on Gwo-bao Min:* Arlen Specter, US Senate, *Report on the Investigation of Espionage Allegations Against Dr. Wen Ho Lee* (Specter Report), March 8, 2000, p. 6, http://www.fas.org/irp/congress/2000_rpt/specter.html.

*"Lee thought [Min] was in trouble for doing the same sort of thing that Lee had been doing for Taiwan":* US Senate, Committee on the Judiciary, Redacted Transcript of Closed Hearing with Attorney General Janet Reno Regarding the FISA Process in the Wen Ho Lee Case, June 8, 1999, p. 15.

*the FBI was worried that "Lee might be acting on behalf of a Taiwan intelligence service":* US Department of Justice, *Final Report of the Attorney General's Review Team on the Handling of the Los Alamos National Laboratory Investigation* (Bellows Report) (May 2000), declassified version released December 12, 2001, p. 23.

61 *Lee lied to the FBI and although asked several times, said that he "had never attempted to contact" Min:* Redacted Transcript of Closed Hearing with Attorney General Janet Reno, p. 15.

*Lee . . . "provided truthful answers only when confronted with irrefutable evidence":* Bellows Report, p. 41.

*the FBI had enlisted Lee's help:* Bellows Report, p. 37.

62 *"She was a very kind of mysterious person":* Federico C. Sayre interview, March 2, 2009.

*"The Chinese Ministry of Materials asked my help to get scrap metals":* Chien Ning interview, March 26, 2009.

63 *"According to Cleveland, Leung initiated their relationship":* OIG DOJ, p. 8.

## 7. RIDING THE TIGER: CHINA AND THE NEUTRON BOMB

65 *The committee issued an unclassified version of its . . . report:* Final Report, unclassified version, of the Select Committee on US National Security and Military/Commercial Concerns with the People's Republic of China, H.R. Rep. 105-851 (Cox Report) (1999).

*"has stolen classified design information" . . . enabling the PRC to develop and test strategic nuclear weapons "sooner than would otherwise have been possible":* Cox Report, Overview, p. 2.

67 *"the PRC stole design information on the U.S. W-70 warhead from Lawrence Livermore Laboratory":* Cox Report, p. 87.

*"further information about these thefts cannot be publicly disclosed":* Ibid.

69 *a thirty-six-page angry rebuttal to the Cox Report:* Information Office of the State Council, China, "Facts Speak Louder Than Words and Lies Will Collapse on Themselves," July 15, 1999, http://www.china-embassy.org/eng/zmgx/zmgx/Political%20Relationship/t35103.htm.

*"China Masters Neutron Bomb Technology":* Seth Faison, "China Proclaims It Designed Its Own Neutron Bomb," *New York Times,* July 15, 1999.

*China "had successfully stolen" more secret information about the neutron bomb:* Cox Report, p. 87.

70 *because the Chinese test in 1988 was not successful:* Shirley A. Kan, *China: Suspected Acquisition of US Nuclear Weapon Secrets,* CRS Report for Congress, February 1, 2006, p. 4.

*"including . . . the neutron bomb":* Central Intelligence Agency, "Key Findings: The Intelligence Community Damage Assessment on the Implications of China's Acquisition of US Nuclear Weapons Information on the Development of Future Chinese Weapons," April 21, 1999, https://www.cia.gov/news-information/press-releases-statements/press-release-archive-1999/key-findings.html.

## 8. THE WALK-IN

72 *He threw the duffle bag out of a second-story window:* Interview with US counterintelligence officer, 2009.

73 *CIA headquarters officials then gave provisional operational approval to enroll the walk-in:* Interview with CIA Directorate of Operations officer, 1999.

74 *the Chinese secret document . . . gave the exact diameter of the W-88's primary, 115mm, or about four and a half inches. . . . the W-88's primary was "two-point aspherical" . . . the radius of the round secondary [w]as 172mm, or just under 7 inches, and . . . the primary of the W-88 was at the tapered tip of the warhead, forward of the secondary. . . . the overall length of the warhead [w]as 1522mm, or 5 feet:* Ibid.

76 *"its most survivable and enduring nuclear strike capability":* Website of the US

Navy, Fact File, "Fleet Ballistic Missile Submarines," http://www.navy.mil/navy data/fact_display.asp?cid=4100&tid=200&ct=4.

*"A single broadside from such a submarine — all 24 missiles fired at the same time — can destroy any nation on the face of the earth"*: Captain Edward L. Beach, USN (ret), "The Submarine Mission Today," *Undersea Warfare* 2, no. 3 (spring 2000).

77 *"his answer went off the charts"*: Interview with CIA Directorate of Operations officer, 1999.

*"We didn't like the way this whole thing looked"*: Interview with former US intelligence official, September 2008.

*"She must have a big 'No' stamp"*: Interview with former FBI special agent, 2009.

78 *"There is a high possibility of failure unless you understand these weapons"*: Interview with CIA Directorate of Operations officer, 1999.

*"whatever they got saved them time, maybe two to fifteen years"*: Ibid.

*"has stolen classified information on all of the United States' most advanced thermonuclear warheads"*: Final Report, unclassified version, of the Select Committee on US National Security and Military/Commercial Concerns with the People's Republic of China, H.R. Rep. 105-851 (Cox Report) (1999), p. 60.

79 China was *"capable of producing small thermonuclear warheads based on the stolen U.S. design information, including the stolen W-88 information"*: Ibid, p. 61.

*"the PRC had conducted only 45 nuclear tests in the more than 30 years from 1964 to 1996"*: Ibid., p. 76.

*"China obtained at least basic design information on several modern US nuclear reentry vehicles, including the Trident II (W-88) . . . and weaponization features, including those of the neutron bomb"*: Central Intelligence Agency, "Key Findings: The Intelligence Community Damage Assessment on the Implications of China's Acquisition of US Nuclear Weapons Information on the Development of Future Chinese Weapons," April 21, 1999, https://www.cia.gov/news-information/press-releases-statements/press-release-archive-1999/key-findings.html.

## 9. KINDRED SPIRIT: WEN HO LEE

81 *Counterintelligence at the department was "little more than a joke"*: Notra Trulock interviews, August 5, 1999, and July 23, 2009.

82 *China, in achieving a small warhead in a very short time, probably gained its success through espionage*: Notra Trulock, *Code Name Kindred Spirit: Inside the Chinese Nuclear Espionage Scandal* (San Francisco: Encounter Books, 2003), p. 72.

*In September, DOE opened a formal investigation*: US Department of Justice, *Final Report of the Attorney General's Review Team on the Handling of the Los Alamos National Laboratory Investigation* (Bellows Report) (May 2000), p. 275.

83 *[Footnote] A secret Justice Department report*: "Executive Summary of the OPR Report on the Investigation and Prosecution of Wen Ho Lee," p. 255. The report, produced by the Justice Department's Office of Professional Responsibility, was classi-

fied SECRET/NOFORN/RESTRICTED DATA but later declassified. It was released to the author under a Freedom of Information Act request.

*"There were Americans of Chinese origin and not of Chinese origin on the list"*: Trulock interviews, August 5, 1999, and July 23, 2009.

*"An initial consideration will be to identify those US citizens, of Chinese heritage"*: Daniel J. Bruno memorandum, quoted in Trulock, *Code Name Kindred Spirit*, p. 111.

*"there are seven Chinese restaurants in Los Alamos"*: Bellows Report, p. 385.

*"no evidence of racial bias" by DOE*: Ibid., p. 342.

84 *"a virtual indictment of the Lees"*: Ibid., p. 341.

Wen Ho Lee *"was the only individual identified during this inquiry"*: Ibid., quoting the DOE report.

*"Wen Ho Lee was its man"*: Bellows Report, p. 378.

*the scientist was singled out "because Lee is ethnic Chinese"*: Declaration of Robert Vrooman in United States v. Wen Ho Lee, 99-CR-1417, August 10, 2000, http://www.fas.org/irp/ops/ci/vrooman.html.

*the cause was not "ethnic profiling or racism"*: PBS, *The NewsHour with Jim Lehrer*, September 13, 2000, http://www.pbs.org/newshour/bb/law/july-dec00/wenholee_9-13.html.

*he read "in a popular Chinese-language magazine" that "a Taiwanese nuclear scientist was fired from Lawrence Livermore"*: Wen Ho Lee, with Helen Zia, *My Country Versus Me: The First-Hand Account by the Los Alamos Scientist Who Was Falsely Accused of Being a Spy* (New York: Hyperion, 2001), p. 24.

85 *"Ko Pau Ming," whom he knew was from Taiwan, "was having trouble with some men in China" and "out of curiosity" had telephoned him*: "Psychophysiological Detection of Deception (PDD) Examination of Wen H. Lee," Wackenhut polygraph report to Edward J. Curran, director, DOE Office of Counterintelligence, December 28, 1998, Defendant's Exhibit A, United States v. Wen Ho Lee.

*Min was later identified by name*: Dan Stober, "How FBI Wiretap Launched Spy Case China Probe: Wen Ho Lee Phoned Nuclear Espionage Suspect, Now Identified," *San Jose Mercury News*, April 13, 2000.

*Lee went up to Hu and was warmly embraced by the top Chinese weapons scientist*: Matthew Purdy, "The Making of a Suspect: The Case of Wen Ho Lee," *New York Times*, February 4, 2001, p. 18.

*"We know him very well. He came to Beijing and helped us a lot"*: Arlen Specter, US Senate, *Report on the Government's Handling of the Investigation and Prosecution of Dr. Wen Ho Lee*, December 20, 2001 (Specter Report II), http://www.fas.org/irp/congress/2001_rpt/whl.html.

86 *"he did not know the answer" and did not wish to discuss the matter*: Affidavit of FBI special agent Michael W. Lowe in support of search warrant to search the home of Wen Ho Lee, April 9, 1999, p. 3. The quote describes Lee's answer when questioned by the FBI on January 17, 1999 about the hotel room episode. http://www.fas.org/irp/ops/ci/lowe_affidavit.html.

*Lee . . . omitted any mention of his hotel room meeting with Hu Side*: Robert S.

Vrooman interview, August 15, 2009, and Robert S. Vrooman, "Clinton's Scape-goat: The Persecution of an American Scientist," unpublished manuscript, p. 68 (Robert S. Vrooman Collection Pertaining to Wen Ho Lee and Los Alamos National Laboratory, Center for Southwest Research, University Libraries, University of New Mexico). Vrooman writes that his notes from his interview with Wen Ho Lee after the 1988 trip show that "Lee did not tell me about the incident with Hu Side. It was not just an oversight, because the entire purpose of my meeting with him was to learn if something like this had happened. He answered no to a direct question. He lied to me."

*on May 30, 1996, at the request of DOE, the FBI opened a full-fledged investigation of Wen Ho and Sylvia Lee:* Bellows Report, p. 290.

*In 1999, months after Wen Ho Lee was fired from the Los Alamos lab, a broader investigation was finally begun by the FBI:* Bellows Report, p. 364; Stephen W. Dillard interview, October 16, 2009.

*"the FBI investigated the wrong crime":* Bellows Report, p. 336.

*With his brothers and sisters, he caught fish and frogs each day for dinner:* Wen Ho Lee biographical details are from Lee, *My Country Versus Me*, pp. 21, 97–99, 100, 165–68.

87 *She also reported to the FBI and the CIA on what she gleaned from those contacts:* Purdy, "Making of a Suspect."

88 *An FBI agent who was a Chinese American telephoned Lee, claiming he was "a representative of the 'concerned department' from Beijing":* Specter Report II. Other details of the failed "sting" operation against Wen Ho Lee are cited in the same report.

90 *It . . . described "the main suspect" as "a Los Alamos computer scientist who is Chinese-American":* James Risen and Jeff Gerth, "China Stole Nuclear Secrets for Bombs, U.S. Aides Say," *New York Times*, March 6, 1999, p. A1.

*Trulock had leaked the story to the* Times, *a fact he later publicly confirmed on CBS's* 60 Minutes: Notra Trulock, interview by Lesley Stahl, *60 Minutes*, December 17, 2000, CBS News Transcript, p. 4. "Mr. TRULOCK: I reached out to the New York Times. . . . Yes, I did."

*"There's a person at the laboratory that's committed espionage and that points to you!":* Excerpts from the FBI interrogation of Wen Ho Lee are from the Bellows Report, pp. 649–51, and "Executive Summary of the OPR Report on the Investigation and Prosecution of Wen Ho Lee," pp. 152–61.

93 *operation* SEA CHANGE: Dan Stober and Ian Hoffman, *A Convenient Spy: Wen Ho Lee and the Politics of Nuclear Espionage* (New York: Simon & Schuster, 2001), p. 213.

94 *"I feel like a pariah in this department":* Trulock interview, August 5, 1999.

*"The truth is I'm innocent":* Wen Ho Lee, interview by Mike Wallace, *60 Minutes*, August 1, 1999, CBS News Transcript, p. 1.

95 *"change the global strategic balance":* Matthew Purdy with James Sterngold, "The Prosecution Unravels: The Case of Wen Ho Lee," *New York Times*, February 5, 2001, p. A1.

96 *"I believe you were terribly wronged"*: "Statement by Judge in Los Alamos Case, With Apology for Abuse of Power," *New York Times,* September 24, 2000, p. A 21.

97 *the suit was settled for $1,645,000:* Paul Farhi, "U.S., Media Settle with Wen Ho Lee," *Washington Post,* June 3, 2006, p. A1.

## 10. SEGO PALM

100 *"I got a phone call out of the blue from Bob Bryant"*: Stephen W. Dillard interview, August 28, 2009.
    *an "overall investigation" . . . "to examine other potential areas of compromise"*: Ibid. *Dillard put together a task force of three hundred people in eleven government agencies:* Ibid.

101 *the information in the walk-in document "had to have come from X Division"*: Ibid.

103 *"the FBI's own lack of investigative interest in looking beyond Wen Ho Lee"*: US Department of Justice, *Final Report of the Attorney General's Review Team on the Handling of the Los Alamos National Laboratory Investigation* (Bellows Report) (May 2000), p. 342.

104 *the information obtained by China had come from more than one document:* Dillard interview, August 28, 2009.
    *four scientists at the lab believed that the documents originated with a defense contractor in Colorado Springs:* Robert S. Vrooman, "Memo for the Record," September 21, 1999, Operation Fallout, Robert S. Vrooman Collection Pertaining to Wen Ho Lee and Los Alamos National Laboratory, Center for Southwest Research, University Libraries, University of New Mexico.

105 *"It is clear that you did not give proper attention to your driving"*: J. Edgar Hoover letter to Kenneth J. Schiffer, March 16, 1970. Schiffer showed the letter, framed on the wall of his study, to the author during an interview at his home on August 13, 2009. *Schiffer was required to learn Toishan:* Kenneth J. Schiffer interview, May 26, 2009. *the walk-in's document on the W-88 appeared to match a 1986 "interface" document:* Ibid.

106 *"If you translated the US document . . . back to inches there could be a slight discrepancy"*: Raymond H. Wickman interview, October 27, 2008.

108 *"the compromises were likely to have been made by either multiple personnel or multiple means over a several-year period from the '70s to the early '90s"*: Dillard interview, August 28, 2009.

## 11. TROUBLE IN PARADISE

110 *"Secretary Jiang asked, 'What are President BUSH's chances of being reelected?'"*: This and the other quotes from the Chinese leaders and Leung are from J.J. Smith report to headquarters on Leung's 1991 meeting in Beijing, FBI Leung Asset File, US Department of Justice, Exhibit 18, United States v. Katrina Leung.

112 *Lei Feng Day, named for the national hero: People's Daily Online* (English), "Lei

Feng Remembered throughout China," March 3, 2003, http://English.peopledaily
.com.cn.

113  *she had acquired the code name Luo from none other than Zhu Qizhen:* RT2, p. 21.
   PARLOR MAID *asked an official in the Chinese consulate in San Francisco to call her
   from a pay phone:* OIG DOJ, p. 7.

114  *the FBI received the information that* PARLOR MAID *had tipped off the Chinese to
   the FBI's bugging of China's consulate in Los Angeles:* Multiple interviews with former FBI counterintelligence agents; and OIG DOJ, which obliquely refers to the
   consulate bugging as information received by the FBI "indicating that Leung had
   disclosed to PRC officials the existence and location of a then-active sensitive technical operation."
   PARLOR MAID *could not have informed the Chinese of the electronic eavesdropping of
   the Los Angeles consulate, because J.J. himself did not know about it:* OIG DOJ, p. 9.
   *At the very time that J.J. was investigating Miller:* OIG DOJ, p. 7.

115  *The videotape showed the entrance and then a courtyard inside the spy headquarters:*
   Interview with former US intelligence agent.
   *It was, one of the CIA officers remarked, "too good to be true":* Ibid.
   *Kelly was startled to see both J.J. and* PARLOR MAID, *whom she knew, going through
   customs:* OIG DOJ, p. 12.

116  *the supervisor "was overly dependent on Smith, reluctant to confront him, and inappropriately deferential to him":* Ibid.
   *a woman named "Katrina" was a double agent "working in the FBI":* OIG DOJ, p. 13.

117  *"We really like your President," General Ji said, according to Chung:* David Johnston,
   "Committee Told of Beijing Cash for Democrats," *New York Times,* May 12, 1999.
   *General Ji fared less well:* Erik Eckholm, "China Widening Crackdown on Corrup-
   tion," *New York Times,* December 23, 2000.

118  *China's most popular cigarette, Hongtashan, marketed abroad as the Red Pagoda
   Mountain brand:* K. Connie Kang and David Rosenzweig, "Entrepreneur Formed
   Ties to China, Then Politicians," *Los Angeles Times,* May 18, 1997, p. 1.
   *"If China needed a good agent":* Ibid.

119  *several assets originally recruited by the bureau had been seized and interrogated in
   China:* OIG DOJ, p. 16.
   *an informant . . . reported that Leung was working for a PRC spy service and had a
   source inside the FBI:* Ibid.
   *the same informant reported that Leung was "in bed with" the FBI's LA division:* Ibid.

## 12. ETHEREAL THRONE: THE SPY WHO NEVER WAS

123  *Unknown to Jeff Wang and his wife, he had been under investigation by the FBI for
   more than a year:* Interviews with former FBI agents.

125  *she was told to renew their friendship, to take advantage of it, and become close to Jeff:*
   Jack Keller interview, June 13, 2003.

126  *she greatly impressed her boss:* Ibid.

127 *Although the informant could not see what was inside the envelopes, he assumed that cash had been exchanged for secret documents:* Interviews with former FBI agents, and OIG DOJ, p. 15. The Justice Department review describes the informant's claims, without identifying Jeffrey Wang or Denise Woo.

129 *an informant it had relied upon for years had concealed the fact that his wife was Jeff Wang's cousin:* Interviews with former FBI agents.

131 *"She was a fantastic agent. . . . She was outstanding, extremely diligent and conscientious":* Marc S. Harris interview, March 12, 2009.
*took the case pro bono:* Mark C. Holscher interview, March 30, 2009.
*the bureau fired her:* OIG DOJ, p. 15.
*In the indictment of Woo, Wang was not identified. He was referred to only as "J.W.":* United States v. Denise K. Woo, US District Court for the Central District of California, 04-CR-1141, December 2, 2004, p. 2; and David Rosenzweig and Greg Krikorian, "Ex-Agent Indicted in Spying Probe," *Los Angeles Times,* December 11, 2004.

132 *"discussed with and thereby disclosed to J.W. confidential information concerning the identity of an FBI confidential informant":* United States v. Denise K. Woo, "Binding Plea Agreement for Defendant Denise K. Woo," p. 3.
*"This is a kind of bittersweet ending to a long and continuing tragic injustice":* Greg Krikorian, "Ex-FBI Agent Is Sentenced in Plea Agreement," *Los Angeles Times,* October 31, 2006, Metro, p. 3.
*"She was put in a horrible position of investigating a family friend":* Holscher interview, March 30, 2009.
*J.J. had briefed Katrina Leung on the Jeff Wang investigation and consulted her on all details of the case:* OIG DOJ, p. 15. The Justice Department report refers to Jeff Wang only as "a Chinese American employee of a defense contractor."

133 *accusing her of having told the MSS about his relationship with the FBI:* OIG DOJ, p. 16. The Justice Department report does not identify the informant.
*He also claimed that Leung had told Beijing about the . . . investigation:* Ibid.
*he was dropped from the FBI payroll for lying:* Interviews with FBI officials and a former FBI counterintelligence agent.
*"A truly innocent man and his family suffered some very damaging consequences":* Brian A. Sun interview, August 26, 2009.

## 13. STORM CLOUDS

135 *In 2001 the Chinese uncovered twenty-seven satellite-operated listening devices that the National Security Agency and the FBI had planted in the Chinese version of Air Force One:* John Pomfret, "China Finds Bugs on Jet Equipped in U.S.," *Washington Post,* January 19, 2002.

136 *[Footnote] "My client flat-out did not talk about the plane with her":* James Risen and Eric Lichtblau, "Spy Suspect May Have Told Chinese of Bugs, U.S. Says," *New York Times,* April 15, 2003.

*Gallagher flew to Los Angeles to talk to Ron Iden:* Neil Gallagher interview, October 13, 2008.

*the relationship between J.J. and Leung was "more than friendship":* OIG DOJ, p. 18.

137 *he went ballistic:* Interview with former FBI agent, June 24, 2003.

*The atmosphere was beyond tense:* OIG DOJ, p. 18. The report euphemistically notes that the FBI director "expressed concern about the pace and scope of the investigation."

*"Who's in charge?" Mueller demanded:* Interview with former FBI agent, June 24, 2003.

*she was in the bull's-eye and received the full fury of Mueller's wrath:* David Johnston, "F.B.I. Agent Ousted Over Her Handling of a Spying Inquiry," *New York Times,* January 30, 2002.

## 14. THE COUNTERSPY

141 *a yellow Post-it note that proved to be the smoking gun in the case:* David Wise, *Nightmover: How Aldrich Ames Sold the CIA to the KGB for $4.6 Million* (New York: HarperCollins, 1995), p. 237.

143 *there was a "big problem" with their bankruptcy plan:* Affidavit of FBI special agent Sharon Gardner Lawrence for search warrant for Leungs' bookstore and home, December 9, 2002, p. 18.

*"she could go to jail for filing a fraudulent bankruptcy petition":* Ibid., p. 19.

*bulging with magazines, newspapers, videos, and books:* Ibid., p. 27.

144 *"probably have, uh, faxed them":* Ibid., p. 15.

*"she stated that 'if one forges a signature, that's a very serious crime'":* Ibid., p. 25.

*Katrina Leung . . . had contacted Ron Iden:* RT2, p. 14.

145 *on November 5, 2002, the FBI videotaped J.J. Smith and PARLOR MAID in a Los Angeles hotel room:* RT, pp. 16–17.

*"The electronic surveillance revealed Smith and LEUNG having sexual relations":* Ibid., p. 17.

146 *"he had probably told LEUNG too much":* Ibid., p. 16.

*Smith replied, "She's, she was there":* Ibid., p. 17.

147 *Leung began describing classified documents she said she had secretly taken from J.J.'s briefcase and copied:* Ibid., pp. 14–15.

*she had first become intimate with him in the early 1980s, "Very long ago, but I cannot tell you what year":* Ibid., p. 9.

148 *the code name Luo Zhongshan had been assigned to her by none other than Zhu Qizhen, the Chinese ambassador to the United States:* RT2, p. 21.

*"I think I sneaked it":* RT, p. 14.

*J.J. "would leave his briefcase open":* Ibid.

149 *she "admitted that she provided intelligence she gained in this manner to the MSS":* Ibid., p. 15.

PARLOR MAID *admitted that China had paid her $100,000 because Chinese president Yang Shangkun "liked her":* RT2, p. 22.

150 *The document, dated June 12, 1997, was one of four discovered . . . in a bookcase on the second floor:* RT, p. 13.

*"to intercept the same intelligence":* Declassified FBI legat report, quoted in Bill Gertz, "China Sought System to Intercept U.S. Spy Data," *Washington Times,* September 12, 2005.

*The document said the MSS had offered a $1 million reward:* Ibid.

*the agents also found three other documents:* RT, pp. 12–13.

152 *At this initial interview, however, he did not reveal his own affair with Leung:* Ibid., p. 18.

*Not until a second meeting . . . did Cleveland confess to his own long-term sexual relationship with* PARLOR MAID: Ibid.

153 *"The FBI must now re-assess all of its actions and intelligence analyses based on her reporting":* RT2, p. 24.

*conducting a surveillance . . . for a corporate client of the Emerald Group, a private security firm:* Thomas R. Parker interview, June 10, 2003.

## 15. ROYAL TOURIST

154 *a miniature bug, a microphone that had been disguised to pick up conversations in the room:* Interviews with former FBI counterintelligence agents and statement of Jonathan S. Shapiro, assistant US attorney, Los Angeles, United States v. Peter Hoong Yee Lee, US District Court, Central District of California, Western Division, 97-CR-118 TJH, March 26, 1998, p. 23: "The defendant's wife found the bug which somewhat compromised its value to law enforcement."

155 *"at breakfast he tells a colleague that the strangest thing happened":* Paul Moore interview, August 19, 2008.

*the Joint UK/US Radar Ocean Imaging Program . . . to detect submarines moving underwater:* Arlen Specter, US Senate, *Report on the Investigation of Peter Lee,* prepared for the Senate Subcommittee on Department of Justice Oversight, December 20, 2001, p. 1, http://www.fas.org/irp/congress/2001_rpt/peterlee.html.

156 *he said the technology could also be used to detect submarines moving below the surface: The Peter Lee Case: Hearings Before the Subcommittee on Administrative Oversight and the Courts of the Committee on the Judiciary,* U.S. Senate, 106th Congress (March 29, April 5, and April 12, 2000), pp. 51, 252.

*he erased the graph and tore the photograph into small pieces:* Ibid., p. 252.

*Cordova interviewed Lee, who insisted, as he had on his travel form for TRW, that he had paid his own expenses:* Ibid., p. 21.

157 *Lee now admitted he had lied:* Specter, *Report on the Investigation of Peter Lee,* p. 5. The author reached Peter Lee by telephone at his home in California on March 23, 2009, and asked to interview him for this book. He twice said, "I'm not inter-

ested" and then hung up. Lee did not reply to a follow-up letter asking him to reconsider.

*Lee submitted the phony receipts to the FBI:* Specter, *Report on the Investigation of Peter Lee.*

*ICF, the use of lasers to attempt to trigger what amounted to miniature, tabletop thermonuclear explosions:* Final Report, unclassified version, of the Select Committee on US National Security and Military/Commercial Concerns with the People's Republic of China, H.R. Rep. 105-851 (Cox Report) (1999), p. 89.

158 *Lee met with Chen Nengkuan. . . . Chen told Lee he did not need to speak, he could just nod yes or no:* Specter, *Report on the Investigation of Peter Lee,* p. 4.

*For two hours, Lee answered questions and drew several diagrams, including sketches of hohlraums:* Ibid.

159 *"what I thought was a dead-bang case":* Jonathan S. Shapiro testimony, *Peter Lee Case: Hearings,* p. 71.

*"I strongly advocated for . . . pursuing Mr. Lee on charges of espionage":* Ibid., p. 70.

160 *With a narrow exception . . . the statutes do not penalize disclosure of classified documents as such but of information "relating to the national defense":* See David Wise, *The Politics of Lying* (New York: Random House, 1973), chap. 4 and pp. 65–66.

*in 2008 the government classified 23,421,098 documents:* Information Security Oversight Office, *Report to the President for Fiscal Year 2008,* p. 7.

*the Pentagon classified the fact that it was sending monkeys into space:* Wise, *Politics of Lying,* pp. 67–68.

161 *he could claim he was only trying to help persuade China not to conduct tests of nuclear weapons in the air:* Michael Liebman testimony, *The Peter Lee Case: Hearings,* pp. 125–26.

*the article discussed Livermore's role in the joint US/UK program:* "Radar Ocean Imaging," Lawrence Livermore National Laboratory website, http://www.llnl.gov, March 29, 1995; Ibid., p. 128.

*"important progress in the development of methods to detect submarine signatures with remote sensing radars":* Richard E. Twogood testimony to the Research and Technology Subcommittee, House Armed Services Committee, April 1994, *Peter Lee Case: Hearings,* p. 130.

162 *"my immediate response was that it is at least confidential, and I thought it was likely . . . secret":* Twogood testimony, *Peter Lee Case: Hearings,* p. 23.

*"Dr. Twogood, in my view, would have gone down in blue flames on cross-examination":* Shapiro testimony, *Peter Lee Case: Hearings,* p. 78.

*"I wasn't allowed to hook Mr. Lee up":* Ibid., p. 85.

163 *he opposed "a prosecution that might risk exposure of . . . ASW [antisubmarine warfare] information":* John G. Schuster testimony, *Peter Lee Case: Hearings,* p. 45.

*"the Navy's reluctance was a problem":* Jonathan S. Shapiro interview, January 14, 2009.

164 *"the FBI is much more interested in the intel yet to be garnered than in punishing*

*felons"*: Michael P. Dorris memorandum, November 25, 1997, *Peter Lee Case: Hearings*, p. 74.

*"I'm a one-trick pony"*: Shapiro testimony, *Peter Lee Case: Hearings*, p. 75.

*Lee thus was pleading guilty to revealing information in 1985 . . . on inertial confinement fusion. There was no mention in the plea bargain of the data he had revealed in 1997 about detecting submarines by radar:* Peter Lee Case: Hearings, p. 258.

165   *"to threaten previously invulnerable U.S. nuclear submarines"*: Cox Report, p. 88.

    *"had the potential of creating a widespread misperception"*: Peter Lee Case: Hearings, p. 38.

    *It was just "a scientific thing"*: Ibid., p. 315.

166   *the prosecutor displayed a hohlraum in court:* Ibid., p. 323.

    *"Please, your honor, don't put me in jail"*: Ibid., p. 333.

    *Hatter was skeptical of Lee's explanation:* Ibid., p. 332.

    *The Pentagon asked the Naval Criminal Investigative Service to conduct a "Project Slammer" interview with Lee:* Statement of Thomas A. Betro, NCIS, to U.S. Senate, Subcommittee on Administrative Oversight and the Courts, Senate Judiciary Committee, March 29, 2000. "Based on FBI recommendations, a Project Slammer interview was not conducted."

    *"the only reason it was classified was to get funding from Congress"*: James D. Henderson interview, July 16, 2009.

## 16. RICHARD NIXON AND THE HONG KONG HOSTESS

168   *"Intelligence was a cottage industry in Hong Kong"*: Milton A. Bearden interview, December 8, 2008.

    *"He said there's all kinds of reports about her working for the other side"*: Dan Grove interview, October 28, 2008.

    *"Spanos said she spent last night with Nixon"*: Grove interview, July 27, 2009.

    *" 'but Nixon is a US politician and just had a* TOP SECRET *briefing here' "*: Grove interview, October 28, 2008.

169   *"Spanos says, 'I understand you spent the night with the big man last night.' She giggles"*: Ibid.

    *"She said, 'Myself and Teresa entertained Nixon' "*: Perry J. Spanos interview, January 14, 2009.

    *"She swears they never even touched, and I believe her"*: Grove interview, October 28, 2008.

    *"The Brits said it's been reported to us several times she was a possible CHIS [Chinese intelligence service] agent"*: Ibid.

170   *"a regular bedmate of Vice-President Nixon when he visited Hong Kong"*: FBI memorandum, July 1976.

    *"Sullivan thought with this information Nixon would never get rid of Hoover"*: Grove interview, July 27, 2009. Sullivan's reaction, as related by Grove, that "Mr. Nixon's

private life is of no concern to this bureau," was both hilarious and ironic, given Hoover's exactly opposite reputation as an avid collector of personal gossip about political figures, one of the weapons the FBI director used successfully to maintain his power.

*he had asked Hoover to remain as FBI chief:* Robert B. Semple, "Nixon Will Retain Hoover and Helms," *New York Times,* December 17, 1968.

171 *Hoover dropped by the White House for a private lunch with President Kennedy:* "Alleged Assassination Plots Involving Foreign Leaders," An Interim Report of the Select Committee to Study Governmental Operations with Respect to Intelligence Activities, U.S. Senate, 94th Congress, 1st Session, S. Rep. 94-465 (1975), p. 130.

*"the last telephone contact between the White House and the President's friend [Judith Campbell] occurred a few hours after the luncheon":* Ibid. The Senate report adds, deadpan: "There is no record of what transpired at that luncheon."

*"'I'll handle this one,' Hoover said gleefully when I passed the letter on to him":* William C. Sullivan with Bill Brown, *The Bureau: My Thirty Years in Hoover's FBI* (New York: W. W. Norton & Co., 1979), p. 198.

172 *"From that time on the senator's right in his pocket":* Jack Nelson, "Wiretap Files Were Kept From Hoover, Aide Says," *Los Angeles Times,* May 15, 1973, p. A10.

*she confirmed that she and the other hostess had spent time with Nixon and Rebozo at the Mandarin Hotel:* Marianna Liu interview, December 12, 2008.

*"no love affair. We were friends. . . . I did not spend the night with Nixon":* Ibid.

*she thought they had seen each other on his trips to Hong Kong in 1964, 1965, and 1966:* John Crewdson, "F.B.I. Investigated Hong Kong Woman Friend of Nixon in '60's to Determine If She Was Foreign Agent," *New York Times,* June 22, 1976, p. 19.

173 *"I did not give information to PRC":* Liu interview, December 12, 2008.

*"He was shot somewhere in Shantung":* Liu interview, February 20, 2009.

*Liu moved to Whittier, California, Nixon's hometown:* Ibid.

174 *"Warren got me papers to take care of his wife":* Ibid.

*"Nixon Romanced Suspected Red Spy":* National Enquirer, August 10, 1976, p. 1.

*Liu denied many of the assertions in the tabloid's account:* Liu interview, February 20, 2009.

175 *although the Liu file had not been forwarded to Attorney General Edward H. Levi, he was aware of its contents:* FBI memorandum, July 1976.

*"I took some friends to see Mr. Nixon's grave":* Liu interview, February 20, 2009.

## 17. ANUBIS

176 *He was born in Shanghai in 1949:* Wen Ning biographical details are from James Geis brief, United States v. Ning Wen, United States Court of Appeals for the Seventh Circuit, Appeal from the US District Court for the Eastern District of Wisconsin, 04-CR-241, filed April 24, 2006, pp. 7–9.

177  *the family was forbidden to bring their only child, Sharon, with them to the United States*: Ibid., p. 7.

*Johnson persuaded Wen to remain as a diplomat in the consulate, providing information to the FBI*: Ibid.

*The FBI then arranged for Sharon to come to Washington, DC*: Ibid., p. 8.

178  *documents that he smuggled out of the consulate*: Interviews with former FBI counterintelligence agents.

*he began shipping computer chips to China*: Geis brief, p. 8.

179  *"He thought he might never get out again"*: Interview with former FBI counterintelligence agent.

*"make actual contributions to my motherland"*: Wen Ning resignation letter to Chinese consulate, Los Angeles, March 15, 1992, Exhibit 65A, United States v. Ning Wen, US District Court for the Eastern District of Wisconsin, 04-CR-241, September 28, 2004, p. 1.

*Fuqua had worked counterintelligence most of his career, in Boston and Kansas before Milwaukee*: Melvin D. Fuqua interview, August 12, 2009, and Fuqua testimony, United States v. Ning Wen, trial transcript, p. 758.

180  *Wen began shipping computer chips to Qu and Wang Ruo Ling*: Third Superseding Indictment, United States v. Ning Wen (a/k/a Wen Ning), August 8, 2005, pp. 4–5.

*they would typically falsify invoices*: Geis brief, pp. 9–10; and Criminal Complaint, United States v. Ning Wen, September 28, 2004, p. 21.

*In 2000 the company sent Wen back to China as president and general manager of its refrigeration company in Hangzhou*: Charlie Mathews, "Globetrotters: Manitowoc Co. Employees Travel the World," *Manitowoc Herald Times Reporter,* May 16, 2004, p. B1.

181  *between 2002 and 2004, almost $2 million was wired to Wen Enterprises from China*: Criminal Complaint, United States v. Ning Wen, p. 8.

*"They will need ice machines"*: Mathews, "Globetrotters."

*the "54th Research Institute"*: Criminal Complaint, United States v. Ning Wen, pp. 12–13.

*posing an "unacceptable risk in the development of missiles"*: Ibid., p. 13.

182  *The bureau recorded thirty-seven hours of conversations between Wen and his wife*: Geis brief, p. 25.

*"I was shocked and just about fell out of my chair"*: Fuqua testimony, United States v. Ning Wen, trial transcript, p. 764.

*Lin agreed, replying, "Risk, yeah"*: Criminal Complaint, United States v. Ning Wen, p. 19.

*"You get money from the bank, the bank won't know. You get money directly from ATM"*: FBI special agent Ryan Chun testimony, United States v. Ning Wen, trial transcript, p. 277.

*"Yeah, I have to make up the figure every time"*: Ibid., p. 290.

183  *"China now is desperately purchasing weapons"*: Ibid., p. 296.

*when the couple from Beijing, both Chinese nationals, got off a Greyhound bus in Mil-
waukee, the FBI arrested them. Other agents arrested Wen and his wife at their home
in Manitowoc:* US Department of Justice, "Four Arrested in Scheme to Export Restricted Electronic Equipment to the People's Republic of China," press release,
September 30, 2004, and Gina Barton, "Manitowoc Couple Charged in China Export Scheme," *Milwaukee Journal Sentinel,* October 1, 2004, p. 1.

*"The charges against the Wens are unrelated to the Manitowoc Company or Mr.
Wen's responsibilities as general manager of Manitowoc Hangzhou":* Tara Meissner,
"Two Face Export Charges," *Manitowoc Herald Times Reporter,* October 1, 2004,
p. A1.

184 *Lin Hailin . . . pleaded guilty to conspiracy and money laundering and was sentenced
to three and a half years in prison and fined $50,000:* Department of Justice, United
States Attorney, Eastern District of Wisconsin, "Manitowoc Resident Sentenced to
Prison for Exporting Restricted Electronic Components to China," press release,
December 22, 2005.

*Wen claimed diplomatic immunity:* United States v. Ning Wen, Order Granting Ex-
tension, Judge William C. Griesbach, July 29, 2005.

185 *He then sentenced Wen to five years in prison and fined him $50,000:* "Ning Wen to
Spend Five Years in Prison," *Manitowoc Herald Times Reporter,* January 19, 2006,
p. A1.

*a federal judge in Oregon struck down the expanded provisions of the Patriot Act that
Geis had contested:* Susan Jo Keller, "Patriot Act Sections on Search and Surveillance Are Ruled Unconstitutional," *New York Times,* September 27, 2007, p. A29.
The decision by Judge Anne L. Aiken came in the case of Brandon Mayfield, a Port-
land lawyer arrested and jailed after the FBI erroneously linked him to the Madrid
train bombings in March 2004 that killed 191 persons and injured 2,000.

186 *"will not be tolerated":* "Ning Wen to Spend Five Years in Prison."

*"Just who am I?":* Mathews, "Globetrotters."

## 18. ENDGAME

187 *PARLOR MAID sat in the courtroom with her head in her hands:* Erica Werner, "Former FBI Agent Charged with Allowing Chinese Agent Access to Classified Documents," Associated Press, April 9, 2003.

*J.J. Smith was charged with "gross negligence in handling documents related to the
national defense":* Ibid.

188 *"This is a sad day for the FBI":* Ibid.

*The charges . . . "are very serious":* Jerry Seper, "Mueller Orders Probe of Major FBI
Division," *Washington Times,* April 11, 2003, p. A4.

*"Katrina Leung is a loyal American citizen":* Werner, "Former FBI Agent Charged."

*Brian Sun . . . called his client a "loyal, patriotic, and dedicated former agent":* Greg
Krikorian, David Rosenzweig, and K. Connie Kang, "Ex-FBI Agent Is Arrested in
China Espionage Case," *Los Angeles Times,* April 10, 2003, Metro, p. 1.

*"a thorough review of his work is now under way"*: Houghton did not mention Cleveland by name but referred to him delicately as "the employee in question." Curt Anderson, "Ex-FBI Agents Suspected Woman of Spying," Associated Press, April 11, 2003.

189 *on May 7, J.J. was indicted on charges of "gross negligence" for allowing classified documents to end up in Leung's hands*: Eric Lichtblau, "Ex-F.B.I. Agent Indicted on More Serious Charges in Spy Case," *New York Times*, May 8, 2003, p. A34.

*A federal grand jury handed down a five-count indictment*: Dan Eggen, "Accused Double Agent for China Indicted," *Washington Post*, May 9, 2003, p. A2.

190 *appeared in federal court in downtown Los Angeles for a bail hearing before Judge Florence-Marie Cooper*: The author attended the June 19, 2003, bail hearing at the federal courthouse in downtown Los Angeles, and the description of the scene in the courtroom and the quotes are from the author's notes taken at the hearing.

*she had "reached a tentative decision to grant release with a $2 million bond"*: Ibid.

191 *"if necessary it can be increased to 1 billion"*: United States v. Katrina Leung, US District Court for the Central District of California, 03-CR-434, government's Memorandum of Points and Authorities, June 2003, pp. 15–16.

193 *"whether to publicly disclose 20 years worth of spying secrets"*: Susan Schmidt and Kimberly Edds, "Ex-Handler of Alleged FBI Spy Cuts Deal," *Washington Post*, May 13, 2004, p. A3.

*On May 12, 2004, J.J. pleaded guilty to only one felony count, lying to the FBI*: Eric Lichtblau, "F.B.I. Agent Pleads Guilty in Deal in Chinese Spy Case," *New York Times*, May 13, 2004, p. A16.

194 *"to have no further sharing of information relating to this case with Leung"*: United States v. James J. Smith, US District Court for the Central District of California, 03-CR-29, Plea Agreement for Defendant James J. Smith, May 12, 2004, p. 7.

*"Owens did the first draft of the plea agreement"*: Rebecca S. Lonergan interview, August 24, 2009.

*"That clause was never intended to stop the defense from interviewing J.J."*: Ibid.

*the government had engaged in "willful and deliberate misconduct"*: United States v. Katrina Leung, Order Granting Defendant's Motion to Dismiss, January 6, 2005.

195 *"Smith is being told not to talk to Leung or her attorneys"*: Ibid., p. 3.

*"The goal of the clause was to prevent Smith's lawyers from helping Leung's lawyers"*: Michael W. Emmick interview, February 23, 2009, and e-mail, August 22, 2009.

197 *there were discussions between Los Angeles and Washington "about whether more serious espionage charges were supported by the evidence"*: Emmick interview, January 9, 2009.

*"When a case has high-level attention, it follows that high-level people will be involved in the decision making"*: Lonergan interview, August 24, 2009, and e-mail, August 31, 2009. Lonergan quotes that follow are from the same interview and e-mail.

198 *"We wanted to reduce the risk of being graymailed"*: Emmick interview, January 9, 2009, and e-mail, August 22, 2009.

*"when you declassify, you lose jury appeal"*: Emmick interview, June 18, 2009.

*"an agent for the PRC," and . . . "she began to work for the Ministry of State Security ('MSS')"*: United States v. Katrina Leung, Memorandum of Points and Authorities, pp. 7–8.

*"admitted that she provided intelligence she gained in this manner to the MSS"*: RT, p. 15.

199 *The judge decided on no jail time for J.J. Smith*: "Ex-F.B.I. Agent Convicted," *New York Times*, July 19, 2005, p. A16.

*It charged that she had failed to pay taxes on at least $435,000 . . . she had received from the FBI*: RT, p. 26.

*the complaint charged that she had paid no taxes on $1.2 million that Nortel had paid to her*: Ibid., p. 22.

*the government contended that Leung had engaged in a tax scheme to take annual deductions on mortgage interest of about $40,000 on her home*: Ibid., pp. 22–23.

200 *She pleaded guilty to lying about her love affair with J.J. . . . In addition, she pleaded guilty to failing to report $35,000 in income from the FBI*: United States v. Katrina Leung, Plea Agreement, pp. 8–9, December 13, 2005; David Rosenzweig, "Judge OKs Plea Deal in Spy Case," *Los Angeles Times*, December 17, 2005, p. B3.

PARLOR MAID *stood before Judge Cooper for the last time*: Judge Florence-Marie Cooper died seven years later on January 15, 2010, at age sixty-nine, after suffering a stroke. *Los Angeles Times*, January 16, 2010, Metro, p. 26.

*"I love America"*: Linda Deutsch, "Ex-FBI Informant Takes Deal in Spy Case," Associated Press, December 17, 2005.

*"With my luck the judge's husband just ran off with his thirty year old secretary and I'll get five years breaking rocks"*: This and following quotes are from an e-mail J.J. Smith sent to friends May 21, 2004, United States v. James J. Smith, Exhibit 2.

201 *"As though I were put in the cosmos to take care of her"*: Kam Leung interview, June 25, 2003.

# 19. EAGLE CLAW

202 *The FBI learned that an American spying for China, his identity not yet certain, had stayed in room 533 of the Qianmen Hotel in Beijing*: Tom Carson interview, September 18, 2009.

203 *the FBI searched his luggage at Dulles International Airport and found a key to room 533*: Ibid.

*he was hired as a translator for an Army liaison office in Fuzhou, China*: Chin biographical details from Tod Hoffman, *The Spy Within: Larry Chin and China's Penetration of the CIA* (Hanover, NH: Steerforth Press, 2008), pp. 47–48.

*he passed that information to the Chinese, for which he was paid $2,000*: Stephen Engelberg, "The Multiple Characters of Suspect in Spy Case," *New York Times*, December 8, 1985.

*he met with his Chinese handler, Ou Qiming*: Ibid., and Hoffman, *Spy Within*, pp. 158, 237.

*Chin later said he might not have passed if the questions had been asked in Chinese:* Stephen Engelberg, "Man Accused of Spying Passed His Only Lie Test," *New York Times,* February 4, 1986, p. A17.

204 *he explained his wealth by saying that he played blackjack and was an expert card counter:* Ruth Marcus, "Accused Spy's Property Valued at $700,000," *Washington Post,* January 11, 1986, p. A4.

*he squirreled them in his clothing or briefcase and walked out of the building:* Hoffman, *Spy Within,* p. 173.

*Chin . . . passed the films to Chinese agents in a series of meetings in a Toronto shopping mall:* Carlyle Murphy, "Chin's Motives Debated at Spy Trial's Opening," *Washington Post,* February 5, 1986, p. A16.

*The meal included "Bears' feet" and "muttonpot":* Carlyle Murphy, "Chin: 'Nothing to Regret,'" *Washington Post,* February 11, 1986, p. A5.

*classified memos on President Nixon's secret preparations in 1971 for the historic opening to China:* Carlyle Murphy, "Accused Spy Says He Meant to Promote U.S., China Ties," *Washington Post,* February 7, 1986, p. A11.

*the agency's deputy director, Bobby Inman, personally presented the Career Intelligence Medal to Chin at a retirement ceremony:* Hoffman, *Spy Within,* p. 43.

*A week later, Chin flew to Hong Kong, met with a Chinese intelligence contact, and was paid $40,000:* Murphy, "Chin's Motives Debated at Spy Trial's Opening."

205 *His name was Yu Zhensan:* Hoffman, *Spy Within,* p. 19.

*Yu's father had reportedly been married to Jiang Qing:* Kenneth J. Schiffer interview, August 13, 2009.

*He contacted the CIA and warned the agency that Beijing had a spy inside American intelligence:* Ibid.

*Smith gave Yu Zhensan the code name* PLANESMAN: I. C. Smith interview, August 26, 2008.

206 *Yu Zhensan . . . said that the mole had flown to Beijing on a Pan Am flight that left New York:* Schiffer interview, August 13, 2009; Carson interview, September 19, 2009.

*The passenger was Larry Wu-Tai Chin:* Schiffer interview, August 13, 2009.

207 *"We delayed the flight at Dulles enough to take the luggage":* Carson interview, September 18, 2009.

*"We found the hotel key. . . . It turned out to be the smoking gun":* Ibid.

*Chin suggested to Ou that the Chinese might want to try to recruit Victoria Liu Morton, a woman he had known at the CIA:* Carson interview, September 18, 2009; Murphy, "Chin's Motives Debated at Spy Trial's Opening."

*a Chinese sleeper agent named Father Mark Cheung, a Roman Catholic priest:* Carson interview, September 18, 2009.

208 *"Mark Cheung was a real priest":* Ibid.

*"He rifled his colleague's desk":* Schiffer interview, August 13, 2009.

209 *he bought a copy of* The Puzzle Palace: Hoffman, *Spy Within,* pp. 61–62.

*A moment later the wiretap picked up Cathy screaming, "He's killing me! He's killing me!":* Hoffman, *Spy Within,* p. 58.

*it was not a spying device, but a sex toy, a battery-operated vibrator*: I. C. Smith, *Inside: A Top G-Man Exposes Spies, Lies, and Bureaucratic Bungling in the FBI* (Nashville, TN: Nelson Current, 2004), p. 41.

210 *"We sat on the case — we could not move on Chin for about a year until* PLANESMAN *got out"*: Schiffer interview, August 13, 2009.

*Late in the afternoon of November 22, 1985, the trio knocked on the door of Chin's condominium in Alexandria*: Hoffman, *Spy Within*, pp. 118, 121.

211 *"He realized somebody on the inside had betrayed him"*: Schiffer interview, August 13, 2009.

*"You have details that only Ou knew"*: Stephen Engelberg, "High Chinese Defector Is Linked to Spy Charges against Analyst," *New York Times*, January 1, 1986.

*"He thought Ou Qiming had defected and was the one who had dimed him out"*: Schiffer interview, August 13, 2009.

212 *Chin took the stand during the four-day trial, and claimed he had spied to improve relations between the United States and China*: Murphy, "Accused Spy Says He Meant to Promote U.S., China Ties."

*because Ou was in prison*: Murphy, "Chin's Motives Debated at Spy Trial's Opening," *"stealing documents from the CIA and giving them to the Chinese?"*: Murphy, "Accused Spy Says He Meant to Promote U.S., China Ties."

213 *He had tied a plastic trash bag over his head with a shoelace*: Carlyle Murphy, "Spy Larry Chin Dies in Apparent Suicide," *Washington Post*, February 22, 1986, p. A1.

*"So, Little Fish, don't worry about me"*: Hoffman, *Spy Within*, p. 267.

## 20. RED FLOWER

214 *"I work for Red Flower of North America"*: Edward M. Roche, *Snake Fish: The Chi Mak Spy Ring* (New York: Barraclough Ltd., 2008), p. 3.

*The phone call to Zhongshan . . . was answered by Pu Pei-Liang*: Bill Gertz, "Fumbled China Spy Probe an Intelligence Failure," *Washington Times*, September 18, 2006, p. A1; for background on Pu, see Roche, *Snake Fish*, pp. 134, 143.

*had been secretly passing sensitive Navy data on US weapons systems to China for more than twenty years*: Gillian Flaccus, "Brothers Accused of Being Agents for China Are Denied Bond," Associated Press, November 29, 2005.

215 *the Quiet Electric Drive, or QED, a propulsion system designed to allow the Navy's submarines to run silent*: Roche, *Snake Fish*, pp. 12, 197.

*"are certainly against the law"*: FBI special agent James E. Gaylord affidavit, in support of complaint and arrest and search warrants for Chi Mak, Tai Mak, and their wives, p. 15.

*The FBI concluded that these were "tasking lists" from Chinese military intelligence*: Ibid., p. 11.

216 *after Chi Mak was arrested he admitted passing to China . . . data about the Aegis combat system*: David J. Lynch, "Law Enforcement Struggles to Combat Chinese Spying," *USA Today*, July 23, 2007, p. A1.

*Chi Mak, his wife, and his brother were indicted:* United States v. Chi Mak, US District Court for the Central District of California, MJ-05-394, November 15, 2005.
*none of it was classified:* John Pomfret, "Engineer Indicted As Chinese Agent; Case Didn't Meet Espionage Standard," *Washington Post,* November 16, 2005, p. A3.
*surprise testimony that tied Chi Mak to Dongfan "Greg" Chung:* Roche, *Snake Fish,* pp. 87–88.

217 *Chung, an engineer who worked at the Boeing plant in Huntington Beach on the space shuttle:* Indictment, United States v. Dongfan "Greg" Chung, US District Court for the Central District of California, SACR 08-00024-CJC, February 6, 2008, p. 5.
*"I hope these products will be flying sky high soon":* Roche, *Snake Fish,* p. 88.
*"This channel is much safer than the others":* Quoted in Lynch, "Law Enforcement Struggles to Combat Chinese Spying."
*the jury . . . found Chi Mak guilty:* H. G. Reza, "Engineer Guilty of Trying to Give Documents to China": *Los Angeles Times,* May 11, 2007, p. B3.

218 *"I am regretful for not contributing anything":* Indictment, United States v. Dongfan "Greg" Chung, p. 8.
*"We are all moved by your patriotism":* Ibid., p. 9.
*the Chinese sent him elaborate tasking lists, with detailed questions:* Ibid., pp. 12–13.
*the Chinese asked for "aircraft design manuals":* United States v. Dongfan "Greg" Chung, Memorandum of Decision, US District Judge Cormac J. Carney, July 16, 2009, p. 10.

219 *He looked forward to a trip "of several weeks to take a good look at the motherland with my own eyes":* Ibid., pp. 8–9.
*"It is your honor and China's fortune":* Indictment, United States v. Dongfan "Greg" Chung, p. 15.
*"collect information on . . . the development of the space shuttle":* United States v. Dongfan "Greg" Chung, Memorandum of Decision, p. 11.
*a "small setting, which is very safe":* Ibid.
*as a cover story for his trip:* Ibid.
*they were astonished to find three hundred thousand pages of Boeing documents:* Dan Whitcomb, "Ex-Boeing Engineer Guilty in Space Shuttle Spy Case," Reuters, July 16, 2009.

220 *"He was a spy for the PRC":* United States v. Dongfan "Greg" Chung, Memorandum of Decision, p. 5.
*"purely a fabrication":* "China Dismisses US Spy Charges as Fabrication," Agence France-Presse, July 20, 2009.
*he was sentenced to fifteen years and eight months in prison:* Department of Justice, "Former Boeing Engineer Sentenced to Nearly 16 Years in Prison for Stealing Aerospace Secrets for China," press release, February 8, 2010.
*"stop sending your spies here":* Don Whitcomb, "Ex-Boeing Engineer Gets 15 Years in Spy Case," Reuters, February 8, 2010.
*The three people arrested in February 2008:* Jerry Markon, "Defense Official Is Charged in Chinese Espionage Case," *Washington Post,* February 12, 2008, p. A1.

221 *Bergersen, fifty-one, longed after he retired to move into the world of "beltway bandits"*: Neil A. Lewis, "Spy Cases Raise Concern on China's Intentions," *New York Times*, July 10, 2008, p. A1.

*"where I can pay you three, four-hundred thousand a year, you come out"*: United States v. Tai Shen Kuo, US District Court for the Eastern District of Virginia, 08-CR-179, Statement of Facts, May 18, 2008, pp. 2–3.

*"his associate introduced him to Lin Hong"*: Plato Cacheris and John F. Hundley interview, October 2, 2009.

*"It didn't take him long to realize that Lin was in the Chinese government"*: Hundley interview, October 2, 2009.

222 *Yu Xin Kang moved to New Orleans in 2007 to work as a secretary for Kuo*: United States v. Tai Shen Kuo, Statement of Facts, p. 3.

*Kuo handed Bergersen $3,000 in cash to play poker*: Ibid., p. 9.

*"I don't want CIA, I got CIA's paper"*: United States v. Tai Shen Kuo, Gregg William Bergersen and Yu Xin Kang, Affidavit in Support of Criminal Complaint, February 6, 2008, p. 18.

223 *"I don't wanna go to jail"*: Ibid., p. 21.

*his wife went through his wallet*: Ibid., pp. 24–25.

*He was sentenced to almost sixteen years, later reduced to five for cooperating with prosecutors*: Department of Justice, "New Orleans Man Sentenced to More Than 15 Years in Prison for Espionage Involving China," press release, August 8, 2008; "La. Man Who Spied for China Gets Sentence Slashed," Associated Press, June 25, 2010.

224 *whom he gave the code name Fang*: United States v. James Wilbur Fondren Jr., 09-CR-263, Affidavit in Support of Criminal Complaint, May 11, 2009, p. 5.

225 *Fondren replied, "I can't talk about uh — that stuff over the phone"*: Ibid., p. 11.

*"Let people find out I did that, it will cost me my job"*: Ibid.

*"didn't take notes"*: United States v. James Wilbur Fondren Jr., Superseding Indictment, p. 19.

226 *The chief witness against him . . . was Tai Shen Kuo*: Matthew Barakat, "Retired AF Officer Goes On Trial in Spy Case," Associated Press, September 21, 2009.

*Fondren was sentenced to three years in federal prison*: "Former AF Officer Gets 3 Years for China Spying," Associated Press, January 22, 2010.

## 21. THE CYBERSPIES

227 *Canadian researchers at the University of Toronto called "Chinese cyber-espionage" a "major global concern"*: Information Warfare Monitor, *Tracking GhostNet: Investigating a Cyber Espionage Network* (Munk Centre for International Studies, University of Toronto, 2009), http://www.infowar-monitor.net/ghostnet.

228 *"if a computer has a webcam"*: Nart Villeneuve interview, October 27, 2009.

*the code name TITAN RAIN*: Bradley Graham, "Hackers Attack Via Chinese Web Sites," *Washington Post*, August 25, 2005; Nathan Thornburgh, "Inside the Chinese Hack Attack," *Time*, August 25, 2005.

*Shawn Carpenter . . . studied a series of break-ins at Sandia:* Nathan Thornburgh, "The Invasion of the Chinese Cyberspies," *Time,* August 29, 2005.

*won a whopping $4.7 million jury award:* Scott Sandlin, "Sandia Hacker Gets $4 Million; Analyst Fired for FBI Contact," Albuquerque Journal, February 14, 2007, p. A1. Sandia appealed, and in 2007 Carpenter and the laboratory reached a reportedly substantial settlement, although neither side would comment on the amount. Scott Sandlin, "Analyst, Sandia Settle Suit," *Albuquerque Journal,* October 14, 2007.

*defense networks were taking a million suspicious "hits" a day:* Jim Garamone, "General Lays Out Challenges of Defending Cyberspace," Department of Defense, American Forces Press Service, March 14, 2008.

229 *cyberspies from China, Russia, and elsewhere had penetrated the power grid:* Siobhan Gorman, "Electricity Grid in U.S. Penetrated by Spies," *Wall Street Journal,* April 8, 2009.

*"Taking down the grid for months comes as close to a nuclear attack":* Woolsey quoted in Joshua Brockman, "Cybersecurity on Display in D.C.," NPR, October 7, 2009, http://www.npr.org/templates/story/story.php?storyId=113575765&ft=1&f=1019.

*the CIA's chief cybersecurity official:* Shane Harris, "China's Cyber-Militia," *National Journal,* May 31, 2008, pp. 15–24. Donahue did not identify the country where he said hackers had caused a power outage, but he was apparently referring to Brazil, whose officials disputed that a hacker attack had caused blackouts there in 2005 and 2007.

*the Tennessee Valley Authority . . . was criticized by the Government Accountability Office for lax security:* Ibid.

*a startling video released by the Department of Homeland Security:* See Clay Wilson, *Botnets, Cybercrime, and Cyberterrorism: Vulnerabilities and Policy Issues for Congress,* CRS Report for Congress, November 15, 2007, http://www.fas.org/sgp/crs/terror/RL32114.pdf; Ted Bridis and Eileen Sullivan, "US Video Shows Mock Hacker Attack," Associated Press, September 26, 2007.

*"cyber intruders have probed our electrical grid . . . plunged entire cities into darkness":* White House, Office of the Press Secretary, "Remarks by the President on Securing Our Nation's Cyber Infrastructure," May 29, 2009, http://www.whitehouse.gov/the-press-office/remarks-president-securing-our-nations-cyber-infrastructure.

*CBS News reported . . . an attack in Brazil:* The cyberattacks on Brazil were reported on *60 Minutes,* November 8, 2009, CBS transcript, p. 3.

230 *but the CBS report was disputed by Brazilian officials, who blamed the blackouts on sooty insulators:* Marcelo Soares, "Brazilian Blackout Traced to Sooty Insulators, Not Hackers," *Wired,* November 9, 2009, http://www.wired.com/threatlevel/2009/11/brazil_blackout/; Seymour M. Hersh, "The Online Threat," *The New Yorker,* November 1, 2010, p. 48.

*"The Chinese government has always opposed any Internet-wrecking crime, including hacking":* Timothy L. Thomas, "China's Electronic Long-Range Reconnaissance," *Military Review* (November–December 2008), p. 52. Jiang Yu's statement was issued in Beijing on September 4, 2007, and carried by Xinhua, the official Chinese

news agency. For the full text, see "China Denies U.S. Charge It Hacked Pentagon Network," Embassy of the People's Republic of China in the United States, http://www.china-embassy.org/eng/xw/t358639.htm.

*a sort of "Hacker U," with courses on "Computer Virus Program Design and Application"*: Thomas, "China's Electronic Long-Range Reconnaissance," pp. 50–51.

231   *"we do not know whether we are dealing with a spy, a company insider, or an organized criminal group"*: Robert S. Mueller III, speech to the Commonwealth Club of California, San Francisco, October 7, 2009, http://www2.fbi.gov/pressrel/speeches/mueller100709.htm.

*a program code-named* AVOCADO: Keith Epstein and Ben Elgin, "The Taking of NASA's Secrets," *Business Week*, December 1, 2008.

*a war game called Digital Pearl Harbor*: Wilson, *Botnets, Cybercrime, and Cyberterrorism.*

*"China is actively developing an operational capacity in cyberspace"*: Information Warfare Monitor, *Tracking GhostNet*, p. 7.

*"The PLA has established information warfare units to develop viruses"*: Department of Defense, *Annual Report to Congress: Military Power of the People's Republic of China 2008*, p. 28, http://www.defense.gov/pubs/pdfs/China_Military_Report_08.pdf.

232   *Two Republican members of Congress claimed . . . their offices on Capitol Hill had been penetrated by hackers they believed were in China*: Richard B. Schmitt, "Chinese Suspected in Capitol Hacking Cases," *Los Angeles Times*, June 12, 2008, p. A10.

*robbed, beaten, tied up, and blindfolded*: Peter Yuan Li interview, October 27, 2009; Paul Wiseman, "In China, a Battle Over Web Censorship," *USA Today*, April 23, 2008.

*surprise "that in the US they could do such things"*: Li interview, October 27, 2009.

*"They block e-mails, but we can still send some, either through e-mail or Skype"*: Ibid.

233   *only about 2 percent of the integrated circuits purchased every year by the military are manufactured in the United States*: John Markoff, "Old Trick Threatens the Newest Weapons," *New York Times*, October 27, 2009. Counterfeit chips from China have in fact been sold to the US military. In 2009 three members of a California family were charged with selling fake computer chips imported from China to the US Navy and other government agencies. In 2010, the owner and manager of a Florida company were indicted on charges they sold nearly 60,000 counterfeit chips from China to the Navy for use on warships, missile systems, and fighter jets. Prosecutors said the fake chips could cause weapons systems to fail, putting lives at risk. Del Quentin Wilber, "3 Charged with Selling Counterfeit Computer Chips to Navy, Others," *The Washington Post*, October 10, 2009; Spencer S. Hsu, "Case targets microchips sold to Navy," *The Washington Post*, October 15, 2010, p. A19.

*why the Syrian air defenses did not respond*: Ibid.

*"hackers gained access to emails and a range of campaign files"*: White House, Office of the Press Secretary, "Remarks by the President on Securing Our Nation's Cyber Infrastructure."

234 *"are clearly linked to Chinese foreign and defence policy":* Information Warfare Monitor, *Tracking GhostNet,* p. 52.

*"trace back in at least several instances to Hainan Island":* Ibid.

235 *Perhaps the strongest evidence linking China to cyberspying against the US was provided by WikiLeaks:* James Glanz and John Markoff, "Vast Hacking by a China Fearful of the Web," *New York Times,* December 4, 2010, http://www.ny times.com/2010/12/05/world/asia/05wikileaks-china.html; http://www.nytimes .com/interactive/2010/11/28/world/20101128-cables-viewer.html#report/china -99BEIJING999.

## 22. AN AFTERWORD

236 *The technology giant threatened to pull out of China:* Andrew Jacobs and Miguel Helft, "Google May End Venture in China Over Censorship," *New York Times,* January 13, 2009, p. A1.

*Google turned to the National Security Agency:* John Markoff, "Google Asks Spy Agency for Help with Inquiry Into Cyberattacks," *New York Times,* February 5, 2010.

237 *[Footnote] Six months later:* David Barboza and Miguel Helft, "A Compromise Allows Both China and Google to Claim Victory," *New York Times,* July 10, 2010, p. B1.

*A week went by before Secretary of State Hillary Clinton made a speech calling for global "Internet freedom":* Cecilia Kang, "Clinton Calls for Internet Freedom," *Washington Post,* January 22, 2010, p. A14.

*Clinton's "groundless accusations" were "harmful to US-China relations":* Steven Mufson, "Chinese Government Hits Back against Clinton's Call for Internet Freedom," *Washington Post,* January 23, 2010, p. A14.

*China held more than a trillion dollars of US debt:* Department of the Treasury, "Major Foreign Holders of Treasury Securities," www.treas.gov, and Department of the Treasury, Office of Public Affairs. Data as of September 2009 consists of $798.9 billion in Treasury bonds, bills, and notes, plus agency securities such as Fannie Mae and Freddie Mac, as well as private sector corporate bonds.

240 *"After PARLOR MAID, one of the procedures we put in place, you should not run a source for more than a couple of years":* Rudy Guerin interview, July 22, 2009.

*"when working espionage and someone sets up a US citizen, you can't do that":* Ibid.

*"We have lent a huge amount of money to the U.S.":* Michael Wines, Keith Bradsher, and Mark Landler, "China's Premier Seeks Guarantee from U.S. on Debt," *New York Times,* March 14, 2009.

241 *"China is stealing our secrets":* Agence France-Presse, "Chinese Spying a 'Substantial' Concern: FBI Chief," July 26, 2007.

*"Penetrating the US intelligence community is a key objective of the Chinese":* Report to Congress on Chinese Espionage Activities against the United States, 1999, p. 1, http://www.fas.org/irp/threat/fis/prc_1999.html.

*"the Chinese are surpassing the Russians"*: Harry J. Godfrey III, quoted in William Overend, "China Seen Using Close U.S. Ties for Espionage," *Los Angeles Times,* November 20, 1988, Metro, p. 1.

*they have encouraged people to apply to the CIA:* In October 2010, Glenn D. Shriver, a 28-year-old Michigan man, pleaded guilty to accepting $70,000 from Chinese intelligence officers to try to get a job with the CIA or other government agencies that would provide him access to secret documents. Shriver, according to government documents, applied to the CIA and spent two years going through the agency's hiring process. He was approached by Chinese intelligence while living as a student in Shanghai.

*"It's pervasive, ubiquitous, constant"*: Porter J. Goss interview, September 4, 2009.

242 *"You can get to know the dragon by its claw"*: Neil A. Lewis, "Spy Cases Raise Concern on China's Intentions," *New York Times,* July 10, 2008, p. A1.

*"They're in our knickers and there's maybe one under the couch"*: Interview with Harold M. Agnew, conducted by Mary Palevsky, Nevada Test Site Oral History Project, University of Nevada, Las Vegas, October 10, 2005, p. 36.

*"There are no walls which completely block the wind"*: This and the other quotations from the handbook are in Huo Zhongwen and Wang Zongxiao, *Sources and Techniques of Obtaining National Defense Science and Technology Intelligence* [Guofang Keji Qingbaoyuan ji Huoqu Jishu] (Beijing: Kexue Jishu Wenxuan Publishing Co., 1991), chap. 4, sec. 5, par. VII. The publication of this handbook for intelligence gathering was first disclosed in Bruce Gilley, "China's Spy Guide: A Chinese Espionage Manual Details the Means by which Beijing Gathers Technology and Weapons Secrets from the United States," *Far Eastern Economic Review* 162, no. 51 (December 23, 1999), p. 14. The term *qingbaoyuan* used in the title and text can mean both "information" and "intelligence." But the preface and eight chapters make clear that much of the contents relates to intelligence collection. It also contains an astonishingly detailed list of books, materials, and publications available from Congress, the Pentagon, NASA, and DOE, and notes that subscriptions to most are maintained by one or more of the five Chinese agencies involved in science and technology. The full text, in English translation, can be found on the website of the Federation of American Scientists: http://www.fas.org/irp/world/china/docs/sources.html.

# INDEX